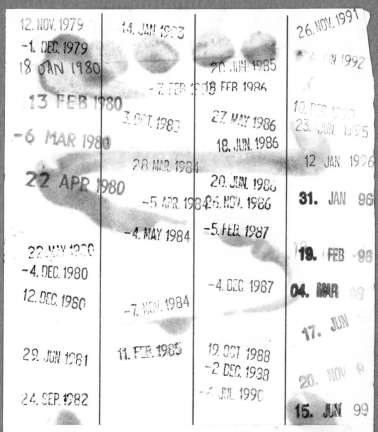

HERE'S LOOKING AT YOU, KID

HERE'S LOOKING AT YOU, KID

by James R. Silke

50 years of fighting, working and dreaming at Warner Bros.

Little, Brown and Company   Boston—Toronto

Library of Congress Catalog Card No. 75-22747

First Edition
Second Printing

Library of Congress Cataloging in Publication Data

Silke, James R.
  Here's looking at you, kid.

  1. Warner Brothers Pictures, Inc. I. Title.
PN1999.W3S5   791.43'0973   75-22747
ISBN 0-316-79131-8

Designed and produced by Chanticleer Press, Inc., New York
Designer: Roberta Savage

Published simultaneously in Canada
by Little, Brown & Company (Canada) Limited

Printed in the United States of America

Special thanks to Les Harsten, who first had the idea for this book and because he said yes to everything, to my wife, Lyn, who is also a snake charmer, and to the following:
Research associates Rory Guy, Roberta Ostroff, Rudy Behlmer, Ron Haver, David Chierichetti, Max Lamb and Joanne Pagliaro.
Graphic research coordinator Ron Haver.
Stan Cornyn and Warner Bros. Records.
Mort Lichter, head of the Still Department for Warner Bros. Pictures and his staff, Jack Kingsley, Sylvia Rabin, Karl Hibbler and Jess Garcia. And to the Oral History Division of the American Film Institute as well as all those participants in the Warner Bros. story who gave so freely of their time and their memories.

The author is grateful to the following publishers and individuals for permission to quote extracts from previously copyrighted materials:
G. P. Putnam's Sons, for *My Wicked, Wicked Ways* by Errol Flynn. Copyright© 1959 by G. P. Putnam's Sons.
Houghton Mifflin Company, for *Raymond Chandler Speaking* edited by Dorothy Gardiner and Kathrine Sorley Walker. Copyright© 1962 by the Helga Greene Literary Agency.
Random House, Inc., for *My First Hundred Years in Hollywood* by Jack L. Warner with Dean Jennings. Copyright© 1964, 1965 by J. L. Warner.
Bette Davis, for *The Lonely Life* by Bette Davis. Published in 1962 by G. P. Putnam's Sons. Copyright© 1962 by Bette Davis.
Delacorte Press for *A Life on Film* by Mary Astor. Copyright© 1971 by Mary Astor.
Hawthorne Books, Inc., for *All My Yesterdays* by Edward G. Robinson with Leonard Spigelgass. Copyright© 1973 by the Estate of Edward G. Robinson and Leonard Spigelgass.

Magazine covers are reprinted by permission of the publishers as follows: *Photoplay* (pages 45, 177, 178) and *Motion Picture* (page 177) courtesy of Macfadden Bartell Corporation. *Modern Screen* (page 178) courtesy of Dell Publishing Co., Inc. *Movie Mirror* (page 177) courtesy of Sterling Magazines.
Chapter headings are from *Casablanca*, screenplay by Julius J. Epstein, Philip G. Epstein and Howard Koch, and from *The Wild Bunch*, screenplay by Wallon Green and Sam Peckinpah.
All photographs, posters and advertisements are materials issued at the time the films were released and from the private collections of John Kobal, David Chierichetti and the author.

Contents

For Sam Warner, who added sound to the magic lantern, but never heard the applause . . . and for Barbara, a snake charmer.

DAMES, DICKS AND DREAMERS

Prologue

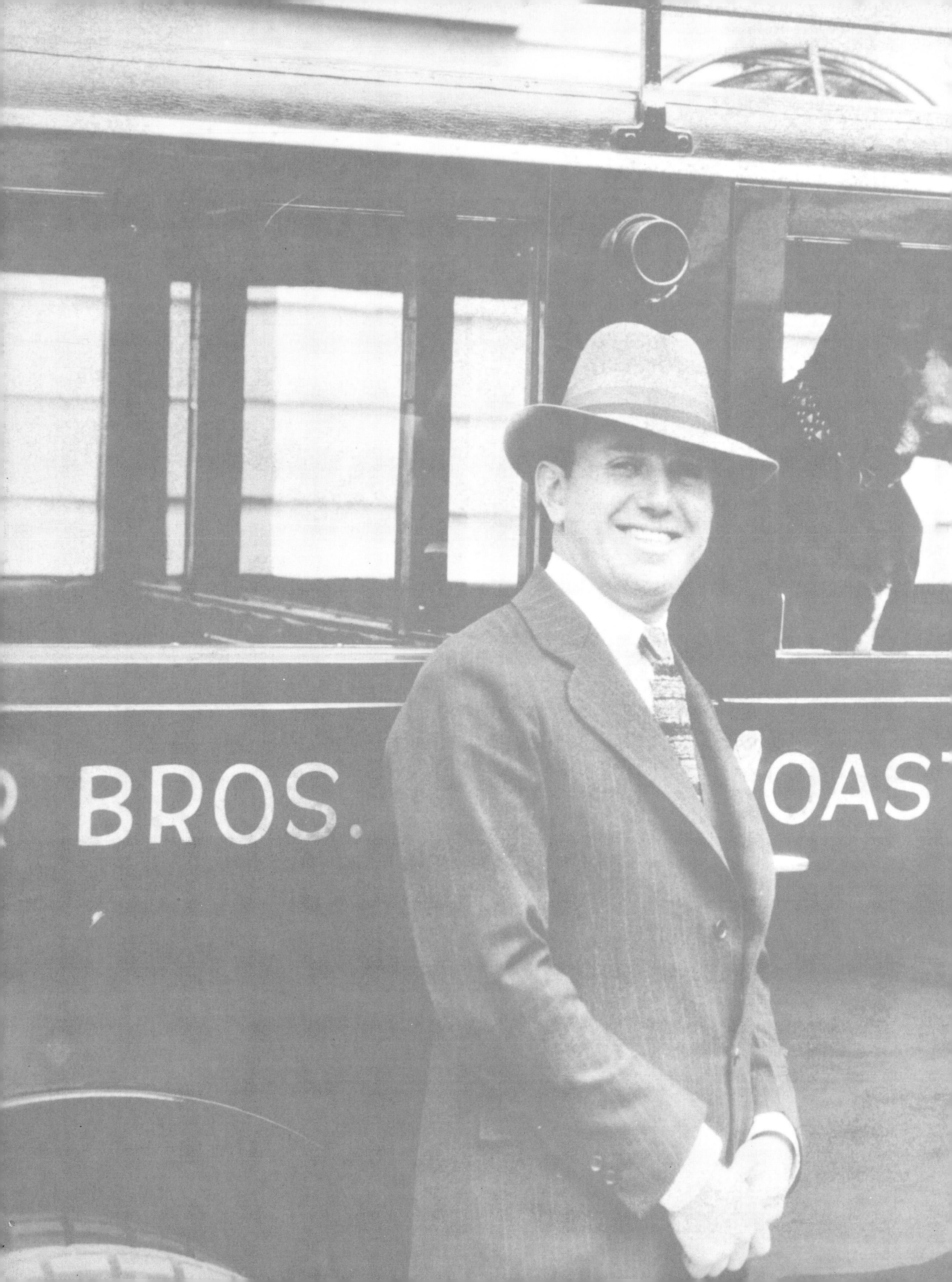
R BROS.
OAST

"Play it once, Sam, for old time's sake."

There are essentially two ways to tell a story. In the first the audience has no idea of how the story will end and their attention is held with either suspense or surprise. In the second the audience knows the ending at the beginning of the story, as in a ballet or the story of The Christ and their attention is held by the attractions of the color, costume, dialogue, humor and choreography of each event, by "how" the story is told. Warner Bros. is the second kind of story.

Five generations of filmgoers have seen the Warner Bros. films either in theaters or on the "Late Late Show." The result of the fifty years of daily suspense, surprise, and hard work at the Warner Bros. studios is common knowledge. Literally everyone who goes to films knows what ended on the screen.

Bogart with a cigarette and a good woman, "Awful good," and Bette Davis with a dozen men at her feet, several dead.

Olivia de Havilland in love and Errol Flynn in Lincoln green.

Ingrid Bergman who, of all the gin joints in all the towns in all the world, had to walk into Rick's. Ruby Keeler in satin scanties and Celluloid. George Raft in prison stripes, Mary Astor in pursuit of the "black bird," Paul Muni in a laboratory, James Cagney in an electric chair, Ida Lupino in a flower print dress, Marlon Brando in a torn undershirt, and Ann Sheridan in blood-red lipstick and no brassiere.

And for a brief moment James Dean, in just three pictures, only a glimpse at tomorrow.

The images are sharp, made of asphalt and silver, indelible.

The audience remembers the Warner Bros. stars even if it only met them on the pale gray tube late at night in a lonely apartment. They were and are good friends, easy to know and care for. Comfortable. Many know the character players: Sydney Greenstreet, Claude Rains, Allen Jenkins, Alan Hale, Peter Lorre, Ruth Donnelly, Frank McHugh, Walter Huston, Hugh Herbert and dozens of others. Some know directors like Raoul Walsh, William Wellman, John Huston and Michael Curtiz. The buffs can even recall composers like Max Steiner, Erich Wolfgang Korngold and Harry Warren.

But there are those who have been forgotten: Henry "Heinz" Blanke, Robert Lord, Brynie Foy, Al Dubin, Casey Robinson, Robert Buckner, Solly Baiano, Harvey Perry, John Bright, Orry-Kelly, Milo Anderson, Sol Polito, Tony Gaudio, Leo Forbstein, and many, many more.

And while the world knows the name of Jack Warner, few know the man: "Sporting Blood," "Creep," "Genius" or "Tyrant." Mogul, fool, friend. A distant figure on the throne of dreamland.

There were many performers in the Warner Bros. story: inlaws, strangers, nomads, drunks, failures, foreigners and here and there a prince in search of a sleeping beauty. Many were without fear, unashamed of turning their cardboard souls into cardboard castles . . . of boasting that they could save the world . . . of digging night and day for a few bits of treasure, a few scraps of the soaring human spirit. Others thrived on fear. They all arrived in Hollywood, however, at a time when the nation was still innocent, just waiting and willing to pay for whatever story they had to tell.

By 1975 Warner Bros. had made over eighteen

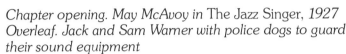

Chapter opening. May McAvoy in The Jazz Singer, *1927*
Overleaf. Jack and Sam Warner with police dogs to guard
their sound equipment
Top. Humphrey Bogart and Ingrid Bergman on the set of
Casablanca, *1943*
Bottom. James Cagney

hundred films. Some are lost, forgotten, most
naturally forgettable. In the thirties and forties, during
the great days of the motion picture industry, the
classic age of film as the French film critics call it,
Warner Bros. ground out approximately sixty films a
year, slightly more than one a week. Out of that grind,
however, came a great many films that will always
be remembered, that will always play.

Today, many look back at American films as
amusing but inconsequential fluff. Honorable but
unbelievable middle-class morality plays structured
on a world where good and bad were too easily
identified. Camp. Pop culture. Interesting sociology.
Impossible dreams.

For others, the old films are like the Sunday
funnies, old detective pulps, dime comics and Glenn
Miller's "Moonlight Serenade," the only dreams
left alive. Particularly the old Warner Bros. films.

Warner Bros. had a style, a look.

The heroes handled every hard case, four-time
loser, cow town, taxi dancer, bootlegger, prison
guard, bad king and good woman they could find,
and most of World War II. They could smell poison
on a broken shot glass, perform an appendectomy
with a razor blade, return Richard the Lion-Hearted
to his rightful throne, discover a cure for syphilis, die
with their boots on, free South America, steal the
"letters of transit" and then give them up to the
man who had stolen their woman.

The women were even tougher. At Warner Bros.
the heroines, dames, wives, tramps, gun molls and
sweet, unspoiled, down-to-earth girl friends had to
survive in a male world. And if they didn't know
how, they soon learned. They took the best and
worst of men with money, bad intentions, the best

of intentions and most often, men with guns. Some followed their guys, others stayed at home as their men served in foreign wars and behind prison bars. Some were loyal, true. Others would do most anything to help their guy "crash out." They handled every male star the studio shoved at them, the best in the industry.

Olivia de Havilland made them love her and Bette Davis ate them alive.

Back in the twenties when Warner Bros. was still hunting for the talent that would eventually supply its unique success, a good part of the world wanted to join those incredible shadows they saw on their local theater screen. And in those days there were jobs available in the motion picture industry, thousands of them. And with each job there was the possibility of tinsel and gold, good-looking men, better-looking women and glory like the world had never known before. As early as 1915 movie stars had been seen by more people, more often, than any other human animal had been during mankind's life span. There were logical, accurate reasons to call them "stars" and seemingly better ones to be one. And if you couldn't be a star, you could do something better. You could make them, set them free; create shooting stars.

Hollywood seemingly had been built for those driven by quixotic dreams, for people eager to fight over contracts, larger dressing rooms, hand props, better parts, brighter lipstick and more close-ups so they could tilt at windmills. It had been built for those who were convinced they were filled with that essential inner chaos which dies if it doesn't have a stage, if it is never seen. The town lured and seduced manicurists and millionaires, girls from

ATHOS FILMS présente

HUMPHREY BOGART

LE TRESOR DE LA SIERRA MADRE

WALTER HUSTON • TIM HOLT • BRUCE BENNET
SCÉNARIO DE JOHN HUSTON D'APRÈS LA NOUVELLE DE B. TRAVEN . MUSIQUE DE MAX STEINER
MISE EN SCÉNE DE

PRODUIT PAR
HENRY BLANKE
JOHN HUSTON

Overleaf. James Dean as Jeff Rink in director George Stevens' Giant, *1956*

Pocatello, Idaho, and Stockholm, Sweden; corner boys from the Bronx and English gentlemen. Most of all, it seduced talent; performers, hairdressers, photographers, trumpet players, makeup artists and dancing girls. Hollywood offered them a stage. It was irresistible.

The girls arrived in crowds by bus, train and thumb. They were certain they had what it took. They had read all about it in the fan magazines: *Photoplay, Shadowland, Motion Picture Classic, Snappy* and *Film Fun.* They wore Phantom Red lipstick just as actress Mary Philbin advised and used Stillman cream every night to make the freckles go away. They had written away to Mary Dunne, Dept. T-4 in New York, to "enlarge your chest-line," and to Doris Kent, Dept. T-4 in New York to "reduce your chest-line." They knew what the studios wanted.

Writers came with reams of original scripts neatly typed with borrowed Underwoods; directors with polished riding crops and leather boots tucked in their initialed luggage; and musicians with dented brass horns and stirring sounds, as yet unheard, deep in their lungs.

The numbers that came were staggering, but there were few jobs with tinsel and gold and the competition was rough and reckless.

Still they came. Whether they had heard it on a legitimate stage or in a Kansas City beer parlor—"And Mama said, 'You're on your own.' And Papa shouted, 'This is it, kid, sing!'"—they had heard the message. They were bitten with an ancient dream. They were going to feed on the food of the gods, on tears and laughter, and they were going to drive Pierce Arrows and have three servants to polish the chrome.

A few actually had genuine talent, some a small chunk, most none at all. Some even had what it was going to take.

Whether they worked or not, however, whether they were to ever get close to even being a small part of the silver on the screen wasn't up to them. Metro-Goldwyn-Mayer, Twentieth Century-Fox, Paramount Pictures, RKO Radio Pictures, Universal Pictures, Republic Pictures, Monogram, Pathe and others made the decisions.

And if they were going to be part of the Warner Bros. story, the decision was going to be Jack L. Warner's. If he said, "Stick with me, kid, I can get you in pictures," he could. But his choices were unpredictable, often adventurous and, as we look back, often made with an instinctive or conscious sense of just who and what was entertaining. "No lecherous boss was he!" recalls Bette Davis. "His sins lay elsewhere. He was the father. The power. The glory. And he was in business to make money."

Jack Warner picked people like a fight promoter putting together a championship fight. Then, with most of them, he started fighting . . . and hard . . . for whatever it was he wanted. And the talent fought back. They were certain they could conquer all comers. With lies, courage, threats, religion, money, magic, violence and sheer labor they would either join or beat the devil.

There were even those who dreamed that the vulgar toy called the talking picture show could be an art form, a form for individualistic expression. They would look for ways of taking creative control of a film away from the other participants, of taking total artistic control and imprisoning their own personal vision of the world with its shadows.

Dreamers, fools, who thought they could even beat Jack Warner.

Whoever they were, they were in a hurry. Warner Bros. provided them with a chance to take hold of their dreams and get rich doing it. It was too good to be true and they wanted their share regardless of how they got it. A few may have even understood that the golden moment of opportunity might pass, that the entire studio system just might collapse. They knew the century was also in a hurry.

The photographs in this book, the stills from the films, the gallery portraits, the magazine covers, the posters and the lobby cards represent what the audience saw during those great days of Warner Bros. films. Hopefully they will slow the films down, imprison those elusive shadows on the screen so the memory can indulge itself. The words are the story of how the writers, directors, hairdressers, producers, powdermen, conductors, performers, etc., put those images and sounds into the theaters—at least part of their story.

Efficient film history got started late, in some cases too late. Many of the participants at Warner Bros. are gone, their memories and their stories buried with them. Some wouldn't talk, a few didn't want to be quoted but wanted to talk, and others had to be coaxed. As Joan Blondell said, "I don't care much for looking back."

Creative people seldom do, and if a performer, writer, supervisor, director or any of the expert craftsmen that came to Hollywood in the twenties and thirties was looking back, he or she was looking the wrong way.

And, if they were afraid of a fight, of competition, or of their dreams, Warner Bros. didn't hire them.

"How" the Warner Brothers films got made is a story built from the lives of ambitious, bitter, tragic, humorous, talented and fighting men and women. It was a rough neighborhood. But, as Bogart said, "I kind of miss the arguments I had with Warner. I used to love those feuds. It's like when you've fought with your wife and gotten a divorce. You kind of miss the fighting." And if Bogart missed it, it had to be good.

"Awful good."

BENT NAILS
AND
LIGHT SWITCHES

1893 to 1930

"Can I tell you a story, Rick?"

"Has it got a wow finish?"

"I don't know the finish yet."

"Well, go on, tell it. Maybe one will come
to you as you go along."

Chapter opening. Corinne Griffith in Prisoners, *1929, a First National Vitaphone production*
Overleaf. The Warners in front of the Cascade Theater
Below. Jack Warner mugging at an early age
Bottom. Jack Warner in the twenties
Facing. Darryl Zanuck, Jack Warner, Mal St. Clair and Rinty in 1926

On July 14, 1967, Jack Warner sold his shares in Warner Bros. Pictures to Seven Arts Ltd. He was finished, no longer the studio boss. Officially he had been with the company for forty-four years, ever since it was incorporated in 1923. Unofficially he had been with it since 1903. He was one of the last movie moguls left alive and a rich man. In round figures he was paid thirty-two million dollars.

In 1903 it was different. When the brothers Warner opened their first movie show at the Cascade Theater in New Castle, Pennsylvania, Jack's sister, Rose, played piano, Sadye collected the tickets, Sam handled the projector and Harry and Albert counted and banked the nickels as Jack sang.

Between shows, as the reels of *The Great Train Robbery* were being rewound, Jack marched onstage, acted out short skits and sang illustrated songs. He was fourteen, his boy soprano voice was changing, and his brothers figured that its cracking sound would drive the customers out so they wouldn't stay for a second show, a "free" show. Even then their business judgment was sound and Jack's youthful career in show business took a profitable if unglamorous direction.

Several years earlier, Sam had advised his talented brother, "Get out in front where they pay the actors." Jack did and first sang "Sweet Adeline" at lodges, churches, benefits and at the Dome Theater. Then, he made a calculated show business decision, took for himself the only kind of name a real boy soprano should have, Leon Zuardo, and went on the road.

Before that, all Sam and Jack saw of a stage were nickel theaters, carnivals and fairs. But amid those loose, fast-change amusements the lures of the "muse" grew soft and tempting. Jack was crazy for a girl singer named Rae Samuels who clerked in father Ben Warner's butcher shop and was later billed as "The Blue Streak of Ragtime." Sam had even crazier dreams: he fronted for a snake charmer. A Barbara. Already the two brothers were working their way around the crude but colorful edges of their future.

Thinking back in his autobiography, *My First Hundred Years in Hollywood*, Jack Warner remembers picking up ideas of what show business was about, even "... on the sandlots where kid pitchers went into an extra twist if there was a crowd around."

Jack had an eye for talent. It was young, untrained, naïve, but it was looking in the right direction. And he had a special

love for Sam: "He was the dreamer, he could see
things coming."

In 1903 the brothers Warner were a long way from their
family roots, but those roots were deep and durable. The
brothers were born prepared to take and hold whatever the
still new, unused America offered them.

Jack Warner's life started as a fight. Krasnostow, Poland,
was the Warner homestead, a little village near the border
of Germany too small for Jack Warner to learn how to spell
or pronounce. It was cold, tough and hostile. Poland was under
Russian domination before the turn of the century and not a
healthy place for Jews. Benjamin and Pearl Warner, however,
were too young and vital to be afraid of life and began their
family with Harry in 1881. Eleven more children followed over
the years. In 1887 father Benjamin made the migration across
the Atlantic to the mythical land called America. A friend had
written, "The streets are running with gold."

Benjamin went alone, settled in Baltimore, didn't find gold
and set up shop as a shoemaker. It was the first of its kind as
Ben was the only cobbler to stand up as he worked. The novelty
paid off. In time he cut enough leather and pounded enough
nails to send for his wife and children and resume building
his family. Several of the Warner children, however, were not
strong enough for the fight and did not survive infancy. Harry,
Sadye, Rose, Albert, Anna, Dave, Sam and Jack did. Jack was
born in 1892 and was among those members of the Warner
family that took their second step into America. The family
settled in Youngstown, Ohio, in 1895.

Bicycles were the craze in '95 and the family set up a
bicycle shop. The craze died, however, and the family experi-
mented with various other ways to make the family fortune:
meat, gambling, ice cream cones, stunt cycling, soap, railroad
firemen. And Sam discovered a magic lantern.

A friend named George Olenhauser had an Edison Kinetoscope in his machine shop and Sam spent hours with him
learning how to run it and repair it. With his new skill, Sam
soon got a new job as a projectionist. He ran a brief
travelogue called *Yosemite National Park,* a novel variation
on the standard "sea wave" carnival amusement. The customers
sat in the rear seat of a touring car, which was placed inside
a tent, and watched the film as the owner heightened the
thrill by rocking the car.

The slight shadows attracted hundreds of customers to the
Idora Amusement Park. Sam, through his many connections
with the low life, greasepaint types who self-righteously called
themselves thespians, soon found where a Model "B"
Kinetoscope projector could be purchased for a thousand
dollars. The owner had gone broke trying to tour with it,
the machine didn't work and the legal rights to its use were
cloudy. The family, however, wanted it. Sam saw something
in the magic lantern they couldn't, but he was the son with
vision, the one to take a chance on.

The family hocked their prized watch that Benjamin had
brought from Poland, put their dollars together and then
pawned their only horse, "Bob," to meet the price. Sam took
possession, soon had it working, and the brothers went on the
road with it to project magic shadows on the walls of beer
parlors and deserted churches. They offered "Refined
Entertainment for Ladies, Gentlemen and Children. Continuous
performance. Admission 5 cents."

In their first show at Niles, a carnival town only a few miles
from Youngstown, they rented a room and chairs from a
funeral parlor. During funerals they shut down. They made
three hundred dollars in the first week, more than "Pop" did
in a month.

In 1903 they opened their own ninety-nine-seat theater in
New Castle, where Jack sang. It was a small store with an
altered front. The chairs again came from the leading under-
taker. It wasn't prophetic.

In 1904 the brothers formed the Duquesne Amusement &
Supply Company when they found there was more money
in distributing pictures to theaters for a rental fee or
percentage of the gate than in showing them themselves. They
branched out with distributing exchanges in Baltimore,
Pittsburgh, Norfolk and Atlanta.

Good years followed. Harry and Albert kept counting the
money while Sam blew it on a Buick White Streak and Jack
worked in the shipping room of the Pittsburgh exchange.
Always looking for a way to get ahead, Jack secretly rented
the negative of a film deposited with him for safekeeping.
On the screen the faces of the performers naturally appeared
black instead of white, but the exhibitor billed his show as
having "The First Negro Movie Stars" and cleaned up. Jack

made an extra twenty-five dollars a week for three weeks.

In 1908 the major film producers, Vitagraph, Kalem, Lubin, Selig, Essanay and others, formed an alliance with Thomas A. Edison to protect his invention of the picture machine as well as their own investments. Together they created the Motion Picture Patents Company which, in 1909, formed the General Film Company, which in turn began to buy out exhibitors or cut off their supply of films. The cloudy legal rights had become clear and the brothers Warner soon found themselves forced to sell out at a ridiculously low figure.

Sam quickly found a way back in. In 1910 he bought the New Jersey and Connecticut rights for a five-reeler called *Dante's Inferno* and the brothers went on the road again. Sam projected, a college professor read Dante Alighieri's poem, and Jack, cranking a homemade machine, made wind and thunder.

Film was a perfect medium for Jack, a boy whose only adventure with education was to have done the bumps and grinds as he sang "Doing the Grizzly Bear" at a Rayen High School function in Youngstown. It was a vulgar medium, a cheap popular attraction and Jack had always made the kind of wind and thunder the audience liked. The boy backstage liked the same things as the folks "out front."

Sam and Jack lost the fifteen hundred dollars they made from *Dante's Inferno* in a midtown Manhattan crap game, but Harry had checked their combined bank accounts and decided there was still enough surplus to take a risk. He suggested that Sam and Jack make a couple of two-reelers. They followed their older brother's advice, rented an abandoned foundry in St. Louis for a studio, hired a soft lovely named Dot Farley as their leading lady and shot a story written by Jack titled *Peril of the Plains.*

It was a "turkey."

Undaunted, they made more films and spread out to escape the detectives employed by the New York General Film Company to harass independents. Jack opened an exchange in San Francisco and Sam opened one in Los Angeles. Eventually they split their company into two units, production and distribution. Sam and Jack settled in Los Angeles, with the production company, and Harry and Albert in New York, with the distribution business—and the money. It was 1915.

In France, World War I was raging across hundreds of miles of mud, trench and men. It was an ocean away and America wasn't in the fight yet, but the conflict was barbershop and beer hall conversation. America was watching Europe. So were the brothers Warner and to them it looked like war pleased the folks "out front."

In 1917, Jack bought the West Coast distribution rights to a Civil War film, *The Crisis,* for one hundred thousand dollars. It opened to good reviews on April 5. On April 6, the United States entered the war and theaters were deserted for weeks. The investment was a total loss. Their second attempt to capitalize on the war was *Open Your Eyes,* a film made to warn young warriors against the evils of syphilis. Jack played a forlorn GI. Theater owners refused to play it and it failed.

War films became the rage with other Hollywood producers, but costs were going up. An average film cost between twenty-five thousand and fifty thousand dollars. Salaries of performers had risen from three dollars a day to three thousand dollars a week in only three to four years. Ticket prices were ten, twenty and thirty cents and quality houses were asking fifteen, twenty-five and thirty-five cents. In 1915 the annual motion picture industry payroll was twenty million dollars. Most of the money, however, was in New York and in 1917 the Hollywood banks could only claim $4,692,882 in assets. It would grow to $7,102,949 within a year, but the banks were holding on tight and took few risks in the vulgar business of picture shows, particularly with newcomers, with dreamers and adventurers like Sam and Jack.

At that time the *Los Angeles Examiner* was running a serialization of James Gerard's *My Four Years in Germany.* As the United States ambassador to Germany, Gerard had written in his diary the firsthand account of his abortive dealings with Kaiser Wilhelm II to stop submarine warfare. Sam and Jack liked the idea of making the book into a film. In 1917 they approached Gerard, who also liked it and agreed to help with the scenario. Jack and Sam then turned the deal over to Harry and Albert in New York and they closed it.

At that time, the brothers Warner had not made a major, feature-length motion picture. They didn't have a studio and they didn't have the money to produce the property they had just purchased. They were what Wall Street money then called "plungers."

Harry, however, quickly found another "plunger" named Mark M. Dintenfass in New York and raised fifty thousand dollars. The initial amount arrived in a shoebox.

Sam and Jack rented the old Biograph Studio in the Bronx and, amid the asphalt gray light of New York and under the sun at Arthur Brisbane's New Jersey farm, which had a replica of a German town on it, director William Nigh shot the film. A deal was made with the First National Exhibitor's Circuit and the film was released in 1918.

The film included such attractive scenes as Frederick William I kicking a young girl until she is crippled, a smirking Prussian officer dragging another soft child away from her family to rape her and a dying German soldier who manages to raise just enough strength to put his knife in the back of a man who is trying to help him. The folks out front loved it. The film grossed one million five hundred thousand dollars.

Now full-fledged producers with success tucked in their smiles, Jack and Sam returned to Los Angeles and took up residence in the Alexandria Hotel. It was the headquarters for agents, flesh peddlers, out-of-work actors, exhibitors, hookers, clowns, bookers and song merchants. Deals were made in bedrooms, at bars and on the curb.

Hollywood was thriving. The nation wanted silver, spangles and silk and the film merchants were giving it to them. Stars were being paid up to five thousand dollars a week to mince and bounce and fall down for the cameras. There were four-bit frails, fast-buck chasers and soda jerks everywhere. The streets were alive, but not exactly running with gold. It was 1919.

The brothers rented a run-down studio next to the Ince Studios in Culver City and made it pay for itself with two serials, *The Lost City* and *Miracles of the Jungle.* This time they featured a variety of wild animals.

Then they built their own studio on Sunset and Bronson in Hollywood. They finally had a fully equipped sound stage and were convinced they could write and direct their own material; but they needed performers, spangles and silver, and stars. They tried to hire Charlie Chaplin, Norma Talmadge, Fatty Arbuckle, Tom Mix and Harold Lloyd, but made comedy shorts with Monte Banks and Al St. John.

At one time Jack signed Gloria Swanson to a two-thousand-dollar-a-week contract, but she got married and canceled it before she found out he didn't have the money to pay her for the first week. He also hired a press agent, for $18 a week, Hal Wallis.

The brothers contracted with Louis B. Mayer for seventy-three hundred dollars to borrow one of his studio directors. The man never showed up for work and Jack ended up directing the picture. Mayer insisted it wasn't his obligation to see that the director came to work and he collected his money. The brothers learned quickly that the town wasn't going to lie down for their brassy competition.

The Warners took out incorporation papers in 1923, made *School Days, Tiger Band, Beautiful and Damned, Why Girls Leave Home*—and Harry managed to get theatrical genius David Belasco to sell him the rights to his latest Broadway hit, *The Gold Diggers.*

The first real star they finally managed to sign was a dog. Rin Tin Tin. The animal was found in the trenches of France by Lee Duncan, an American army lieutenant. He adopted the German shepherd puppy, brought him home to California and trained him to obey commands effortlessly. The Warner brothers contracted with him to make *Where the North Begins,* made a profit and then made nineteen more films, all profitable.

Unknown to Jack and Sam, Lee Duncan had two dogs, one that would work and one that wouldn't. Duncan brought the second one when he felt like quitting early. Eventually Jack had the director secretly clip the hair off one dog so they could tell the difference. Later, Jack gathered over fifteen Rin Tin Tins so the actor could work every day. It was only the beginning of Jack's trouble with performers.

To add some class, Jack and Sam produced *Main Street* from the Sinclair Lewis novel, and *Brass,* both of which were critical hits. The brothers were deepening their roots in "tinsel town." They wanted to stick and hunted for the right talent to make their movies.

In 1924 a one-hundred-and-forty-pound writer named Darryl Zanuck was hired to write for the "Rinty" films. He was twenty-two, but growing fast.

A year earlier they had sent word to nineteen-year-old George Stevens to come to work as an assistant cameraman. Stevens was just breaking into the business: "I came over to replace a guy who fell off a platform on a film Bill Beaudine was directing, a play, *Little Heros of the Street.* They, the brothers, were nobody much then, you know. They had their studio on Sunset then and I went into the foyer; it was

no bigger than a waiting room and this kid stuck his head out from behind the stage door and asked what I wanted. It was Jack." Warner offered him a price, Stevens tried for a little more and Jack closed the door in his face. "But we finally got together."

Stevens would return many years later to produce and direct *Giant,* and ask for more money. "An amazing guy, Jack, a comic at heart. I always enjoyed him."

Jack was a bit more polite with name directors from Europe and he and Harry went into an extra twist to hire Ernst Lubitsch. The director arrived in the rain at the Ambassador Hotel and was greeted by hundreds of veterans carrying signs reading "DON'T LET THE HUN WORK HERE." The next day Louella Parsons called, asked if Lubitsch had been in the trenches, found he wasn't in the army and used her newspaper column "to defend his right to work." Actress Irene Rich brought Lubitsch together with Jack and in 1924 he went to work on *The Marriage Circle.*

During the shooting, Harry learned that Jesse Lasky of the rich Lasky Famous Players studio had settled their contract with Lubitsch by buying him off with a personally signed check for two hundred and fifty thousand dollars. Always in need of cash, Harry blandly asked Lubitsch if he would loan Warner Bros. thirty or forty thousand dollars. He wouldn't.

Arriving with Lubitsch was nineteen-year-old Henry Blanke, his personal secretary, assistant and cutter. The studio hired Blanke for $50 a week. Blanke, however, worked late each night translating everything into German for Lubitsch. Harry also worked every night and weekends, and saw Blanke at his desk both coming and going. He raised his salary to $75 a week. "The stingiest man in the world gave me a raise out of his own pocket. I was very proud."

Lubitsch made five successful films for the studio from 1924 to 1926 before leaving. Blanke stayed. "We were just a shitty little studio then," but he was becoming an essential part of it. When the creditors came looking for something to pay off the debts, "I was the one who took the Bell and Howell cameras home and hid them." He also took coupons instead of paychecks, as did others when the brothers ran out of money, and filled in his financial gap as a correspondent for German fan magazines. He did whatever he was asked to do, did it well and, always a dresser, looked good doing it. In 1926, Blanke was twenty-six, in step with the century.

In 1924 Jack and Sam raided the New York stage and came away with Broadway's top star, John Barrymore. The temperamental matinee idol performed in *Beau Brummel, General Crack, The Beloved Rogue* and several others. With the Barrymore name on the marquees, Warner Bros. was established.

With Barrymore, moreover, the brothers got their first close look at a real acting talent. His contract provided that Warner Bros. would supply him with a four-room suite at the Ambassador Hotel, his meals, an automobile and a chauffeur, and give him approval of his leading lady.

Barrymore, his valet and his monkey, Clementine, moved into what was known as "Siesta 9, 10, 11, 12," a series of upstairs suites in a detached bungalow at the Ambassador. Here he hung fish trophies, maps of sea voyages and a large ornamental cage for Clementine. He covered the walls with blue damask, removed the hotel furniture and selected divans, period pieces, Oriental rugs, and beds from the Warner Bros. property warehouse. He rarely went out socially. There was a large closet piled with burlap-wrapped bundles. Booze.

At the studio, Barrymore's dressing room was packed with gym straps, turning poles, bust developers and a large white icebox. In front of a camera he was brilliant, but he preferred "Siesta 9, 10, 11, 12." In New York, Harry was livid over the price of their star's meals. In Hollywood, Jack was trying to get his star to eat his meals rather than drink them.

Barrymore had "style," and other stars at the studio would try to emulate it, some successfully.

Nobody got rich except Barrymore, but a pattern was formed. A balance between what would one day be called "The Warner Bros. Classics" and money-makers like *Seven Sinners, Red Hot Tires* and *The Love Toy* was to be the studio's exhibition pattern over the years. But in those days the pattern wasn't yet successful and Rin Tin Tin had to bail the brothers out.

Seventeen-year-old Mary Astor came to work as Barrymore's costar in *Beau Brummel.* She was already an experienced screen actress and did as she was told: "You see, I was 'stupid'—I really thought I was—and that was the role I played in life. It was very safe." Mary was perfect for those distant, impossible female creatures of the silent picture shows. During her test for the film a famous collector of female perfection whispered into her ear, "You are so goddamned beautiful you make me feel faint."

Mary was, but during "the next three years he [Barrymore] would teach me that I was a person, that I was somebody in my own right and not just a 'god damn trained seal.'" Little Mary Astor made several films then left. She would return, once more as a girl, then again as an actress . . . a woman.

The right talent and the ability to make it produce at a reasonable price, however, kept eluding the Warner brothers during the early twenties, and on occasion Jack went before the microphones of KFWB, a little radio station they had built on the lot, and again sang as Leon Zuardo.

Sam went East to work at the old Vitagraph Studios in Brooklyn, which they bought with borrowed money in 1925. The technical end of the business fascinated him and he convinced his brothers to sign an agreement with Western Electric, which then merged with Bell Telephone, and together they formed the Vitaphone Company. Sam was one of the few people in the industry with the outrageous idea that there would someday be synchronized sound and pictures.

But the movies didn't need any tricks, they were doing fine in their silent form. By 1925 Hollywood had accumulated nineteen studios and two hundred and fifty producers. The town itself had grown from thirty-five thousand people in 1919 to over one hundred thousand. In 1926 the silent film was reaching its peak. Wall Street estimated two billion dollars was invested in the industry. There were twenty thousand theaters and twenty million daily patrons. Hollywood made over seven hundred films a year, 90 percent of the films made in the United States. Its weekly payroll was over two million dollars and the motion picture had become the sixth largest industry in the nation. MGM and Lasky Famous Players were the big studios and Warner Bros. was barely visible. But the brothers had plans.

Harry was in charge of the money and overall company policy and spent most of his time in New York. Albert was the treasurer. Jack was in charge of production. He had to find and hire the performers, writers, directors, producers, craftsmen, cameramen, stunt men, casting directors, costume designers, art directors, lighting technicians, and all the other skilled and unskilled employees who went into making films. He also had to find the key executives who would be necessary to economic, expeditious and successful productions. But he was still

treating talent as if it were either fragile or culturally superior to himself and taking other people's word for just what talent was. At the studio it was Mr. Barrymore and Miss Astor and the pace was leisurely, courteous on the sets. Jack hadn't found his style yet.

Sam, however, had found his snake charmer to front for. She was petite, vivacious, brunette and a member of what was billed as a National Institution, the Ziegfeld Follies. She wore ermine, pearls, peacock feathers and was every bit as unreal as Sam wanted her to be. Her name was Lina Basquette and Sam married her. He was about to touch his dream.

Investment money from Wall Street was still timid about the film business, particularly Warner Bros., but Los Angeles banks were now able to compete with New York and were finally becoming interested in such competition. Harry Chandler of the *Los Angeles Times,* Motley Flint of Pacific Southwest Savings Bank & Trust Company and A. P. Giannini, president of the Bank of Italy, took a look at Harry's reputation, at how Jack ran the studio and at Sam's experiments and then made it possible for the brothers to raise a much needed million dollars. With it the brothers put more money into Sam's sound equipment and upped production in 1925 to thirty-one films as opposed to eighteen in 1924. By 1926 they were up to thirty-five.

Meanwhile, in New York, Los Angeles and points between, the talent was emerging, on its own.

Ruby Stevens (Barbara Stanwyck) was getting $35 a week and a lot of bruises at the Club Anatol in New York's furious fifties to do the Black Bottom. Ruby Keeler was a Texas Guinan dancer. Humphrey Bogart, in a pair of flannels, was waltzing on New York stages in *Hell's Bells* and *Cradle Snatchers* while carrying a wooden racket and asking, "Tennis anyone?" Lucille Le Sueur (Joan Crawford) was dancing the Charleston at the Club Richman for $40 a week and a lot of false promises.

Max Steiner was a pit conductor in New York doing *Rio Rita.* Robert Lord had graduated from Harvard's English 47 Workshop and was a working playwright in New York. He was also a college boxing champion at one hundred and thirty-five pounds. Solly Baiano was playing violin for the Beverly Wilshire Hotel Orchestra and, with his friend Eddie Frazier on organ, was playing "sob music" for silent films. "I was really getting down on that G string and playing for kissing sequences,

door-knobs-opening-slowly and fiddling like hell for sword fights."

James Cagney, Allen Jenkins and Frank McHugh were hanging around Broadway working as chorus boys, at anything else they could get and watching the "ponies," the smallest chorus girls in *Pitter Patter,* prance by. Jimmy married one, Frances Vernon.

Erich Wolfgang Korngold was in Vienna writing his opera *The Miracle of Heliane.* John Bright was being thrown out of college for leading a strike against freshman hazing. Bette Davis was dropped from a summer stock company in the East and worked the summer as an usherette. Director Lloyd Bacon was already at work on the Warner lot and Mervyn LeRoy had already been fired by Jack and was working as a "gagman" at First National in Burbank.

Errol Flynn was in Australia staring at the sea.

Emmanuel Goldenberg was performing in Atlantic City in *The Kibitzer.* "For the first time I was given billing. The play was with Edward G. Robinson." The G was for Goldenberg, an unforgettable reminder of the young Jewish boy who had arrived in steerage from Rumania.

Jack Warner was at Sunset and Bronson, cocksure and certain that whatever was wrong he could make better. He was thirty-five.

Oblivious, dedicated, lost in his dream, Sam continued to spend time and money at the old Flatbush studios of Vitagraph, and Harry let him. He had been convinced that the beautiful orchestra music that accompanied the films in the major New York theaters could be placed on disks and be heard even in the smallest theaters across the United States. It would be a major move to improve both the films and their sales. During Sam's sound tests, the sole concession to the spoken word was to be an introductory speech by Will Hays, the then somewhat ineffective president of the Motion Picture Producers' Association.

Sam Warner and Major Nathan Levinson, who was the head of the Warner Bros. Sound Department, were concentrating on synchronizing only musical sound, not dialogue. The traffic noises, the hiss of the Klieg lights and pigeons scratching and plopping on the glass roofs of the studio, however, made recording impossible. Sam moved the company to the Metropolitan Opera House, but again the noise of trolley cars and

the subway being dug under the building delayed the work. The tests were finally completed and the sound mixed with the picture, *Don Juan,* which Jack had produced in Hollywood.

On August 6, 1926, the *Vitaphone Prelude,* eight sound shorts featuring Giovanni Martinelli and other musical notables, was followed by a feature film and the sounds of an original orchestral score merged with the sound effects of John Barrymore, as Don Juan, crossing blades on the grand staircase in the palace of the Queen of Spain. The next day the daily trade paper, *Variety,* devoted a special edition to Vitaphone. The paper predicted a sweeping change in the motion picture industry to sound films. *Photoplay* editor James Quirk, however, announced, "Talking pictures are perfected . . . so is castor oil."

Don Juan didn't do anything surprising at the box office and the industry stood still waiting for more proof even though private detectives were seen snooping around the Warner Bros. sound equipment and sound stages. Jack Warner mounted armed guards to keep away those who were too curious. He closed the studio gates. The professionals in the business knew what was coming.

The Warner family was celebrating. On August 25, 1926, Mr. and Mrs. Benjamin Warner celebrated their golden wedding anniversary in their old hometown, Youngstown, Ohio. "All the boys were there," the family album reads, "Harry, Abe, Sam, Jack! All the wives were there and the children! All the best of the old friends and the best of the new! The hardships of the half-century had faded out! Happiness had faded in! It was a glorious scene! Sun up! Not like afternoon at all! Like morning! New fires lit! Old fires rekindled! A reawakening of everything! A re-blossoming! A scene that might have been aptly titled: 'Come the Dawn.'"

Back in Hollywood, however, Jack wasn't dealing in dreams or in talking films. By February, 1927, he announced on the back pages of *Motion Picture World* that all production on silent films was being rushed. He was personally supervising the preparation of a script for a new Patsy Miller feature. Five companies were at work and five more of next year's "26 winners" were scheduled for completion within the month. And Rin Tin Tin was barking successfully but silently in *Tracked by Police.*

In the same month, *Motion Picture Classic* reported that the Warner Bros. and their impressive studio "are the joking stock of our little suburb." Everybody wanted to know what they were using for money. "Certainly their pictures don't make any." Their books showed a total loss for the previous year of ninety thousand dollars.

But Sam kept working. The brothers convinced Al Jolson to make another try at pictures after George Jessel, the star of Warner Bros. *Private Izzy Murphy* and *Sailor Izzy Murphy,* turned Jack down. The singer finally agreed. They purchased Samson Raphaelson's stage play, *The Jazz Singer,* and Sam went into production.

Jolson's irrespressible vitality made him insist on ad-libbing in a few places and Sam wisely left the takes of dialogue on the sound track. The line, "You ain't heard nothing yet!" was blatantly prophetic. On October 6, 1927, *The Jazz Singer* was premiered at the Warner Theater in New York. The reaction was violent, an era ended, and another began.

Warner Bros. competitors were immediately forced to lease from them the patents for sound equipment. Silent stars were dropped right and left when strange accents, stutters and sheer fright made their voices squeak and shrill. In 1927 only one hundred theaters had been wired for sound, by the end of 1928 there were over a thousand. The other studios were panting to catch up to the plunging brothers.

Sam Warner, however, had made another kind of investment and it didn't show on the budget sheets. Overwork had made him tired and listless. He had lost weight. Finally he had a cerebral hemorrhage after he was hospitalized in the California Lutheran Hospital. Then on October 5, 1927, twenty-four hours before the premiere of *The Jazz Singer,* Sam died, only one step short of what he could see coming.

The brothers took Sam's death hard and somewhere inside Jack Warner, imperceptible perhaps even to himself, he did precisely what it was hardest for him to do: he changed. The clothes were still tailor-made, the shoes white leather, the ties hand-painted and the hat a Panama, but some of the brassy shine on his smile had faded. The youngest brother was growing up. He was still only thirty-five, but seemed older. Harry and Albert were still there to handle the money, the studio was expanding, the theaters were waiting and all he had to do was put on a picture show. He had to light the darkness, find a snake charmer to front for and do the impossible: he had to be both Sam and Jack Warner.

In 1929, Harry borrowed money from Goldman, Sachs and

Hayden and S. Stone & Company to purchase the Stanley Chain of theaters and First National Studios, a sprawling lot in Burbank. They had a list of established names: Colleen Moore, Richard Barthelmess, Loretta Young, Billie Dove, Edmund Lowe, Alice White, Constance Bennett, Lila Lee, Conrad Nagel, Kay Francis, Milton Sills and Basil Rathbone as well as director Mervyn LeRoy. The studio was a significant addition, but the theaters were a necessity; they moved Warner from an "also ran" to the "top studio" in the industry. The company was on the move.

Robert Lord was immediately transferred from Sunset Boulevard to Burbank. "First National was a country club, nobody worked much. Their only real star was Colleen Moore. They made pictures leisurely over there. Zanuck was then the bright young man at Warners who did the leg work and the dirty work. He sent me out there to get them off their ass. They took five months to write a script and we took four weeks. I went out like the new broom to sweep them clean, to make them hate me and the new regime."

Lord was good at writing and producing, however, and too good to waste as an executive. Besides, Hal Wallis swept harder and made people madder. By 1929 Wallis was working at First National in the same capacity Zanuck had at Warner's.

Jack was finding his style.

So was Zanuck. A song plugger remembers, "Even if he went from his office to the lunchroom on the lot, he had six or seven people with him all the time, every day, like clockwork. And he always had a little baton in his hand." Wallis, on the other hand, "never had anybody around. They were afraid to be around. They thought if he saw them, he'd fire them."

After the success of *The Jazz Singer,* a young gag writer and director on the lot, Brynie Foy, approached Jack to make a feature talkie. Foy had been working as a gagman on the studio's Syd Chaplin films and had helped on the Vitaphone shorts. He recalls, "Jack said, 'Go ahead, but make it a two-reeler' and left for Europe." Foy went to work with Hugh Herbert, the comic who was also an active screenwriter, and developed a script for *The Lights of New York.* "But we did it as a feature. They wouldn't know. Jack left Lou Halper, his brother-in-law, in charge and he wouldn't know what we were doing."

When they had almost finished, Foy told Harry and Jack that he had overshot and, "Harry said, 'What did it cost, eighteen

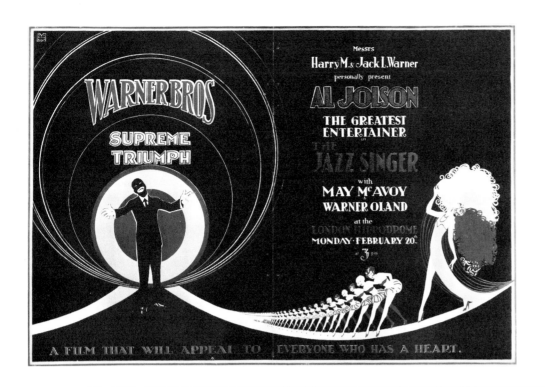

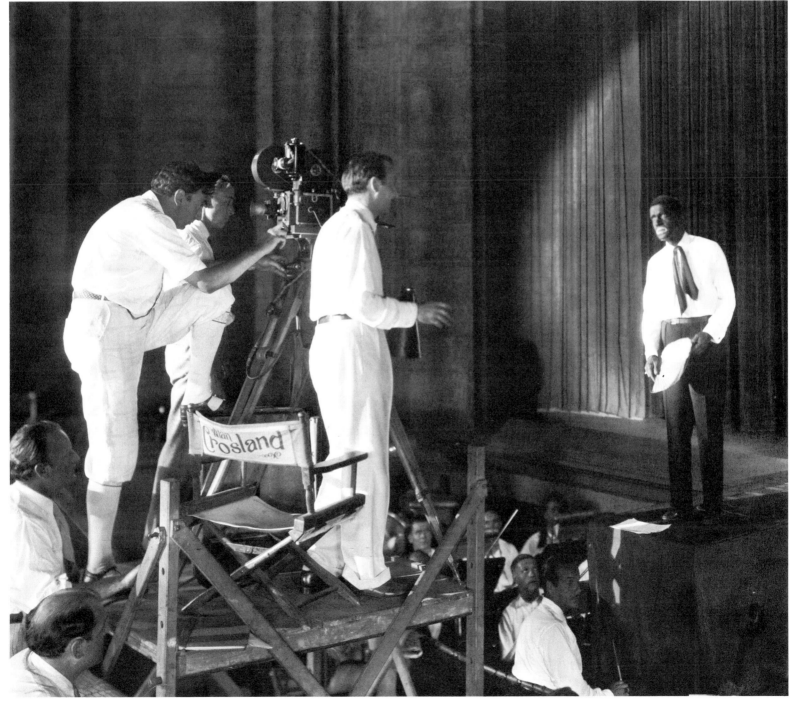

thousand dollars? Cut it to two reels, you're not going to put us out of business.' Neither Jack or Harry would look at it." After Foy offered to buy it for twenty-five thousand dollars, however, Harry and Jack sent Albert to look at it. Albert loved it and Jack said, "Go ahead and fix it, but do it at night so Zanuck won't know it." Zanuck wanted to make the first all talking picture.

"I got it cut, scored and we previewed it in Pasadena," recalls Foy. "There was a line around the block and the theater had a huge sign announcing the FIRST ALL TALKING PICTURE. We showed it in New York at the Strand, and the Skouras brothers, Charles and George, and the exhibitors began to bid for it by the third reel. So Jack stopped the film and made a deal right then. In the first week at the Strand it did forty-seven thousand dollars." Foy fit Jack's factory; he got things done.

The studio released Jolson's second film two months later, in September of 1928, and it reached its peak net income of $13,912,605 in 1929. Then the money stopped.

On October 29, "Black Thursday," Wall Street crashed and across the country the film customers tightened their grip on their nickels and dimes. The studios, which had grown fat on the surge of profits from sound films, were suddenly faced with the first major crisis in their business. They reached down, not up, and clutched at the fading audience with what they believed was an old show business staple, a basic attraction, wild women.

Eleanor Boardman, the most demure and ladylike heroine in pictures at that time, blossomed as a gangster's moll in *Diamond Handcuffs.* Meek and merry Mary Philbin went vampire in *Drums of Love* and did some "high fancy necking" according to the trade papers. Even Marian Nixon, Hollywood's sweetest little girl, went jazz in *Red Lips* and "proceeded to wildcat all over the place." At Warner Bros. the classic beauty of Dolores Costello became an underworld ornament in *Tenderloin,* but she wasn't cut out to play hard-boiled little eggs with one black eye and one green.

Profits slipped at Warner Bros. Times were so bad that when the Lux Toilet Soap Company ran an advertisement claiming, "96% of all the lovely complexions you see on the screen are cared for with Lux Toilet Soap," only one of the thirty female faces featured in the advertisement belonged to Warner Bros., Thelma Todd of First National.

Paramount's answer to their financial problems was Clara Bow. She understood the type in style. Boyish bobbed hair, perfumes and cushions were her tools. "An audience wants its heroines rough and ready," she said. "It's come to the place now where I can count the number of black and blue marks on me at the end of a picture and then prophesy exactly how big a success that picture will be at the box office."

At Metro-Goldwyn-Mayer, Lucille Le Sueur had changed her name to Joan Crawford and was bringing in customers with a lot of hot dancing, satin lingerie and a pair of dark eyes bigger than bank notes.

Jack fought the competition by contracting performers from Broadway: Fannie Brice did *My Man,* Texas Guinan, *Queen of the Night Clubs,* Sophie Tucker, *Honky Tonk,* Marilyn Miller, *Sally* and Ted Lewis, *Is Everybody Happy?* Most, however, returned to "the great white way" after one film. The new wide-mouthed comic Joe E. Brown promised a lot in *Hold Everything,* but his talent was only a promise, and Warner's stayed in the red.

On December 11, 1930, the Depression finally hit the city of Hollywood head on. The secretary of Guaranty Building and Loan announced his personal overdraft of $7,630,000, which he'd lost in the market. The announcement staggered Hollywood and made many of her best citizens penniless. Businesses allied with Guaranty closed their doors, rents continued to drop and stores were vacated. The Depression was in full stride. Hollywood contained two hundred and thirty-five thousand people in 1930, but each day more and more couldn't afford the thirty-five cents it cost to enter a cinema.

The studios were now going to have to take their work more seriously. Film making could no longer be a wild, fancy game. The Warner boys and the Metro boys couldn't go after each other in a drunken brawl on Saturday nights at the Ambassador Hotel like they had back in the early twenties. The fights were going to be settled at the box office, with talent, if it could be found.

Writing in the fashionable intellectual journal of that time, the *American Mercury,* Robert F. Sisk summed up *tinsel city.* "The cheapskate producers who have searched for and produced stuff fit only for the daughters of stevedores seem ordained to be driven out of business. Their fate seems sealed with the successful advent of the talking films, for it is a fore-gone conclusion that these films will be forced to stick to a low intellectual level unless their producers wish to alienate the great audiences already enrolled under their standards."

But Robert Sisk didn't know who was waiting to get on the stages the movie moguls had built, waiting to get into the theaters amid the darkness and become part of the silver on the screen. The first generation of Americans raised on motion pictures was out there, waiting, and Sisk was among them. In a few years he would be in Hollywood as one of those producers he condemned; he would produce both John Ford's classic *The Informer* and Rin Tin Tin's successor, *Lassie.*

From 1930 to 1933, the balance sheets at Warner remained in the red. The staggering overall loss was $113,000,000. The financial turmoil within the industry and the questionable means by which some of the studio owners tried to solve it prompted a senatorial investigation by the Seventy-second Congress. Harry Warner was asked to appear before the Senate Banking and Currency Committee and was questioned as to whether or not he and his brothers had realized a profit of $9,521,454.50 by buying and selling their own stock through Renraw Inc. (Warner spelled backward).

Harry denied it; they made only $7,394,459. They had sold at 54 and bought it back at 23. He blamed the financial columnists for inflating the value of Warner stock, expressed ignorance that dividends to stockholders had been passed, and asserted that "when we traded in the names of Harry or Albert Warner it influenced others." Eventually the stockholders sued and the brothers and Renraw Inc. were requested to transfer one hundred thousand shares of Warner stock to the Warner Corporation; they did. Jack was in business to make money, but he was also in business to make motion pictures.

In June, 1930, *Variety* devoted a special section to Warner Bros. which showed Jack's spirit of adventure in the face of disaster. In addition to the parent company, there were now fifty-one subsidiaries enabling Warner Bros. to handle every phase of their business without calling in outside sources. Stockholders owned shares valued at just over two hundred million dollars and had collected annual dividends of almost twelve million. Employees numbered eighteen thousand five hundred and they carried home an annual payroll of thirty-six million dollars. In addition to five well-equipped studios, the parent firm owned ninety-three film exchanges and eight

hundred and twelve theaters, which seated 932,360,605 paying customers annually. "There is not an instant during the twenty-four hours of the day that Warner Brothers pictures are not being shown in some part of the world," boasted Albert Warner.

Meanwhile, Jack was making selections and picking just what and who he wanted from the flow of flesh and flesh peddlers that swarmed across his path in a continual effort to get something from him. His hide had thickened.

During these four crucial years, 1930 to 1933, Jack Warner hired a group of people, most of them in their early twenties, who would stay at Warner for the next two to four decades. Bill Schaefer went to work as his office boy in 1933 and is still with him, forty-one years later, as his personal secretary. Al Tondreau was hired to run the camera machine shop and would stay forty-five years. Harold McCord was put in charge of Post Production and would stay until his death twenty years later. Perc Westmore was put in charge of the Makeup Department and stayed for twenty-six years. Rudi Fehr was hired in the Sound Department and stayed to run Post Production for thirty-six years; he is still there. Solly Baiano put his fiddle aside, went to work as Jack's personal talent scout, then became head of the Casting Department and retired when Jack retired, forty-seven years later. Walter MacEwen, in charge of finding stories, Leo Forbstein, in charge of the Music Department, Major Levinson and George Groves, in charge of the Sound Department, and many others were also to stay for those classic years, the thirties and forties, and for many more.

Along with the right factory workers the factory was taking shape. There were production meetings every morning, one on Monday for what was to be done by next Monday, one on Tuesday for next Tuesday, and so forth. The work was to be always one week ahead. Everything was covered, requisitions were made in advance, everything from costumes, food, travel time, etc., was outlined and worked out.

The pattern was changing. The fun was over and the serious fun beginning. Each Monday Jack Warner, Bill Koenig, the studio manager, and Darryl Zanuck, who had been made head of production in 1930, toured the back lot to find which sets were still usable so stories could be written to use them.

As the Depression got worse, the cost of production dropped and salaries were cut. The talented personnel were kept on,

but in the first six months of 1931, nine hundred employees were dropped from the payroll. Bill Schaeffer recalls, "Jack was always the first to anticipate hard times and get ready for them."

Jack's background was also showing and he turned off light switches and emptied ashtrays as he moved about the studio. Solly Baiano says, "The stories about him are true, by God. I remember once when we came into the Greenroom [the commissary] on a Saturday and there was this little light no bigger than the end of your thumb left burning and Jack had a fit. 'Those no good sons of bitches, they can't even learn to turn out a light.' It was a fact, he worried about every little thing, but on the big things, when there was real money to be spent on a picture, it didn't even faze him."

When Harry would be in Burbank, he could be seen picking up nails on the sound stages and straightening them with his teeth, out of habit, an old one, dating back to the years at Youngstown and Baltimore. Harry was tough on carpenters. They each had a two-by-four with their names on it secretly stacked in the carpenter shop. They took them with them whenever they went visiting a friend on another stage so Harry wouldn't think they were loafing and fire them on the spot.

The term "bicycling" also started at Warner Bros., another old Warner family business. The bicycles were used so performers, etc., could get from one sound stage to another quickly and thus work on two or three different films in one day.

Jack Warner's instinct for talent was also sharpening. When Harry phoned that he had heard good things about a German picture titled *Moon Over Israel*, Jack went after it. He found it was locked up in the Paramount vaults. Its story was the tale of the Ten Commandments and Paramount had bought it to protect their investment in Cecil B. DeMille's epic about the same story. Jack didn't attempt to buy the picture, but he went after Michael Curtiz, the director, and hired him. Curtiz stayed to direct *Noah's Ark, Captain Blood, Robin Hood, Casablanca, The Sea Hawk, Yankee Doodle Dandy* and others.

Jack believed in going after whom he wanted and instructed Rufus LeMaire, Max Arnow, Steve Trilling, Irving Kumen and Solly Baiano, the heads of the Casting Department during the classic years, to spread out over the town and search for talent. The Bliss-Hayden Theater on Robertson and Doheny was visited regularly, talent scouts from all the studios taking up

JOAN BLONDELL

B-13.

many of its thirty seats. Downtown, the Belasco Theater, the Mayan and the Biltmore were covered and in Hollywood, the El Capitan, Vine St. Theater, Hollywood Palace and the Music Box. The Pasadena Playhouse had three theaters: the Playhouse, its private Playbox Theater and its Lab Theater, where shows were staged with a ten-dollar budget. There the new authors and actors were particularly interesting.

The University of Washington was visited every year. They had three shows, a theater, a repertory company and a showboat on Lake Washington. In Chicago, the Goodman Memorial School of Theater was a good source of talent and in New York it was Lee Strasberg's, Sandy Meisner's and Stella Adler's schools as well as the on- and off-Broadway shows.

The Casting Department screened films, judged beauty contests and talked to agents daily. Sometimes a greedy flesh peddler would charge a girl "with a face like a can of worms" twenty-five dollars just to get an interview at Warner Bros. The girls were usually advised to go home, establish themselves locally and then wait for Hollywood to find them.

It was all business at Warner Bros. "Jack was death against producers putting girls in their films for themselves," recalls an assistant casting director. And from all the hunting, "there wouldn't be one in a month that it would be worthwhile going backstage to see."

In 1930 the talent, the performers, writers, producers, directors and musicians began to arrive. They were riding chance and opportunity, riding hard, and had no idea of who was there in Burbank waiting for them.

By late 1933, the turnabout in management and talent had its effect and the budget sheets showed a meager profit of $105,752. It was a beginning. Buying for productions was centralized, and all furniture and equipment was standardized to obtain uniformity and economy. Each item was analyzed for efficiency before purchase, and Harry made the rules stick. Jack remembers he had "the toughness of a brothel madam and the buzzing persistence of a mosquito on a hot night."

Many of the performers, crews and office personnel didn't like the economy drives, but they often helped give Warner Bros. its look, a look that manifested itself in many small ways. Thousands of still photographs were taken of every starlet at the studio; in bunny costumes, as valentines, leg art and cheesecake. Each girl got the full treatment from the hair-

Right. George Groves and Darryl Zanuck in a sound mixing booth, 1929

dresser, makeup artist, lighting man and still photographer. At Metro-Goldwyn-Mayer, the Publicity Department did the same and sent out double-weight glossy finished photographs of Norma Shearer and their starlets to the fans. But Warner Bros. only sent out thin postcards printed in faded brown ink, even of Bette Davis. Somehow it suited her; and it suited Warner Bros.

The hours were long, the work week had six days and each day consisted of fourteen hours or more, for both staff and talent. Performers were started at $50 a week without a test and $150 with a test. Each was signed to a seven-year contract with six-month options for the studio. The player was to work twenty out of each twenty-six weeks and was raised each six months from $250 to $350, $500, $750, $1,000 and finally $1,500. It sounded wonderful when you started; even to James Cagney; but not for long. Extras earned from $3 to $7.50 a day.

The search for stories was organized. "Plants" were put inside the New York publishing houses to find stories before they were published, readers read *every* book that came out and scripts arrived daily from agents. Certain publishers also secretly sent books to the studios prior to publication to make a few fast dollars on the side. The authors, who were certain their novels would bring astronomical sums if they were offered to Hollywood after they had made the best-seller list, didn't care for the practice.

During the fighting, sweating and film making, Warner Bros. was a family. Many gave the credit to feisty little Darryl Zanuck, who had a zest for success. As much as writer John Bright didn't care for the man, he gave him credit for instilling the initial spirit on the lot. He recalls, "We all liked each other then. We went to each other's previews and when a film was successful, we cheered. We loved it! I thought it was like that at all the studios at first, but it wasn't. I worked at all of 'em. At Metro for instance, when you walked into the commissary after a preview and you saw all the tables smiling except one, you knew the picture was a flop. If all the tables were sour and downcast and only one was smiling, you knew it was a hit."

Jack Warner, however, had his differences with Zanuck. When his head of production argued with Harry, twice, Harry suggested to Jack that Zanuck wasn't the kind of man he wanted around. Zanuck, who had agreed to a salary cut for eight months because the studio was in financial trouble,

wanted his salary restored to its original figure. The eight months were up, but Harry liked Zanuck's salary as it was. Jack agreed with Harry.

Zanuck left in 1933 and in 1934 formed Twentieth Century-Fox with Joe Schenck. The spirit, the family and the "look," however, stayed at Warner Bros.

While he was in charge, Zanuck worked tirelessly, sometimes around the clock. Jack did the same. Both men normally arrived around noon after using the phone for most of the morning and then stayed into the night going over dailies and rough cuts and reading stories.

Memories of Jack Warner, however, vary. "There was one thing at Warner's, there was no place to pass the buck." "Jack Warner would fire his wife if she didn't produce." And he did fire his son. "When he was wrong, he'd never say he was sorry, but he'd ask you to dinner or do something nice to let you know." "I didn't care much for the way he treated many people, but then he was a studio head and perhaps it was necessary. But I didn't like it." "He was only a figurehead. Zanuck and Hal Wallis did the work." "They milked the actors while their salaries were small, then dumped them." "One thing good about those days compared to now, the studios were run by tyrants. They made decisions." And the decisions started fights: with writers, supervisors, directors and performers, even musicians. But at Warner Bros., films couldn't be made any other way, and the fighting styles were limitless.

The thirties had begun and business looked good, but only a dreamer, a man gifted with the magic to see tomorrow, could imagine what was going to happen on all those silver screens that spread across America. But there was no longer the brother who "could see things coming," who could see that the streets would be running with gold. Jack now had to do it his own way, find his own snake charmer.

While he was hunting and fighting, however, the writers were parking their cars next to the fence that contained the Writers' Building, climbing over it, going through an open window and walking over a co-conspirator's desk so Jack wouldn't know at what time they arrived for work.

JUNE

CLASSIC

PICTORIAL of SCREEN AND STAGE

25¢

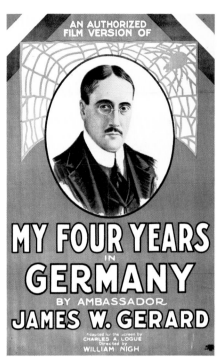

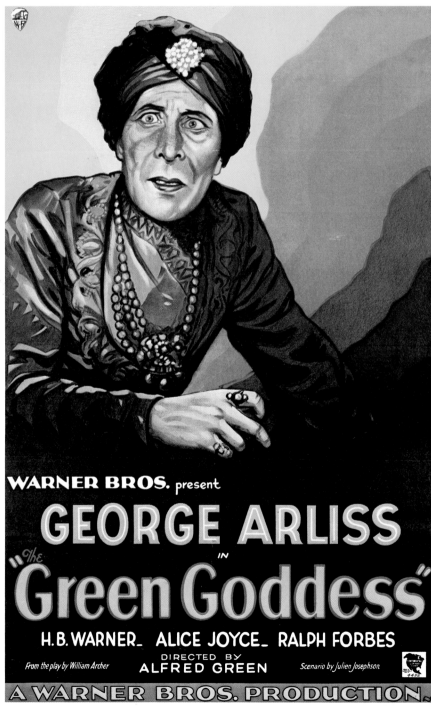

Top. Dolores Costello

KAY FRANCIS
Confession

IAN HUNTER • BASIL RATHBONE
JANE BRYAN • DONALD CRISP • MARY MAGUIRE
Directed by Joe May • Original Screen Play by Hans Rameau
Adaptation by Julius J. Epstein and Margaret LeVino
A First National Picture

Presented by
Warner Bros.

Bette
DAVIS
JEZEBEL

with

HENRY FONDA   GEORGE BRENT
MARGARET LINDSAY   DONALD CRISP   FAY BAINTER

A WILLIAM WYLER PRODUCTION

A WARNER BROS. PICTURE

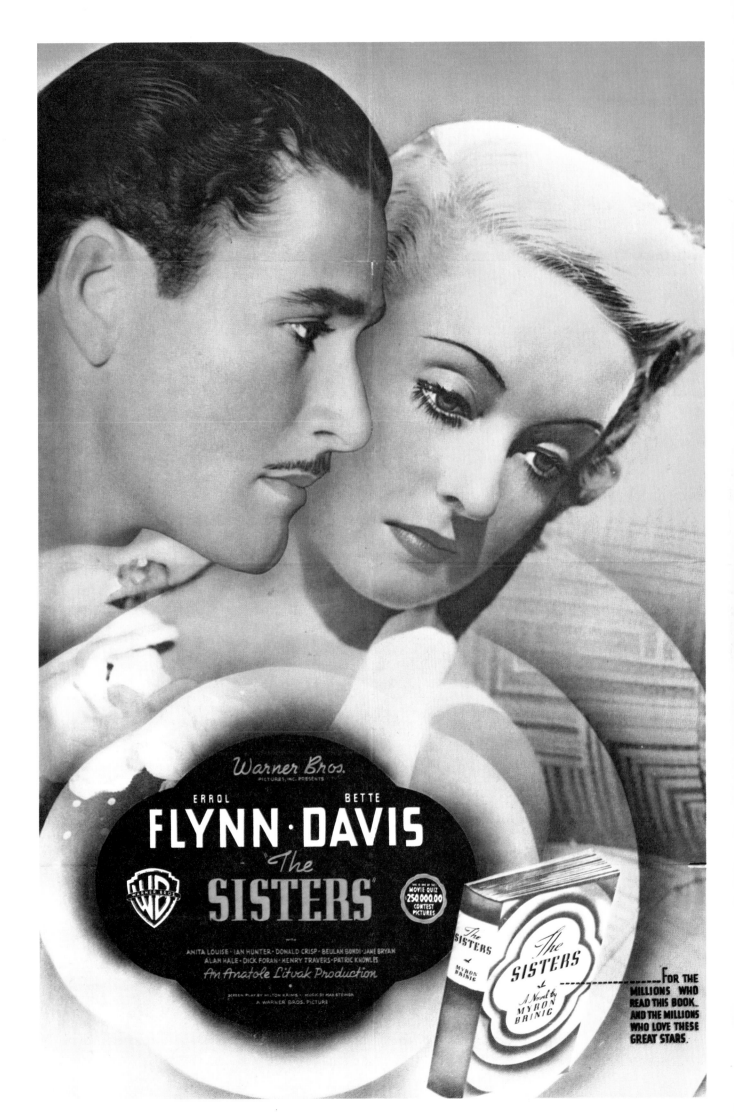

HUMPHREY BOGART in **ACROSS THE PACIFIC**
Presented by WARNER BROS.

BOGART AND LAUREN BACALL

"THE BIG SLEEP"

WARNERS'   MARTHA VICKERS · DOROTHY MALONE   HOWARD HAWKS

ERROL FLYNN in "OBJECTIVE BURMA"

WILLIAM PRINCE · JAMES BROWN · GEORGE TOBIAS · HENRY HULL · WARNER ANDERSON   Directed by RAOUL WALSH   PRESENTED BY WARNER BROS.

JOHN GARFIELD
ANN SHERIDAN

in

they made me a criminal

CLAUDE RAINS
THE "DEAD END" KIDS · Directed by BUSBY BERKELEY
Screen Play by Sig Herzig · From a Novel by Bertram Millhauser and Beulah Marie Dix · Music by Max Steiner
A WARNER BROS.-FIRST NATIONAL PICTURE
RE-RELEASE

WARNER BROS.

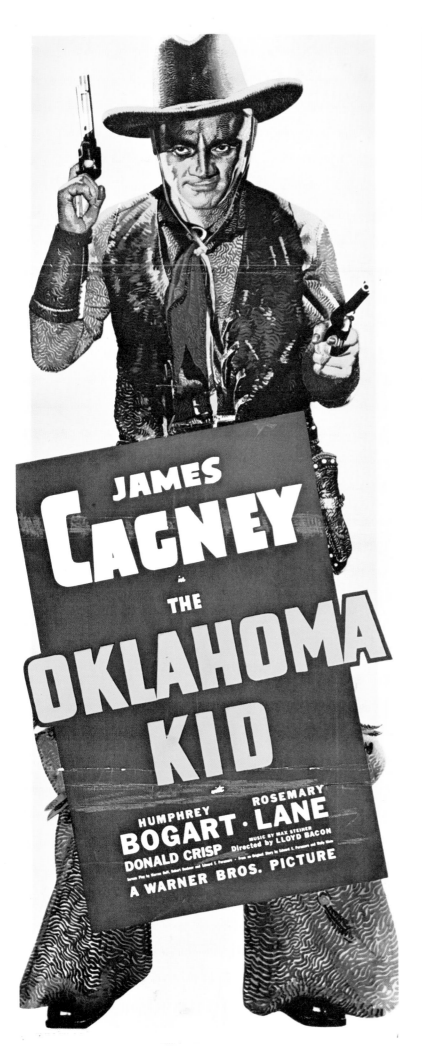

JAMES **CAGNEY** in

THE **OKLAHOMA KID**

HUMPHREY **BOGART** · ROSEMARY **LANE**
DONALD CRISP   MUSIC BY MAX STEINER   Directed by LLOYD BACON

A WARNER BROS. PICTURE

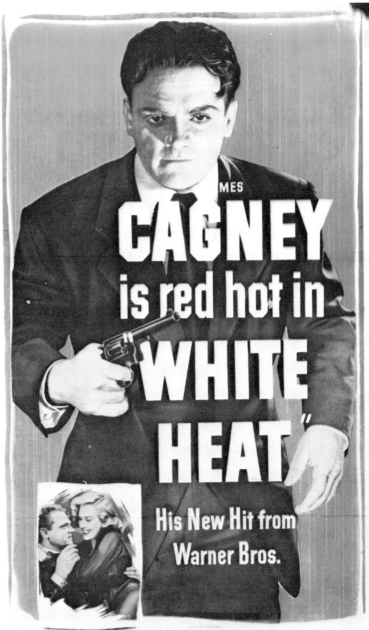

MES **CAGNEY** is red hot in "**WHITE HEAT**"

His New Hit from Warner Bros.

VIRGINIA **MAYO**

EDMOND O'BRIEN   FRED CLARK   DIRECTED BY RAOUL WALSH
Screen Play by IVAN GOFF and BEN ROBERTS

SHMUCKS WITH UNDERWOODS

Writers

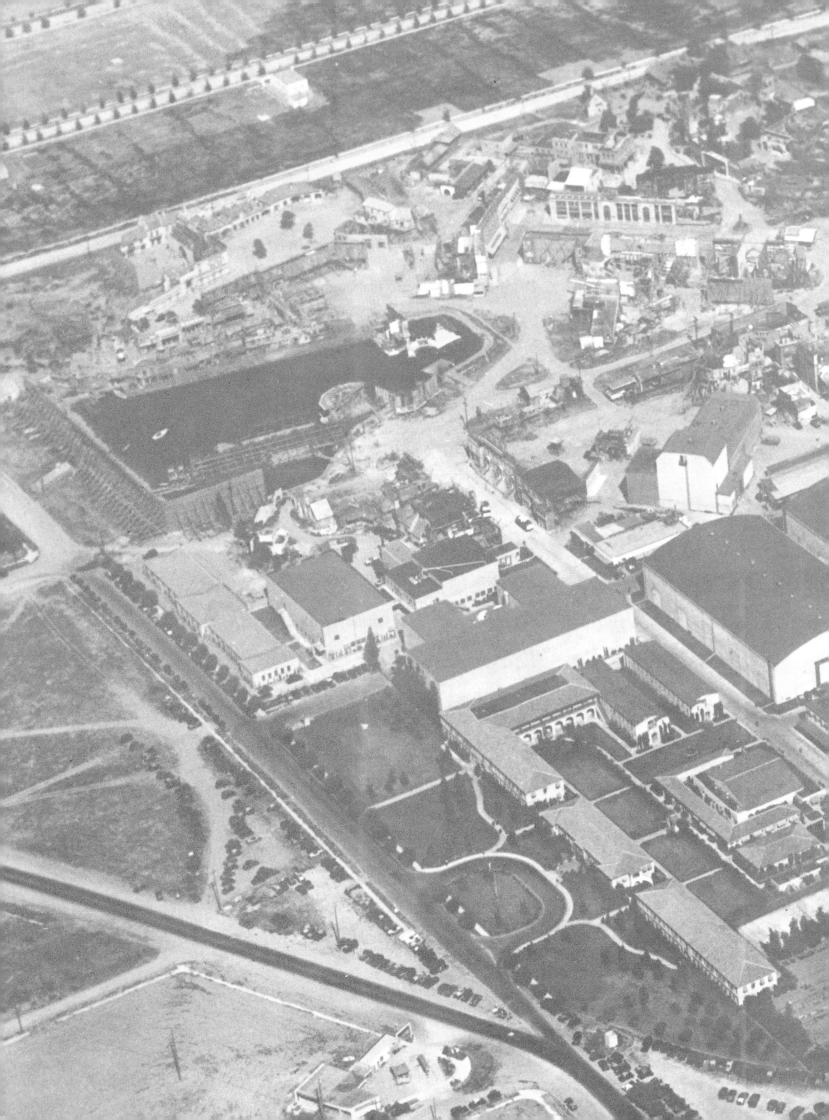

"And what in heaven's name brought you to Casablanca?"

"My health. I came to Casablanca for the waters."

"Waters? What waters? We're in the desert!"

"I was misinformed."

The Broadway, the El Capitan and the Super Chief carried the writers from the East Coast to Hollywood. A long steady stream of young men and a few gutsy ladies: novelists, magazine writers, press agents, crack reporters. The trip was a pleasant thirty-nine and one-half hours on the Chief. Calf's liver and bacon was seventy cents, larded tenderloin of beef in Madeira sauce, ninety-five cents and Malossol caviar, one dollar and seventy-five cents. The writers bought one-way tickets.

In New York, many writers were out of work. The Depression was hard on expendable artists, musicians and writers. The city itself was perfect; it was laced with European culture, the women were silken and sophisticated, the liquor imported; but even when you worked your words were worth only pennies. At the "other end of Broadway," on the coast, there was work. The talking picture was the new attraction and the performers needed something to say. They needed words and even New York writers with steady work headed West. Some were even invited.

The moguls, the tyrants, those despots who ran the dream factories had apparently learned their lesson. They had built a mammoth industry, they had a stage and a screen in every city in the nation, throughout the world, but words were still an aggravating necessity. They had quickly discovered they needed new performers, actors and actresses who could speak clearly, even act, and directors who could control those actors. Finally, they had admitted that they needed words, words that made some kind of sense, that fit the story, that tied the action together, that entertained.

Plush flesh, satin and muscled profiles were not attracting the audience as they were supposed to and the relatives and friends who had written the subtitles for the silent films were just not good enough any more. The moguls needed writers, real ones, whatever that meant.

The writers were the last to come to the new Hollywood, but they came. Only a trickle in the late twenties, a few more in 1930, then in crowds in 1931 and during the thirties.

They came with purpose. Hard times were eroding the nation, eating out its heart, its spirit; but to the literate, educated, thinking man, the Depression was only tearing down the old way to make way for the new. The time was ripe for change, and the socially aware writers needed a stage for their words. One place appeared perfect, Hollywood.

A mighty system of sound stages, laboratories, distribution circuits and theaters was on the coast waiting for the writers, waiting to spread their truth across the dying nation, and across the world if they only had the strength and courage to dream big enough. In Hollywood they could carefully put their words end to end with their great ideas, even with pictures, and restructure the society. They could make the poor rich, bring the dying back from the dead, raise the storyteller to his rightful throne and get paid for doing it.

Hollywood was at last going to have a soul, a social conscience, an intellect. Film was at last going to become an art form; the writers would see to it. And in many cases, the studios were even naive enough to pay train fare.

It was a quiet parade, but steady: philosophers with Model A ideas, reformers in debt, loners who still believed in legends, heros and dreams, one-penny word merchants with million-dollar stories to tell. Screenwriters on the Super Chief.

They had no idea what was waiting for them; a city where ladies went shopping in shorts, wore cotton brassieres made in Arizona and went out at night in baggy slacks, an industry that went to work at 5 A.M., about the time they normally went to bed, censors who rewrote your work before it reached the public, actors who could out-drink them, actresses who could out-shout night-desk editors, and directors who had egos big enough for six-volume obituaries, who worked on horseback, with megaphones and with a version of the English language that had formerly only been used by "China marines." Finally, there were the executives, the movie moguls.

There was no way a writer, not even a good one on his best day, could have anticipated Jack L. Warner, or the young man who worked for him, Darryl Zanuck.

John Bright remembers his first job. "I came to Hollywood because I was chasing a girl . . . and I caught her. And married her. Unfortunately." He arrived in 1930, age twenty-two. Bright had attended the New School for Social Research in New York, written a book about the mayor of Chicago with his partner Kubec Glasmon and had under his arm their unpublished novel about the rackets and hoods of that same city, *Blood and Beer.*

Bright was a curious man. Spangles, silk and satin didn't amuse him; he liked streets. "I remember all those one-legged men selling apples. Near Hollywood and Cahuenga Boulevard. It seemed to be a good spot for them. A busy cross-street.

Chapter opening. Ginger Rogers
Overleaf. Burbank studios in 1932
Left. John Bright, James Cagney and Kubec Glasmon during the shooting of Public Enemy, *1931*
Below. Famed European biographer Emil Ludwig arrives on the Super Chief to write Napoleon *for Edward G. Robinson, but the film is never made*

I wondered where they got the apples and I asked. I found out they hitchhiked clear out to a distant land called San Fernando Valley. They bought the apples there by the lug, which meant as many as you could carry in a mesh bag. About a hundred. The bag cost them twenty-five cents and they sold the apples for whatever the traffic would bear. A nickel or a dime depending on their estimation of the customer."

Bright had worked for his partner, Glasmon, as a soda jerk in a Chicago drugstore, a place where hoodlums hung out. Their book was "based on a great deal that was criminal and organized in Chicago. The drugstore life had sucked both of us into that ambiance." They saw and wrote about that life style a little too well for their publisher, who wanted the obscenity edited out by a lawyer. Bright didn't, and he asked an old friend from Chicago, Rufus LeMaire, who had produced *LeMaire's Affairs,* to take the book to Warner Bros.

In an effort to become a producer, LeMaire showed it to Darryl Zanuck, who had just been made head of production and "Zanuck double-crossed him. He made LeMaire casting director, which didn't make him happy but got him a lot of girls, and decided to produce the book himself, one of his first films as the head of the studio."

Bright and Glasmon were paid fifteen thousand dollars for the novel and signed to one of those "famous seven-year contracts with yearly options. You agreed to begin at a very modest sum because you were looking at the end of the contract which was twenty-five hundred dollars a week." The title of their novel was changed to *Public Enemy* (the film censors didn't care for the word "blood") and they got out their pencils to start the script.

Six months later, Bright and his partner had written the scripts for four films, *Public Enemy, Smart Money, Blonde Crazy* and *Taxi.* They all starred an unknown named James Cagney, but made him a star and helped shove Warner Bros. toward regular profits. Bright was paid $100 a week, which amounted to $600 per film and a total of $2,400. It was the kind of economics Jack Warner liked, but the wage at the end of his contract no longer looked as good to Bright and it was a long way away. He got sick, stayed home and only got well when the studio adjusted his contract.

Money arguments were popular with the writers, but they also had a personal problem, nobody seemed to understand them. The studio wanted them to come to work in the

morning, at 9 A.M., to write all day, then go home at night and come back fresh the next day, including Saturday. The executives weren't interested in the claim that a serious writer became so involved in his story that his mind couldn't stop writing until the story was finished, not even on Sundays, no matter where he was, not even when he was asleep. They had not read the wise, carefully thought-out arguments detailing the idiosyncrasies of a writer's life by Henry Wolfe, James Joyce, H. L. Mencken, Leo Tolstoi and others. They didn't even know the names of those guys and besides, what "their" writers were writing wasn't serious.

It usually took about six months for the writers to find out that although they were needed badly, they weren't wanted.

A few writers quickly got back on the Super Chief and went home, but most stayed, took their money, and kept to themselves. Some even formed a club that met in small apartments, almost secretly, and threatened to become a union. Many even liked to live alone and drink alone, a lot. Even those in the industry who admitted they needed writers didn't know where they fit, what they really wanted or why. The writers didn't act like movie people, didn't even act like they wanted to belong; and a few obviously didn't need to. They were usually the talented ones, loners with strange ideas and behavior patterns that didn't fit any business, anywhere. Hollywood would put up with all kinds of madness, with thieves, magicians, pimps and radicals, but not with men who consorted with the moon, with men who preferred to be alone. Once they were no longer needed, they would have to go.

Most were simply bad writers. Raymond Chandler, when he came out in the late thirties, took a look at his fellow screenwriters and figured they "could not make two cents a word in the pulp market if their lives depended on it." Chandler was a novelist, he knew how to put words end to end so they said what he thought and felt and he expected other writers to do the same. But that wasn't necessary, not in the movies.

Hollywood was cranking out over three hundred films a year in the mid-thirties and most of them were bound to be bad no matter how hard the creative forces tried to make them good. And most of them were supposed to be bad, "B" films, cheapies, programmers, but the opportunities to be good or bad came weekly, sometimes daily.

In time the mistrust, the grind, the annoying, prying crowds

on the studio lots and the inability to get their thoughts and dreams into any recognizable form on the screen began to eat at the writers. Actors rewrote lines, directors emphasized the romance and action instead of the ideas and the executive producers behaved like "low-grade individuals with the morals of a goat, the artistic integrity of a slot machine, and the manners of a floorwalker with delusions of grandeur," just as Chandler said they did. The discontented writers did their job, took their money and ran.

At Warner Bros., Jack Warner took a close look at these strange new additions to his film factory. They arrived at work late, slept on the job and worked on their own stories and for independent film companies on his time. They drank too much coffee, made outside phone calls, didn't turn out the lights at night and were always wandering off. He made a considered pronouncement: "Writers are *shmucks* with Underwoods."

Jack Warner, however, kept hiring them. There were usually thirty to thirty-five on the lot, sometimes as many as eighty. Jack even built them their own building. He liked to know where they were.

Mary McCall (*Craig's Wife, Mr. Belvedere Goes to College, Dancing in the Dark, Women of Glamour, A Slight Case of Murder, Maisie, Slim Carter, Juke Box Rhythm*) came to Hollywood in the early thirties. "I had written a novel called *It's Tough to Be Famous,* and I don't believe that anybody but my mother and the Warner Brothers read it. They bought the book and I asked if I could come to Hollywood and work on the script. They had a policy then that didn't allow writers to work on their own material. Two weeks later they called me out to work on another project.

"In those days, the writers were scattered all over the lot. Then they built the Writers' Building. As soon as we all got settled in, some workmen came and started digging a trench all around the building. I watched them and thought, 'Oh my God, he's going to blow us all up. All together!'

"My first writing assignment was ten weeks on a picture for Kay Francis. It was called *Street of Women*. Darryl Zanuck was in charge of the production. My job was the dialogue. He had two other writers on the project doing the continuity. He gave me a copy of the novel and I read it and thought it was terrible. I knew that I wasn't supposed to do anything but the dialogue, yet I couldn't help thinking about an opening for the film. The story concerned a man and his mistress, Kay Francis, and the man's dog of a wife.

"My idea for the opening was to show the man coming home through New York traffic and to then show the woman eagerly waiting for him at home. He comes in and it's, 'Hi, darling, how was your day?' and the woman fixes him a martini. Suddenly the maid comes in and says to the woman, 'Mr. So-and-So is on the telephone,' and the woman gets hysterical and tells the maid to tell him she isn't at home. Then the man gets up and says, 'I guess I'd better be going.' You then know that the woman, Kay Francis, is not the man's wife.

"I outlined this to Mr. Zanuck and he sent it back with the comment 'It's sensational!' He instructed me to go back to my office and write it. He told me to write it as if it were a novel, to not worry about script form. I wrote. I sent him pages. He would send them back with 'It's sensational!' Then the director of the film, Archie Mayo, came in and said, 'I got a sensational idea for the opening. We fade in on a bed and the bed is mounted on steps and Kay Francis is lying on the bed and we get Wardrobe to make her a sensational-looking negligee that clings to her and sitting on the steps is this man and he is looking up at her as though she is the most wonderful thing in the world.'

"Well, since Archie was the director of the film, I started to work on his idea, on the bed idea. Archie complained that I wasn't getting a very spiritual quality into this particular scene and I explained to him that it was rather difficult to get spirituality into the bed. Now, Mr. Zanuck—who only had one thing to say before, 'It's sensational!'—gets involved in the script. He called us into his office and he said, 'You know what the trouble is with this script? It's lousy, I will construct! We fade in on the structural steelwork of a skyscraper!' And that's how the film started.

"I had one other problem with my first film job. I wasn't a very ardent fan of Miss Francis, and I didn't know that she had a speech impediment and couldn't pronounce words with 'r's' in them. Every character in my script had an 'r' in their name. The grand climax came when she rang for her secretary, Sarah, and said, 'Sawah, I want to have my bwotha's woom wedecowated.'"

On the other side of the trench, inside the Writers' Building, at home or in their sleep, the writers worked out the rules of a new trade, screenwriting. Novelists learned how to write dialogue for actors instead of linotypes, even to write lines for wooden hams and busty starlets that were so lucid and convincing that they were "actor proof." Magazine writers learned how to string out an idea dramatically rather than state it openly and then defend it. The reporters found out they had to know not only what happened, but why it happened, and the pulp writers had found a home that finally paid them what they were sure they were worth. All they had to do was make their old stories longer. The smash, crunch and four-letter-word vernacular with which they had made their two-cents-a-word living was still good; and the rules for writing were the same, at least at Warner Bros.: "When in doubt, have someone enter the room with a gun in his hand."

Robert Lord, who wrote *Manhattan Parade, Fireman Save My Child, It's Tough to Be Famous, The Purchase Price, One Way Passage, You Said a Mouthful* and doctored five other films in 1932, reduced the rules of writing at Warner Bros. to one, "Don't bore the audience, anything goes as long as it's entertaining and interesting."

Lord came from the "bending over the washboard" school of writing. He didn't mind the sixteen-hour day, seven days a week. Even when he left the studio, he would follow the same schedule. The rest of his writing rules came from his knowledge and expertise in boxing: "Set the audience up to expect your right and give them a left." Lord definitely "fit."

The writers that didn't fit, however, began to ask themselves questions at the club and during lunch at the writers' table, aesthetic questions. The writers knew only too clearly they weren't wanted; but after careful consideration, they weren't even sure that they belonged, that film was a viable medium for a serious writer, that their thoughts and their dreams could ever actually get up there on the silver screen. Aesthetics, however, had to wait. The money was getting real good and the writers were settling in place, marrying attractive actresses, even having children. At least for the time, they needed the money as much as they needed to write, or at least thought so.

Even a few loners who would never fit into the business stayed around. When asked why they wrote screenplays instead of novels or plays, they would reply with a line of dialogue they had written often for one of the contract players, "I did it for the money." Few, however, believed them any more than the audience believed Humphrey Bogart. They were

hiding something and it made them even more suspect and peculiar.

Whatever the writers' private or public attitudes, at the studio there was no time to question them. Jack Warner wanted every book, idea, script and short story broken down into a "one-pager" for him to read. His grammar-school vocabulary could get him through that. If he liked it, it was turned into a "sixteen-pager." If he liked that, it was turned into a script which he would read; but he only read the dialogue. No one was sure, however, what Jack wanted; they only knew that it wasn't what they wanted.

Brynie Foy, the producer of the "B" films, also required a constant flow of scripts and rewrites of previous Warner Bros. films. *Tiger Shark*, a story of tuna fishers, became *King of the Lumberjacks,* which became *Bengal Tiger,* a circus story, then *Manpower,* a story of steeplejacks. Finally it became a story about pearl divers. Foy once stole a story idea from Metro; when warned by a writer, he replied, "Don't worry, they stole it from Faith Baldwin."

The studio needed stories, words, and they paid for them. The writer's contract was for twenty-six weeks in the early thirties; later it was for fifty-two weeks with twelve or six weeks vacation. Through hiring and firing, Jack kept the average salary around $650. But the name writers, Casey Robinson, Earl Baldwin and Norman Reilly Raine, received anywhere from $1,000 a week to $1,750. And Seton I. Miller could manage a contract that went from $1,250 to $1,750 in two years, without options. The bottom end was $75 or $100 (Carlton Sand and Ivan Goff) but the top figure was always in sight. You ate at the same lunch table as the high-priced writers, spoke the same language and you were sure you would make it . . . and Goff would (with *White Heat* and *Come Fill the Cup).* Few of the writers, however, could handle all that money once it came.

John Bright remembers, "I reacted like so many others. I got a big house in Westwood, right around the corner from Jimmie Stewart. I had a champion sheep dog and three cars. I remember one of them was a Packard Phaeton, with those chrome cowels on the sides. I had a chauffeur and every time I drove past one of those one-legged men selling apples, I felt terrible."

Despite the drawbacks and the money, the opportunities to one day be a "real writer" stayed a solid attraction; in New

York the writers kept getting on the Broadway, transferring to the Super Chief in Chicago and getting off in Los Angeles, each one brimming over with whatever it was he or she had to say.

"I remember when I came to Warner Bros.," recalls Allen Rivkin. "Zanuck made films out of the headlines. He had just started the gangster cycle. He'd read a headline on Friday, think about it over the weekend, get the story set in his head and call all the writers into his office on Monday morning. He'd say, 'Okay, boys, here's the story, it'll have Jimmy Cagney in it. We'll start shooting four weeks from this morning and we'll open at the Warner's downtown eight weeks from today.'"

The thirties were a time of block-booking. The films were sold far in advance of their actual production, at sales meetings with exhibitors and theater managers. If an exhibitor wanted to show a Cagney film, he had to agree to show all the other films that the studio wanted him to exhibit. That was the deal. Jack Warner, however, "found out you couldn't take bets on public taste" many years earlier and he wouldn't say what he wanted or liked until he read it.

Outlines were continually written for Cagney, Muni, Davis, Robinson, Blondell, Stanwyck and others. There were always fifty to sixty scripts at work and the writers had two good reasons to make them good scripts. If the front office liked it, they would put a star in it; and they'd pick up your option, which insured an increase in salary. It was the ultimate power of the studio held over the writer and it tamed many of them, but not all.

"Mavericks are the exception now," Bright recalls. "They were more common then. Dalton Trumbo was a reader at Warner's when I started, two years older than I, twenty-four. They wouldn't let him become a writer so he wrote sardonic reviews of books like *Lady Chatterly's Lover,* books that couldn't possibly be considered, and submitted them as if they were material for films. And got fired."

To even come close to their dreams on the screen, the writers had to find a way to select the right director and performer for their material. They were obliged to act like mavericks and, like Bright and Glasmon, found it necessary to step into studio politics, an arena populated by street fighters, body peddlers and a twenty-eight-year-old tyrant.

Bright recalls that Zanuck had a great story mind. When they discussed *Public Enemy* he pointed out quickly that *Blood and*

Beer had five stories in it and they could only tell one. They settled on the story of Tom Powers and Matt Doyle, but "when the casting question came up, Zanuck said the lead was going to be played by an actor named Eddie Woods who had just turned in a fantastic performance in a picture called *Mother's Cry*. He asked us to see it and we were impressed by Woods' excellent performance; but Woods was absolutely wrong for our picture. He played a stool pigeon, a cowardly, sniveling, informer. Our character was a swashbuckling, hard-fisted guy, a hoodlum who had come up from the Irish ghetto to the top. He had an income of ten thousand dollars a week or more. Notches on his gun. Been shot at many times. So we were just sick with dismay. We talked with Woods and of course every actor thinks he can play any part. It's part of their childlikeness and sometimes the secret of their success. And they believe it. Others are more skeptical.

"In any event, Jimmy Cagney was to play the lesser part. Up to then he had only played small parts, but in one picture, *Sinner's Holiday,* the screen burst into flames when he came on. When I saw him I said, 'Holy Christ! This guy is good. He should play Tom Powers.'

"Zanuck, we knew by this time, was a terribly imperious man. A man of considerable talent, a man of many abilities, but at that time very weak in the casting department. He just simply couldn't cast things correctly. He learned subsequently how to do it. He was good at editing a script and very creative; for that I gave him a great deal of respect. But his personality was imperious. He was Hollywood's Napoleon.

"We had, however, seen just enough of Zanuck to know he couldn't be disagreed with. If he picked Eddie Woods, it was going to be Eddie Woods. So we thought we were going to make our debut with a bomb. And to have a good story victimized by bad casting is just heartbreaking. So, we ventured into our first studio politics. We were novices at it, but it worked.

"The first step was to get a shift away from the director. Archie Mayo was scheduled to direct because of his success with crime melodramas. He was unhappy about the assignment because he didn't want to be typed as that kind of director; but he didn't have the guts to tell Zanuck. Hardly anybody did.

"So, we had a few subversive, covert talks with Bill Wellman, who rode a motorcycle and was called 'Wild Bill,' He had been fired by Paramount for goosing a girl. She bolted into a twenty-five-thousand-dollar Mitchell camera and smashed it to the floor just as some bankers were walking on the set to inspect the studio for refinancing. Zukor wasn't at all pleased.

"Wellman hadn't worked for a couple of years because of that, but he was a friend of Zanuck's. Wellman fascinated him because he was a big game hunter, because he had so much 'macho.' Zanuck was looking for an assignment to give Wellman, who at that time was sitting around Warner Bros. reading scripts and throwing them in the toilet. Wellman asked us if he could read *Public Enemy* and we gave him the script and told him Mayo was scheduled to direct, 'but personally we felt it was his kind of thing.' He read it and agreed. So, we left it in his hands.

"Wellman exploited his friendship, got the picture and Mayo was relieved. Then we took Cagney to see Wellman and suggested he play the lead, 'but we're new here, we're nobodies, how the hell can the switch in casting be made?' Wellman said, 'Leave that to me.' So, we got an executive summons, the same day, and Zanuck said, and I found this to be typical of all Hollywood, Zanuck said, 'I just got a great idea. I'm changing the casting from Woods playing Tom Powers to Jimmy Cagney playing Powers.' He didn't give Wellman credit and Wellman didn't give us credit. But that was all right. It wasn't all right, however, for Zanuck not to credit Wellman. But he gave credit to nobody."

Jack Warner was not averse to the kind of politics Bright practiced. If a writer, director or actor could get things done, then Jack could use him. That kind of drive was needed in his plant, and the writers who were good politicians like Bright or Lord became supervisors. It was a pattern other writers would follow.

Lord's political position as the supervisor of a production as well as writer gave him the creative strength to get *Black Legion* on the screen just as it was written, and with a promising second-string actor, Humphrey Bogart, in the lead. The year was 1936. Lord took his story from the newspaper accounts of the killing of Charles Poole by a Detroit fascist organization. The *New York Times* called it "editorial cinema at its best." Further praise came in a lawsuit brought by the Ku Klux Klan against Warner Bros. Warners won on a technicality.

In those early days other screenwriters strong on editorial

Facing, left. Claude Rains, Vincent Sherman and "Brynie" Foy
go over script for a "B" film
Facing, right. Young John Huston and Henry Blanke working
on the script for Juarez, 1939

cinema weren't as lucky as Lord. The censors carefully read each script prior to its production, particularly those criticizing politicians, industry and America.

James Wingate, head of the New York Board of Film Censors, had a stifling effect on more than a few screenplays. In 1933, in regard to *Heroes for Sale* (the story of a worker who tries to stop a labor riot and is consequently jailed five years for rioting), Wingate wrote Jack Warner, "We suggest that wherever you can you trim the scenes in which the police are shown as overly officious and unfair in carrying out their duties." The script was altered to comply with Wingate's wish. *Wild Boys of the Road* was changed for similar reasons.

Happy endings replaced sad and the inside of a female thigh was never to be shown. Justice must prevail and sin be condemned. Excessive alcohol was not allowed and even the hack writers knew that wasn't honest. The Writers' Building was miserable, but their problems continued.

In 1935 Hal Wallis wrote Joe Breen, the censor for the Will Hays office of the Motion Picture Producers' Association, that Warner Bros. was proceeding to film *Black Fury*. There had already been much correspondence regarding the controversial coal mining film. Breen replied immediately: "With a view to protecting ourselves against any valid criticism on the part of the organized forces of the bituminous coal industry, we respectfully suggest that in scene 61 on pages 26 and 27 you might insert a line spoken by Mike, to the effect that while the miners may not have ideal working conditions, nevertheless working conditions of the coal industry have vastly improved and are getting better all the time." Breen went on to make it clear that the film should show that the miners have little to complain about. Writers Carl Erickson and Abe Finkel somehow overcame their desire for social reform, put Breen's words into usable dialogue and the film was produced. Editorial cinema!

John Huston went to work as a screenwriter on May 23, 1938. "I don't remember the writers being particularly unhappy at the time, or of wanting to do something besides what they were doing. They were writing and being paid. I was hired for three hundred and fifty or five hundred dollars a week. I can't remember. (It was seven hundred and fifty dollars.) That was good money in those times, but there were writers making fifteen hundred, two thousand dollars a week—maybe more." Huston, however, would change professions in three years' time. There was something else he wanted.

Robert Buckner was one of the writers who appeared content. "I have nothing but praise for Bob," recalls Lord. "He came from a very old, distinguished Virginia family, six-feet-one or six-two, a handsome guy. We became good friends." Was Buckner ashamed of the scripts he wrote, *Dodge City, Santa Fe Trail, Yankee Doodle Dandy,* and *They Died with Their Boots On?* "Never." Buckner also became a supervisor/ producer.

Seton I. Miller (*The Adventures of Robin Hood, The Sea Hawk, The Dawn Patrol*) didn't complain. He also became a supervisor/producer.

Lord recalls, "Nobody was manacled, nobody put a gun to anybody's head. You could leave anytime you wanted to. And we were immensely compensated. All of us were immensely lucky." Lord stayed, put in his hours and kept trying.

Even those writers, however, who got along with Jack Warner fought with him daily, all except one. Jack called him friend—the incorrigible, irreverent Wilson Mizner. He entertained the entire studio.

When Mizner arrived at Warner Bros., they put him to work with Lord. "Somebody got the idea of teaming us up. I was the craftsman, he supplied ideas and dialogue. We worked together a year and became immense friends. He had developed a huge pot belly that made him look pregnant, wore an old brown hat both indoors and out because he was bald and used it as an ashtray. He never wrote, of course; we'd talk; then he'd go to sleep and I'd write."

Mizner was a slim, handsome six feet three inches when he started his wanderings, and a "crook, thief with the most tremendous sense of humor," recalls Lord, "and a real promoter. He came from a real pioneer family, they came with the gold rush and settled across the bay from San Francisco near the Benicia Naval Arsenal. They bought land and became very wealthy. Wilson always had money.

"He had two sisters and two brothers, Addison, who was the oldest, became a famous architect and an immense land promotor, and John, who became an Episcopal bishop and was called the black sheep of the family.

"When Wilson first left home he went to Alaska for gold. He loved thieves and whores, a real bum. He told me he and another guy owned a dance hall and whorehouse in Nome. After that he returned to San Francisco, became a pimp and

had four to six girls working for him. The pimps would meet at 1 A.M. in this restaurant, play Panguini, eat submarine sandwiches and drink steins of beer as the girls came in to pay off. He used to say, 'That was our cocktail hour.'

"Then he married a wealthy San Francisco woman and her family paid him to leave her—he was a terrific womanizer. He then went to Chicago, married a Stokes, a wealthy family, and her family did the same. Then he went to New York and became attracted to Broadway. He wrote *Alias Jimmy Valentine* with a collaborator and it was a phenomenon, it cleaned up, he and his partner split twenty-five thousand dollars a week. They then wrote *Deep Purple*, it was 'only' half the success and they split twelve thousand dollars a week on it. He was rolling in money.

"After that he went to London and became an odd eccentric in high society—a freak—immensely profane, rich and good-looking. They loved him. But he got involved in a scandal about building the London subway and was given twenty-four hours to get out of England. Then he came to Hollywood, met Zanuck, who was also a swinging guy, had nothing to do so became a motion picture writer."

Warner's attraction to Mizner was basic—he made him laugh. "We were writing *Too Hot to Handle*. He wasn't feeling well so he stayed home. He lived at the Ambassador. We worked there. I'd type and he'd sleep. But he got this telegram that Addison was dying. Well, Wilson wasn't much for that kind of thing, he didn't want to go down to Florida, couldn't, didn't know what to do and then decided to send a telegram. And did. 'Dear Addison, stop dying, Bob and I are trying to write a comedy. Love, Bill.'"

Mizner found everything funny, even his own death. In March of 1933 he had a heart attack at the Warner studio and after recovering was asked if he wanted a priest. He replied, "I want a priest, a rabbi and a Protestant clergyman. I want to hedge my bets."

Told his death was only a few hours away, he sent a postcard to a friend: "They're going to bury me at 9 A.M, don't be a sucker and get up."

Coming out of a coma, he saw his brother in his Episcopal robes standing over him, smiled and said, "Why should I talk to you, I've just been talking to your boss." Then he died.

Robert Lord heard the story another way, but, "What does it matter, it's better, it's all legend now anyway."

The writers needed ways to amuse themselves and self-irony was essential in the Writers' Building even if it wasn't allowed in the scripts. You were required to write twenty to thirty pages a day and the studio made it clear that the subject matter would be their choice. Lists of topics were published; Action, Africa (including Foreign Legion), Biography, Costume, Gangster, Industrial Drama, Mystery, Negro Cast, Political (including crooked politics), Prison, Public Service (including FBI—Civil Service—G-Men—Police—Secret Service), War, Western and many others. Jack's affection for President Roosevelt's New Deal was also to appear in each film. The writers, however, found ways to survive.

They drove secondhand cars and new cars, Plymouths and Packards. They lived in Bel Air and Beverly Hills, Toluca Lake and Westwood, at the Hollywood Hotel, in the Wilshire District, in Malibu, and at the Garden of Allah, where the liquor, humor and women were constant. They worked six days a week at the Warner studios in Burbank, but even there they found their way around the factory rules.

Jim Webb (*Montana, Charge at Feather River, South of St. Louis*) recalls, "We were not encouraged to leave the lot at any time. I remember one day leaving the lot for about a half hour. That same afternoon, my producer received a note from Jack Warner. It said, 'Your writer Webb was off the lot from 3:15 to 3:45 this afternoon. See that it doesn't happen again.'"

The writers were to be available even during lunch or coffee breaks. Part of Blayney Mathews' job as chief of security and protection was to keep surveillance on the writers, and he did. Hiding on the roof of the main reception building, he could see the writers escaping to the drugstore across the street for coffee. "He was an ugly man, a plainclothes, political investigating cop," recalls one writer. "The first thing he did when he started at the studio was to have everyone fill out a personal form stating their race, religion, jail record, everything." The writers balked, so did others, but Blayney always knew where the writers were.

Normally lunch was in the Greenroom and the writers made their table "the table." They were the high-flying intellectuals with the grand ideas about saving the world, about art and about what was good and bad in the movies. To the young actresses the men and women who sat at the table were both attractive and threatening. On occasion, however, a writer would condescend to talk to one of the young lovelies who

simply made pretty pictures and populated the cardboard castles; he might even have her for lunch. They made many an actress feel ashamed about the films she was making, but most of the writers married one, some several; Casey Robinson married Audrey Dale and ballerina Tamara Toumanova; Seton I. Miller stage actress Ann Evers, Mark Hellinger the Ziegfeld girl, Gladys Glad.

"We had the best writers' table in town," recalls Allen Rivkin. "We'd allow certain actors and directors to eat with us if they met our standards. Minnelli. Dieterle."

Mary McCall was included at "the table" and recalls being the only woman on the lot; but the writers were a good bunch. "I don't recall ever suffering for it."

Jack Warner made his presence felt despite the writers' best efforts to avoid him; some writers, however, never saw him. "I remember one occasion," says Mary McCall. "The Motion Picture Permanent Charities were soliciting funds. There was a notice that went out to all of the writers to meet at four o'clock in the Greenroom. A great many writers had never met Mr. Warner. He came into the room and said, 'Now, boys and girls, you know why you're here and I've heard every goddamn crappy excuse why you aren't going to give and I'm tired of them. You're going to give and you're going to give plenty and you're going to give fast and get out of here.' I remember thinking that there was not one of us there who didn't want to say no, but on second thought it was a good cause and it shouldn't suffer because our employer was a boor. We signed our pledges and as we were leaving, one of the writers kept bumping into hedges and muttering, 'What manner of man is that?' He couldn't quite believe it."

Other writers knew the vice-president in charge of production only too well—and how to handle him. When Jack Warner decided that too many outgoing calls were being made from the Writers' Building, he stopped them and allowed only incoming calls. You had to go off the lot to place a call. One day one of the writers' wives was having a baby and every time he wanted to call he'd have to go across the street to the drugstore. John Bright decided it was time to fight back.

He organized the writers, all thirty-five of them, and took them to a pay phone on the distant edge of the back lot. It was a Monday morning and Bill Koenig, Zanuck and Jack Warner were paying their scheduled visit to find reusable sets. When they turned a corner, there was the entire staff lined up

Left. Robert Buckner, Delmer Daves before he became a director, Seton I. Miller, Peter Milne
Below. Robert Lord, John Bright, Wilson Mizner and Kubec Glasmon at the Burbank studios in 1931

in front of the telephone booth waiting to place an outside call. John Bright recalls, "I got the position of honor, I was in the booth. Koenig did nothing but Zanuck laughed and Warner hit the sky." The outside call privilege was returned to the Writers' Building.

Katherine Tourney (*A Stolen Life, My Reputation, The Man I Love*) remembers another method of escape. "I believe it was John Collier who started the afternoon tea break. He was English and every afternoon about three or so, we would all break for tea. Then somebody got the idea to lace the tea with a little rum. Soon there was more rum in the tea than tea. I remember we got a letter from the front office to 'cool' it with our tea breaks."

On weekends John Bright recalls going to the Gower Gulch Saloon, which was near the Columbia Pictures lot at Gower and Sunset. Every Saturday night there was a brawl. The stunt men lived near there and "they knew how to have a good time."

On occasion the writers used their work itself to comment on their boss. Norman Reilly Raine, Heinz Herald and Geza Herczeg, using Larue for Warner, paraphrased the writers' dilemma in *The Life of Emile Zola*.

LARUE: Why do you have to write such muckraking stuff when there are so many pleasant things in life?
ZOLA: And so many unpleasant things.
LARUE: That's not your business while you're working for me. From now on you will attend strictly to your work and stop writing trash.

Many of the writers, however, were convinced that what Warner wanted was trash and that they were writing it. They felt they were working for money not art, and they were usually right. It had to hurt. Most had come to Hollywood for the chance to show the world what that world was really like. Their sharp, cynical, rebellious minds had left the romantics, the Lake Poets, the legends and the novelists who wrote of silver stallions, chaste queens and the nobility of the British soldier in Mandalay back with their childhood. They were sick of happy endings, of heros with perfect bodies and transparent souls. The writers were sick of dreams and they determined that the world would no longer hide within them. They wanted to make the world face its own ugliness, face its social injustices, its prejudices, its sweatshops, its murder and they wanted to do it honestly, brilliantly and preferably with four-letter words, the language of the streets.

They couldn't do it without Hal Wallis' and Jack Warner's okay, but they believed they deserved it, believed that approval was their right. Few, however, got it.

As the thirties neared the forties many had become more than competent craftsmen. They had a hundred ways to get the exposition out fast, without the audience noticing. They knew how to set the goals of each character, shape a scene and open the conflict. They knew the difference between the line of action and the inner action. And they knew the basic rule, never bore the audience.

The writers were good at their work; they wanted to show what they could really do, and they wanted to do it with Jack Warner's money.

Some wanted to explore man's criminal nature, the animal within all of us and do it without preaching; they wanted to do it with honesty and with enough courage to examine themselves, their reality, their own animal natures.

What the female writers wanted to say no man understood. Perhaps it was too old, too ancient, too true.

A few writers wanted privately to build cardboard castles. They knew only too well that the world was ugly, that they were merely animals driven by their glands and that it was better to build dreams, to build characters and worlds that would compel the world's imitation. They believed in the old-fashioned romantics and like the modern romantic, James Branch Cabell, believed that "Man could play the ape to his dreams."

One or two writers simply wanted to get into the middle of a script, get into that second act and meet its chaos head on, without any preconceived idea of how the story would end. It's a chancy way of writing, dangerous for the writer since he may find out things about himself he doesn't want to know; but for the writer it is the ultimate adventure. Most aren't up to it. They simply sweep by with colorful action or sit staring at the blank white sheet in the Underwood and reach for the Jack Daniels.

To Jack Warner what the writers wanted was downright dangerous politics, dull philosophy that had nothing to do with show business, stories for faggots in lavender suits and pure foolishness. You don't wing a script, you type it. To Jack a

second act had nothing to do with what a writer believed, dreamed of or with what he was willing to fight for. A second act was simply something a writer had to rewrite because he wasn't good enough the first time. Something Jack had to pay for twice.

That difficult second act was the part of a story no studio boss wanted to hear about and if it ever got on the screen, they were certain it would ruin the business. The writers, however, learned slowly.

When the thirties ended and war came, most of the writers left for the Army Signal Corps or active duty. Some went to Washington, their stories still untold. From 1930 to 1940 Warners had purchased the rights to 1,518 stories. Less than five hundred were originals and of that number, 30 to 40 percent were rewrites. But a total of 602 films had been made.

When the writers left for war, new writers came to the Warner lot. "I don't know quite how to explain it," says Jim Webb. "All the writers that came to Warner's while we were away, all of them disappeared as soon as we came back. It wasn't that they weren't good writers. They were. They just left."

"I don't believe I would have gotten a contract to write at Warner's if it hadn't been for the war," comments Katherine Tourney. "I don't believe that Warner's liked women. It always struck me as a man's studio. Jack Warner seemed to me to be a shy man, particularly among writers, especially female writers. I was there from 1943 until 1948."

The war years were a golden time for the screenwriter. The studio drastically reduced production, from sixty-six films in 1937 to nineteen in 1944, but the public hunger for films was at its peak and good writers were at a premium. "If a screenwriter was sharp," recalls Stephen Longstreet (*The Gay Sisters, Stallion Road, The First Traveling Saleslady, Untamed Youth*), "he could be working on three or four scripts for three or four different studios at the same time."

The living was easy. "Eager beaver writers were discouraged," says Longstreet. "It was understood that no writer should turn in more than ten pages a day. You shouldn't rock the boat. It was a sausage factory and it was grinding out Westerns and melodramas and musicals. We still had the best writers' table in town: writers and novelists like Christopher Isherwood, W. R. Burnett (*Little Caesar, High Sierra*), John Huston (*The Amazing Dr. Clitterhouse, Jezebel, High Sierra*), Richard Brooks (*Cobra Woman, Deadline U.S.A., Battle Circus*), and Somerset

Maugham (*Of Human Bondage, The Letter*). We even had Thomas Mann's brother, Heinrich for a while. I brought William Faulkner (*To Have and Have Not, The Big Sleep, Land of the Pharoahs*) to Warner's to work with me on *Stallion Road.* He was broke and he hadn't won the Nobel yet. He needed the money so he could return home and write his novels. Everybody knew that Hollywood was not the place to come to make your reputation as a writer. Hollywood never produced an O'Casey or an O'Neill. The serious writers came here, did their job, took their money and ran."

William Faulkner had his own ways of dealing with Warner Bros. He worked closely with director Howard Hawks, who did not delude him into thinking his soul would appear on the screen the way it did on the pages of his novels. Instead, both took advantage of the pleasures film making had to offer; they went to Egypt for several months to try and figure out just how an ancient Egyptian should sound speaking the English language. They finally gave up, resorted to the traditional King's English dialect for *Land of the Pharoahs* and saw everything to be seen in Egypt, at Jack Warner's expense. When working on the Burbank lot, Faulkner even got permission to go home and write. When Jack Warner called him he discovered that Faulkner had gone all the way home to Mississippi. Warner would never make that mistake again.

Longstreet recalls why Warner wanted the writers where he could watch them. "They didn't trust us. They needed us. They needed us to sew the dialogue into the action, because basically that was what movies were—action. We had no real power. No writer ever stopped a scene to tell the director it was being done wrong. The studio always put three or four writers on the same project. You didn't know that. You'd be off doing your version and they'd be off doing theirs. Credit stealing was going on all over the place. It was easy to steal a credit from a writer—particularly if you were a smart producer. You would have the writer do all the work and then you would add a few lines to his and convince the head office that you wrote most of the script. It was before the time of a strong writers' union—we had no real arbitration."

The dreams died daily. "We were there to mend story lines, to fix construction. We were not there to write great scripts. I remember writing a Western and watching the director rip the pages out of the script. 'Okay,' he said, 'we just got the chickenshit out of the way. Let's burn down the wagon train.'

Our job was to stand by with a bucket and a broom and a shovel and clean up the elephant crap.

"The only writer the studio could trust was the fellow who had a mortgage on his house and two wives to support."

The mistrust and misunderstanding had only increased. When Jim Webb returned from the army, he considered his position as a screenwriter in a town that needed screenwriters. He decided to free-lance. "I was working at Warner's at the time and when I refused to sign a contract, Jack Warner told my agent that he would fire me. I signed the contract.

"The studio liked to control you. They controlled you through their long-term contracts, through the options. Options were always coming up. As a writer under contract, you would always try to be in the middle of a script when your option was coming up. That was one way of assuring yourself that they would pick it up. Of course, you couldn't always manage to be in the middle of a picture. Then you would lose your option or get fired. The reason for this was to clear the lot of writers who were not currently working. It was not considered unusual to be fired from Warner's on Friday and rehired on the following Monday."

During this period Jack had a tennis court built behind the main reception building. One day, Julius and Philip Epstein walked on the court, played a set of tennis and were fired by five o'clock.

The trench that had been dug around the Writers' Building in the late thirties was filled and replaced with a fence in the forties. The fence had a gate and it was locked up tight. Jim Webb remembers the gate. "To show you how they felt about writers, they wouldn't allow us to park on the lot right next to the Writers' Building. We had to park at the lot across the street. Since the gate was locked, there was only one way to enter and leave the building. The way was by a long cement path on the side of the Administration Building. You had to then go through another gate behind the back lot and then over to the lot where you parked. The only person who had a key to that gate was Jack Warner. I would watch him with his entourage every lunchtime—opening the gate that surrounded our building on his way to his private dining room. It was rumored that the reason the gate was locked was because a writer had once tried to steal a typewriter. The gate remained locked for a good ten years.

"They didn't trust us. We had to clock in and out. We

reported promptly at nine-thirty and left at five-thirty. I remember one writer always took a nap at four in the afternoon and he would never wake up before seven at night. I'm sure Jack Warner really considered that fellow a loyal employee." Of course, writers still had to work on Saturdays. "It was an unwritten law between the writers that we would not do any writing on those Saturdays. We played cards and made up word games. We had a good time.

"You would see Jack Warner if one of your films was being previewed. He would pick you up in his limousine and crack jokes on the way to the preview. If the preview wasn't too good, there wouldn't be too many jokes on the way back home."

With the end of the war, production picked up slightly and in 1949 the studio produced twenty-nine films. But the century was now moving faster than Warner Bros.

Stephen Longstreet sighs as he remembers the change. "Suddenly the pressure was on. You were expected to turn out more pages. The studio was nervous about television. More and more independent film companies were sprouting up on the lot. It wasn't fun any more." But the conflict between what the writer wanted to say and what Jack Warner would pay him to type still existed.

While Raymond Chandler was in Hollywood he spent some careful words trying to figure out just what was wrong between the writer and the motion picture, why the marriage always ended in bitter divorce. "Insofar as the writing of the screenplay is concerned, however, the producer is the boss; the writer either gets along with him and his ideas (if he has any) or gets out. This means both personal and artistic subordination, and no writer of quality will long accept either without surrendering that which made him a writer of quality, without dulling the fine edge of his mind, without becoming little by little a conniver rather than a creator, a supple and facile journeyman rather than a craftsman of original thought."

Chandler's words are not the kind Jack Warner would have understood, even read, just more seeds for misunderstanding. By the end of the forties, most of the writers didn't want to hear them either, but for a different reason. They understood them only too well.

Chandler had his own problems. Warner Bros. bought his novel *The Big Sleep* and made it into a film in 1946. The central character, a detective named Philip Marlowe, had been carefully built by Chandler, word by word, in a series of

novelettes, and in seven novels. Chandler knew his detective: "In everything that can be called art there is a quality of redemption . . . down these mean streets a man must go who is not himself mean . . . a man of honour, by instinct, by inevitability . . . he might seduce a duchess and I am quite sure he would not spoil a virgin; if he's a man of honour in one thing, he is that in all things . . ."

In the darkness at the picture show, however, Philip Marlowe no longer belonged to Raymond Chandler. Fellow novelist William Faulkner and pulp writer Leigh Brackett had worked like journeymen on the screenplay. Philip Marlowe now belonged to director Howard Hawks, to Bogart, to Warner Bros. To the movies.

Howard Koch recalls in his book on *Casablanca* that he wanted the film to be about politics in North Africa, but that director Michael Curtiz kept emphasizing the love angle. The director, of course, got his way.

If, after the attack of the censors, Jack Warner, the directors, the performers and old age, a writer still held onto his dreams, he had two choices: he could become either a supervisor/producer or a director. Some did and submitted to that awkward Hollywood compliment, "You're too good to only be a writer."

Most didn't, however, and other writers continued to arrive: screenwriters on the Super Chief. Most would never learn; they were blinded by the picture show and they could already see their names up there on the silver screen, above the title.

Across the lot from the Writers' Building, the musicians had their offices in the Main Administration Building. There were no trenches, no fences, but the factory rules were the same. Nine to five officially, to ten or midnight unofficially, and six days a week. But in 1931 when lyricist Al Dubin arrived from New York to write the lyrics for the musical *42nd Street* and was told to come in by 9 A.M., he promptly left for San Francisco, which smelt, tasted and sounded a lot more like the New York he loved, and disappeared.

Below. James Cagney and Pat O'Brien in the final scene from
Angels with Dirty Faces, *1938*
Top. Paul Muni in I Am a Fugitive from a Chain Gang, *1932*
Bottom. Eleanor Parker in Caged, *1950*

Top. Edward G. Robinson and Lauren Bacall in
Key Largo, *1948*
Center. James Cagney and George Raft in Each Dawn I
Die, *1939*
Bottom. Humphrey Bogart and James Cagney in Angels with
Dirty Faces, *1938*
*Facing. Lauren Bacall, Humphrey Bogart, Marcel Dalio, George
Suzanne, Walter Szurovy (in bed) and Dolores Moran (on the
floor) in* To Have and Have Not, *1945*

Left. John Garfield in Out of the Fog, *1941*
Center. Street scene from The Sea Wolf, *1941*
Right. Gene Nelson and Sterling Hayden in Crime Wave, *1954*

Below. Edward G. Robinson as Caesar Enrico Bandello in the flophouse scene near the end of Little Caesar, *1931*
Facing, top. Edward G. Robinson and Douglas Fairbanks, Jr., in Little Caesar, *1931*
Facing, center. Street scene from G-Men, *1935*
Facing, bottom. James Cagney and Margaret Lindsay in G-Men, *1935*
Facing, right. Ricardo Cortez and Bebe Daniels in the 1931 version of The Maltese Falcon

Below. "Miss Wonderly, this is Mr. Archer, my partner."
Humphrey Bogart as Sam Spade, Mary Astor as Brigid
O'Shaughnessy alias Miss Wonderly and Jerome Cowan as
Miles Archer in the 1941 version of The Maltese Falcon
Facing, top left. ". . . not an insignificant live bird but a glorious
golden falcon encrusted from head to foot with the finest jewels
in their coffers." Humphrey Bogart and Lee Patrick in publicity
photo for The Maltese Falcon, 1941
Facing, bottom left. "I'm not heroic. I don't think there is
anything worse than death." Barton MacLane, Peter Lorre
and Ward Bond in The Maltese Falcon, 1941
Facing, top right. "We've got it, Angel! We've got it!" Walter
Huston as the dead Captain Jacoby, an uncredited part he
did in his son's first film as director, The Maltese Falcon, 1941
Facing, bottom right. "Be kind to me, Sam." Gladys George
as Iva Archer and Humphrey Bogart in The Maltese
Falcon, 1941

THIRTY - TWO BARS
OF SCHMALTZ

Musicians

"Will you ask the piano player to come over here, please?"

The musicians were often as strangely made as the brass horns they blew, as odd as the clothes they wore. Or didn't wear. They used words like "jive," "hip," "bread," spoke in friendly terms about C sharp major and said, "I just come out of the ether," when they woke up. No reasonable person understood them. And after working hours they'd go to a little nightclub in "dark town" or on Sunset Boulevard and blow their heads off there, for themselves. For nothing! That wasn't at all natural, but Warner Bros. would find a way to live with them. One way or another the musicians were going to work in the factory.

Harry Warner loved fine symphonic music and he trusted that affection for good reasons. It had led him to invest heavily in brother Sam's experiment with sound, the experiment that had saved them, the movie business and consequently given the moving picture show what he wanted in the first place—beautiful music. Now, with sound films in full production at the start of the thirties, Harry wanted the best music men Warner Bros. could buy.

Jack, of course, was Leon Zuardo, a boy tenor at heart. If he had entered the film business with any professional expertise, it was musical. He wanted songs even he could sing.

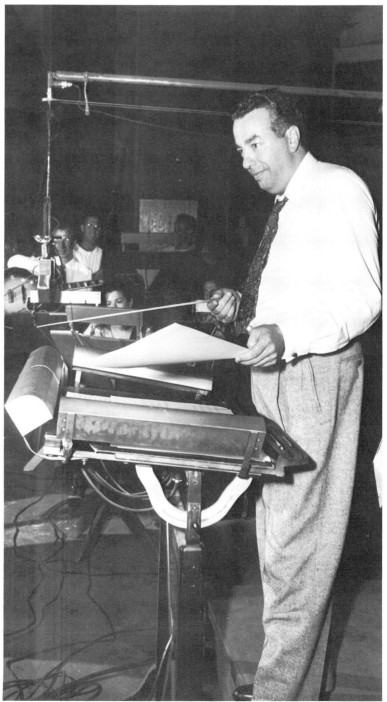

Harry's son, Louis, shared his father's love of music, and when the studio bought the music publishing firms of Remick, Harms and Witmark in 1929, Harry put him in charge. Buddy Norris, the son of the vice-president in charge of foreign exchanges, Sam Norris, was made his assistant. Some felt Harry bought them for Louis. His son was the heir apparent, the potential studio boss who would carry the family name into the century.

The control of their own music publishing, of course, also gave the company the rights to songs without having to make impossible deals with strangers. They also made additional profits. Particularly when a song became a "hit," an evergreen, and Harry wanted nothing less. He was determined to make even nepotism profitable, but he wasn't going to hire the workers. That was Jack's job. He was on the coast with the rest of the creative lunatics in the film business, the risk takers and loud showmen, and among them Jack should be able to find the employees they needed, guys who could play piano, fiddle, conduct and come up with thirty-two bars of *schmaltz* when they needed it for a love scene that didn't play or to make the audience feel sorry for a "four-bit" frail of an

Chapter opening. Lina Basquette
Overleaf. Gold Diggers of Broadway, *1929*
Facing, top. Leo Forbstein
Facing, bottom. Ray Heindorf
Left. Harry Warren

actress without a heart. And in 1929 Jack also needed some-one to help him put together all those musical productions with the Broadway stars Harry had hired: Ted White, Fanny Brice, Sophie Tucker, Marilyn Miller and Al Jolson.

The musicians should be easy to handle. They wouldn't have anything to do with creating the stories. They'd simply help fix them up after they were shot and edited, like Monday morning quarterbacks. Jack wouldn't have to read anything they wrote and he wouldn't even have to talk with them. He'd get a manager to do that. All the musicians had to do was work, perform, and Jack could listen and say yes or no, something he did best.

Jack didn't have to look far. The musicians were drifting in from most everywhere. Some wouldn't tell where they came from, others couldn't remember and more than a few weren't sure. They came on buses, on foot and on the Union Pacific. Train fare from New York was a hundred and sixty-six dollars, about four weeks work in a Bronx bar. They had heard that a "steady date" in a studio was "real fine" and they wanted to try it for size. They didn't care much what studio they worked for, it just didn't matter. They had worked in asphalt holes and the London Pavillion, but in each they provided the sounds, not the place. All they wanted were three things: enough money to get their horns out of hock, a place to tune up, play, sing, orchestrate, conduct or even compose and then to get rich doing it. Good booze, the company of other incredible music men and a "dark town" where the jazz was fine weren't things they wanted, they were necessities.

They would have liked it if their quirks went unnoticed, their different use of drugs, their clothes, loneliness, work habits, food and their women, but they didn't expect it. Most of them had gotten used to being looked at funny by the age of nine.

To the music man, both Hollywood and Warner Bros. appeared acceptable. Scale for members of the orchestra was five dollars per hour with a three-hour minimum. Evenings, Saturdays and Sundays were paid at regular rates and there was no premium overtime, but that didn't matter, "The aim was to be part of a contract," recalls Malcolm Beelby, Busby Berkeley's piano player. "I went to Warner Bros. in the summer of 1932 for *42nd Street* and got a guarantee of a hundred dollars a week for a thirty-three-hour week and overtime for the rest of the week at five dollars an hour. Your

checks went to three and four hundred dollars a week." Later the hourly rate would rise to ten dollars an hour. The movies were in fact a good "gig."

If there were any unseen, unlivable drawbacks in the motion picture business, they weren't obvious. The musicians would simply be doing what they had always done. And for the most part done well. Most had already given the audience music that made them sing. Beelby had been playing piano with Ray West's band at Miller's Lafayette Hotel, doing songs like "Idolizing," "Wistful and Blue." Others came from the Bryant rehearsal hall on New York's Sixth Avenue, from Healy's Saloon in Brooklyn, from the Vienna Opera House and from the Fanchon and Marco Ideas Vaudeville Revue. From pit orchestras, church choirs, high school orchestras and Tin Pan Alley. And more than a few came from movie theaters that no longer needed them because Warner Bros. had developed sound pictures. Horn players, song pluggers, lyricists and symphonic composers. Musicians already drugged on applause.

Leo Forbstein was a fiddle player. He arrived in 1928 from Grauman's Metropolitan Theater in Hollywood. Before that he had been in a Kansas City vaudeville house that ran pictures between stage shows. At Grauman's he was the musical director and he got the same job at Warner Bros. By 1933 he had formed the first studio orchestra, with eighteen musicians. The nucleus was six men hired from Jimmie Grier's dance band, which was a regular at the Coconut Grove.

The piano player with the Grier band was Ray Heindorf. He went to work for the studio in 1931, but kept playing piano nights at the Grove. "Nobody knew he was a genius then, but he had great fingers. Soft lightning," recalls Beelby. Talent, however, wasn't something that frightened Forbstein, it was something he admired, respected, wanted. By 1933 he usually gave the baton to Heindorf when something special was needed and was using his advice to pick additional music men. Before Heindorf, "the songwriters had to correct the musicians when they were wrong," recalls Harry Warren. Forbstein didn't have the ear for it, but he could handle the studio politics. Warren remembers Forbstein running up to Heindorf during a rehearsal and saying, "I'll take the baton for a few minutes; Jack Warner is on his way to the stage." Nobody was annoyed, the musicians knew their jobs at Warner Bros. were much more secure with Forbstein between them and the head of production.

They liked that security because they remembered only too well what it had been like on the bottom edge of show business in New York. "Most of the time," recalls Warren, "lunch for me was a glass of milk and two ginger snaps. On twenty dollars a week, what could you do? And I was married. I lived in one room with a wife and baby. I don't know how, but we did. We had a kitchen table and some plates. No piano, nothing. Who could afford a piano?"

At one point in the early twenties, Warren had considered becoming a movie director, "but there was more mystery in music," and he started to write songs and play piano. He worked at Healy's Saloon in Sheepshead Bay for a dollar fifty a night. "In those days if you knew a lot of Irish songs you could get work." He had also played drums with the Bean and Shippey one-ring circus, sang with a quartet at Vitagraph Studios in Brooklyn, was a candy boy in a theater, an usher, focus puller, finally got a job with Shapiro Bernstein Music Publishers as an "act man" and was hired to plug songs for shows and vaudeville acts in the theaters that lined Broadway from Forty- second Street to Fiftieth, the "New Tin Pan Alley." He played piano, plugged and then wrote.

His songs sold for ten cents at Woolworth's. "And they had beautiful title pages, of a lake with a moon glimmering on it, in color, stuff like that." After he wrote three Broadway shows, the dimes added up.

When Warner Bros. bought Remick, Harms and Witmark, Harry Warren was under contract to Remick and was part of the package, a both unexpected and expensive part at $500 a week.

Lyricist Al Dubin was part of the Harms package. He had already been collaborating with Warren with some success. Born in Zurich, Switzerland, on June 10, 1891, to nihilist Jewish parents who had been thrown out of Russia for their beliefs, he had been writing lyrics for songs and vaudeville acts since he was sixteen. An immense man, over three hundred and twenty pounds, with a larger appetite, Dubin had his own way of working and there was no way Jack Warner could have been ready for him, much less be expecting him.

Symphonic composer Erich Wolfgang Korngold arrived from the Vienna Opera House. Born of wealthy, cultured parents, he was a *cause célèbre* at thirteen and was taught, encouraged and promoted by Robert Fuchs, Gustav Mahler, Richard Strauss and Bruno Walter. By the age of nineteen he had written two

one-act operas, *The Ring of Polycrates* and *Violanta*. He arrived in 1934 to score the Max Reinhardt film production of *A Midsummer Night's Dream* for the studio, with more "class" than Jack Warner had ever seen before.

Maximilian Raoul Steiner, "Max," was born from the union of a theater manager and a chorus girl, on May 10, 1888. A precocious student, he finished a four-year course in one year at the Imperial Academy of Music in Vienna and was also coached and taught by Robert Fuchs and Gustav Mahler. He conducted his first operetta at twelve, *The Belle of New York*. He also wrote an opera, *Beautiful Greek Girl,* but his father refused to stage it.

"He didn't like it," Steiner recalls. "He thought it was lousy. So I went to his greatest competitor, who ran the Orphean Theater. He had been my father's stage manager years before and he liked it . . . and put it on and it ran a year. My father was such a big man and owned all the theaters and everything . . . and nobody thought I could do anything with such a famous father. So I packed up and went to England and started from the bottom playing piano at rehearsal. Almost starved to death."

He spent eight years in England, at the Adelphi, Hippodrome, the London Pavillion and the Blackpool Winter Garden. With World War I, he was interned as an enemy alien, but a fan, the Duke of Westminster, got him an exit visa to America. He arrived in New York with thirty-five dollars in his pocket.

"I played rehearsals in Bryant Hall on Sixth Avenue. It was a rehearsal hall. I got one dollar an hour or something and I used to sit on the steps waiting for some actor to come by, anybody who was rehearsing. And I said, 'You got a piano player?' Or the guy who rented out the hall would tell them if they asked for a piano player, 'There's one sitting right out there.' And that's how I met a dance team. They were famous in those days, Adam and Muse Hughes. They showed up one day and their player was sick and they didn't have anyone so I played for them and they said, 'Can you conduct?' And when I told them, they said, 'Oh, my God!' And I was in."

Steiner spent the next fifteen years on Broadway, then headed for Hollywood and became the head of the Music Department for RKO. After several loud fights with David O. Selznick—"He insulted me and I told him to go and shove

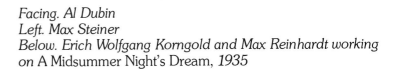

Facing. Al Dubin
Left. Max Steiner
Below. Erich Wolfgang Korngold and Max Reinhardt working
on A Midsummer Night's Dream, 1935

it and walked out"—and offers of fabulous sums from other
studios, he went to Warner Bros. At RKO he had scored,
among others, *Little Women, A Bill of Divorcement, The
Informer* and *King Kong.*

By 1936, however, when Steiner went to work on *The
Charge of the Light Brigade,* Warner was ready for most anybody. His factory was grinding.

"Forbstein was a good executive," recalls orchestrator/
composer Hugo Friedhofer. "He had organized Warner's
Music Department so well it could practically run itself. We
were all cogs in his well-oiled machine. When I was there, I
was servicing Korngold and Steiner to everyone's complete
satisfaction, so why change things? Working conditions were
good, I was well paid, and I suppressed my creative ego until
I could do so no longer."

Heindorf: "Jack L. Warner really was the champion of music
and he encouraged Forbstein to make the Warner Bros. Music
Department the best in Hollywood. He also gave Forbstein a
free hand and considerable control . . . and Forbstein was fair
and understanding. Everyone had great respect and affection
for him. Although not the world's greatest conductor, the men
would give him their best. His ego did not mind others getting
the glory. He was only interested in getting the best people and
keeping them and the studio happy."

Warren: "In those days, Leo Forbstein always wanted music,
music, music. There were plenty of times when Leo would call
me and say, 'Come on in the projection room. I want to run a
scene for you.' And he'd run a scene and say, 'Give me thirty-
two bars of *schmaltz,'* which was his favorite expression. 'Just
the melody for the love scene.' It was always the love scene."

Warren wrote countless thirty-two bars of *schmaltz* for which
he wasn't credited, but he was paid regularly, $500 a week. The
studio was solvent. No one had to shin up the high-tension
poles and tap the wires for electricity because the bills weren't
paid. Those days were over and everything that happened was
accounted for, logged in monthly reports and paid for. "Leo
had two girl secretaries," recalls Warren. "They had to type
down everything that was shot, musical numbers, who did
them, make up the payroll for the musicians, everything. They
had a contractor who hired the musicians."

The factory was running smoothly. Even when it rained and
the bridge in Dark Canyon Pass washed out, the work didn't
stop. "They issued blankets to us. We stayed all night." No

Facing, top left. Roy Obringer, head of the studio
legal department
Facing, top right. Hugo Friedhoffer
Facing, bottom. Harry Warren and Al Dubin working on
The Singing Marine, 1937

problem, temperament, or natural disaster could alter the scheduled productions.

It was the same in all departments and each month Jack received an itemized report on what the talent was being paid, when their next option was coming up and what the special conditions of any particular contract might require of the studio. Maximum salaries were also noted so he could clean house when a department began to cost more than whatever he considered economically feasible. He never hesitated to start over with new employees, with new writers, directors, producers, songwriters, to start over and only pay starting salaries. The department heads and executives were to do the same, keep the salaries down and the factory grinding.

As of November 1, 1938, the executive salaries were $5,000 a week for Hal Wallis, $800 a week for Robert S. Taplinger, who headed the Publicity Division, $350 for Steve Trilling, who headed the Casting Department, $400 for Walter MacEwen, who headed the Story Department, $450 for Anton Grot, who headed the Art Department and $600 a week for Nathan Levinson, who headed the Sound Department.

Robert Obringer, who handled the studio's legal affairs and made the deals with the principal players, had his salary kept secret. So did Tenny Wright, who headed the Production Department. No contract, however, exceeded two years' duration except Wallis', which was for three years.

No one, of course, knew what Jack or Harry Warner made, but they weren't keeping it all for themselves, not quite. Leo Forbstein was receiving $1,500 a week. Max Steiner and Harry Warren also received $1,500. Dubin received $1,350. Johnny Mercer $800 and Ray Heindorf $800.

According to his contract, Korngold was to do "two pictures during 52 weeks' period commencing September 15, 1938, upon seven days' written notice to Composer. $1,041.66 per week for twelve weeks in each picture and prorata thereafter. Option: 52 weeks."

Two men in the eighteen-piece studio orchestra were paid $150 a week, two $125 and the rest $100. There were no no women.

As of November 1, 1938, the Music Department cost $34,874.84 a week. A year later it cost $33,499.84. Forbstein was the prototype of a Warner Bros. department head.

There was no waste, no fat at Warner Bros. The example set by Jack and Harry as they turned out lights and straightened bent nails permeated each department. If you wanted to know what the gossip in the studio was at any one time, you checked with the "incinerator man" who burned the secrets. But even the garbage was checked to see nothing useful was being discarded and that the writers were using their pencils down to the stubs.

By picking the right men to head each department, by giving them a budget and the responsibility and the control to make it work (and firing them if it didn't), Jack's factory managers kept the employees in line and working. But the boss remained the toughest customer the creative people faced.

Louis B. Mayer, Harry Cohn, Jack L. Warner and the other Hollywood moguls had a long experience of failure behind them by the thirties . . . and an ingrained, hidden fear of more failure. They also had a gift. And whatever it cost them in pride, one way or another they acknowledged that gift. "They knew everything, every psychological move you made, they knew how the entire industry of making films worked," recalls producer/director George Stevens. "But they didn't know how to make film . . . and they knew it."

It wasn't a weakness, it was their greatest strength. When Jack Warner found someone who could make films, or any part of one, he dropped on him with contracts, lawyers, managers, foremen, supervisors and spies like wet cement that hardened fast. No matter who they were, no matter how outrageous, how difficult, how insane, or how discomforting to his ego and to his soul. Even musicians.

And with the success of *42nd Street* in 1933, Warner wanted even more from his music men. More dance numbers, more girls, more flesh and satin hot pants, more Busby Berkeley tabloids and more songs.

From the beginning, however, the songwriters had trouble communicating with management. Harry Warren and Al Dubin would attend the budget meeting that preceded each film to find out what was required from them. "They always wanted the love song we hadn't written first," recalls Warren. "It always happened that way. They'd ask for six or seven songs and we'd say five. They asked for five and we'd say four."

The words the musicians and executives used were the same, they used the same twenty-six letters in the same alphabet, but the language was different. "I remember one incident where I said to Hal Wallis, 'The lyrics are wrong. They're singing the wrong lyrics.' He said, 'What difference does it

make? Nobody knows what the right lyric is.' I said, 'Yes, but we're going to print copies of these songs and the lyrics will be on the copies.' He sort of brushed me aside. That was my first experience. Little did I know what was to come after that.

"A lot of things like that happened. Music is always a sort of mystery to most people who want music in their pictures. They hate to pay for it, but they'll listen to it. And they'll never really analyze it and find out what it's all about."

Warren and Dubin, however, found ways to communicate. "We had a gag going between Wallis and Jack Warner. Neither one liked the other. So we called up Jack Warner's office and asked if we could see him. We wanted to play a song for him. I had to audition every song for him, play the piano and sing myself. He had a piano in his office. So we had a gag. We said, 'Mr. Warner, we want to play you a song that Hal Wallis didn't like.' And we'd play it. He said, 'That's great! What does he know about songs?' I said, 'He doesn't want to put it in the picture.' He said, 'It'll be in the picture. Don't worry.'

"Then we used the reverse tactic. Sometimes we'd play a song for Jack Warner. He wouldn't like it. We'd go to Wallis and say the same thing, that Jack didn't like it. We knew they were feuding.

"Another time we had a song called 'A Rose in Her Hair' for Wallis; it was a waltz. He said, 'How long did it take you to write that, ten minutes?' I said, 'Why?' He said, 'It's very short.' I said, 'It's a waltz and it goes fast.' That's an idea of the people you had to bring in your homework for.

"When I played 'September in the Rain' for them, they didn't like it, but I had Bill Elfeldt and Jimmy Melton do it and they loved it a week later, thought they had never heard it before.

"Hal Wallis was a tough guy to work for. He was just ornery all the time. I don't know why. In fact, when we did *Gold Diggers of 1935*, we had a song called 'Plenty of Money and You.' He came in to hear it and he sat down in our office and picked up the newspaper. He said, 'All right, let's hear the song,' and started to read. I said, 'Wait a minute, are you going to read or are you going to listen to the song?' He got very indignant, because being the big boss, we weren't supposed to talk to him that way. Anyhow, he heard the song and then opened the door, walked out and said, 'It stinks, write another song.' So as he walked away, I opened the door and said to him, 'You stink, get another boy!' Wallis just laughed. They didn't fire guys who were producing."

For Zanuck it was easier. "Wilson Mizner hung around Darryl and every time we played for him, Wilson would shout and applaud, 'It'll do two million copies.' He helped a lot."

Erich Wolfgang Korngold had another way of communicating. He maintained his European veneer, surrounded himself with friends and family on the sound stage and spoke German (so the children wouldn't forget their native tongue). It was "Doctor Korngold" or "Professor Korngold" to strangers, fellow musicians and even studio executives. He would allow the producer, director, even Hal Wallis or Warner on Stage 9 when he was recording, but he was still in total command. No one spoke to him or to anyone else unless spoken to by the Professor. Not even Jack L. Warner.

For Harry Warren, Korngold had style: "He was a character. If he didn't like anything, he went home.

"He used to wear this short little Viennese hunting jacket that hit him just above the hips. I called it his 'farting jacket.' He'd stand there conducting, then stop when a musician missed a note and ask, 'The second beat, did I write that note?' The musician would say, 'It's a B flat' and Korngold would say, 'No! Na! Na!' shaking his finger. 'It's A natural.'" Warren also liked his table manners. "He ate with two hands, everything within reach." Boiled beef, noodles and dumplings, braised beef, wiener schnitzel, sacher tortes, marillen knödell, linzer tortes.

Korngold was also misunderstood; he had a subtle sense of self-irony that was difficult for movie moguls to grasp. Henry Blanke remembers watching him walk down the corridor, then stop and listen to another studio composer lifting one of his pieces of music. "He'd stick his head in and say, 'Vy do you steal from me, vy don't you steal from Richard Strauss, whom I'm stealing from?'"

Korngold also mystified Hal Wallis one day in the Green-room as they were lunching together. Those were the days when the studio employed black "boys" to serve coffee to the stars and directors on the sets. They wore ruffled Georgian costumes, white stockings and all. It was Jack's one indulgence, his one concession to opulence. Class! Korngold was working, however, on *Green Pastures*, which featured an all-black cast with Rex Ingram playing De Lawd. Korngold asked Wallis where Ingram was and Wallis explained that the Negros didn't lunch in the Greenroom, but in the cafeteria. Korngold nodded,

gathered up his food, with both hands, headed for the cafeteria and sardonically allowed, "I'm going to eat with the Lord."

Max Steiner's language was more direct: "Nobody *tells* me anything. If they do, I walk right out on them. The minute they open their mouths, 'This is what I want,' this is goodbye. I never come back."

His system of work was similar. "They don't hand me anything. When the picture's ready, I go look at it and do what I want. I never go to the studio from the time I see the picture until it's finished. Jack Warner never told me anything in his life. If he did, I said, 'What the hell do you know?' You know, I have a saying: a motion picture executive is a man who knows everything, but can't think of it."

Steiner spoke plainly, but still didn't communicate. "Nobody understands me, even my wife, she don't understand me. I had to get rid of my dog because he didn't speak English. He was a French poodle. No kidding! You don't even believe me."

"Steiner was a very funny little guy," recalls Warren. "He had a great sense of humor and would make funny remarks to the musicians in the orchestra. Of course, he was very serious about his music, but he was still a very funny little guy. He had sort of 'carte blanche.' He could pick his own pictures. If they were important, he would do them."

Steiner had an approach to the studio. "I never tell the truth." He wanted something, but he would never talk about that. That is what he did. His kind of deceit, the evasive, cordial lie, was developed to a fine art at Warner Bros.

Lyricist Al Dubin, however, had the best working style. Jack Warner couldn't ever find him.

"He was a loner," recalls Warren. "He liked to get off by himself. On our first job, when they told him to come to work at nine, he disappeared for two weeks, then came back with all the lyrics for *42nd Street*. Luckily, Al could read a lead sheet, because he had this habit of disappearing all the time. We never could find him. We finally found out he used to go up to San Francisco, because they had good restaurants up there. John's Rendezvous was one of his favorites. Al loved good food and the restaurants weren't so hot in LA in those days, so I'd just give him the lead sheet and he'd vanish. I was always on the spot, but I never knew where he was.

"They looked for him everywhere. They'd call all over. Just

make random calls, mostly to the border towns and ask if anyone had tipped a bellhop five dollars for a bottle of bourbon and a pitcher of ice water. They found him that way. They had him paged once in the San Antonio Railroad Station, and you know, he was there!

"He called me once from a Juarez brothel where he was writing, 'Where am I, am I in heaven or am I really with you?'"

Malcolm Beelby remembers when Dubin couldn't be found during the shooting of the "Lullaby of Broadway" number for *Gold Diggers of 1935.* "Warren had written the music, but Dubin disappeared. Someone finally found him in a Mexican border town tending bar in a saloon. When he came back, the lyrics were written on the backs of envelopes."

On the lot Dubin also had a style. His wife wouldn't let him drink at home and he claimed, "I don't drink until the sun goes down," so on long summer days he'd pull the shades down at five and break the label on a quart of Mt. Vernon rye. He also chewed tobacco a lot and had spittoons in several places in his office. Once in a while he would hit one, but usually he'd just dirty the wall. He also dirtied the windows of his pink Cord automobile and William, his black chauffeur, who wore a bright red uniform, bought him a big red thermos to spit in. He was a big, gross, loud-laughing man, but when he worked, alone, he was a different man.

> I don't know if we're in a gar-den,
> Or on a crowd-ed ave-nue.
> You are here, so am I,
> May-be mil-lions of peo-ple go by,
> But they all dis-ap-pear from view,
> And I on-ly have eyes for you.

Whenever Jack Warner finally found Dubin, and put his words with Warren's music, he got what Harry Warner wanted. Hits. Standards. And Jack liked the songs. He would often come onto Stage 9 when Ray Heindorf was conducting them. After listening to a playback one day, Heindorf decided to do the song over. "Why?" asked Warner. "It sounded fine to me." "The string bass came in two bars early halfway through," replied Heindorf. Warner didn't care for the answer. "Whoever goes out of a theater whistling the bass part?" Heindorf smiled politely, then proceeded as planned.

Off the stage, Heindorf had another style. Early one dark

morning a producer arrived at Heindorf's home and was met at the door by the arranger/conductor, stark naked. Heindorf was working, drinking and arranging while his wife was standing nude in front of an easel, painting. The producer didn't bother to ask why, it was obvious. Heindorf was a musician.

The musicians in general had a life style that annoyed not only Warner Bros. but most of Beverly Hills. "All the orchestrators in Hollywood would come up to Heindorf's house and have all-night parties," recalls Beelby. "He had the equipment in his house, big speakers and all. He'd blow the windows out."

Every once in a while there was even a musician the musicians couldn't understand. Joe Venuti, a great jazz fiddle player, worked at the Warner lot in those early days. "Nobody liked him," recalls Warren. "He was the first guy to eat a goldfish."

After hours, away from the lot and Jack Warner, the musicians led another kind of life at night in downtown Los Angeles amid the sounds that came from a nightclub across from the Pacific Electric Station on Main Street. Malcolm Beelby remembers: "The Paradise Club, with colored dancers and a two-finger piano man named Lionel Hampton. Great jazz! There was a black line of six or eight girls and Marie Bryant was the featured singer. Different musicians would sit in, Jimmy Dorsey and others. Heindorf played great piano in those days."

There were also clubs on Sunset Boulevard where Art Tatum and others made their sounds with the help of studio musicians who stood in for a "set."

Beelby never figured he was good enough to sit in, but he had already had his pleasure. At the studio. "I was the first one to play all those Warren and Dubin tunes. For two weeks at a time, ten hours a day, sometimes all day and night. They were magic. 'Shadow Waltz,' 'Lullaby of Broadway,' 'September in the Rain,' 'I Only Have Eyes for You,' 'Dames,' 'Lulu's Back in Town,' 'I'll Sing You a Thousand Love Songs' and all the others."

The musicians liked the music but called Warner Bros. "prison." They stayed inside it long enough, however, to get their work done, and for a good reason. The studio took everything they wrote and performed, each note, each lyric, then recorded it and sent it directly to the audience, everything, their best and worst, and the musicians couldn't resist that. They became insatiable. And unknowingly they became perfect factory employees.

"When you worked for Warner's," recalls Warren, "it was a case of working all the time, day and night, night and day. We used to spend nights at the studio, just working. It was just one of those things that's hard to explain. I guess it's because you like to write that you write a lot. If I didn't like it, it would have been impossible. It never seemed like to work to me. I'd stay in the studio till two or three and it wouldn't make any difference. It had been the same when I played at Healy's Saloon. I'd play till three and four. I loved it.

"I worked, usually, away from the piano if I wanted to get a good melody. I don't want to call it a trance, but I'd try to think of something beautiful, a melody, and it would come. The melody came first.

"On the piano I used to get into D flat or G flat, which I couldn't play so well, so the fingers wouldn't just go to the same places again.

"I can't listen to that old stuff now, but my big kicks were when I first heard the orchestra play it. I had been used to a pit orchestra of seven men. When I heard fifty men do it, I almost fell down. It was marvelous."

Dubin picked his own place to work, the Stud Saloon in Tijuana, John's Rendezvous in San Francisco and distant hotels, but his product was the same.

Warren and Dubin were the men who put words and music together so Warner Bros. could sing and Jack Warner didn't really mind how or where they did it. And Heindorf could go naked and spend his nights with a bottle of Five Star Hennessey, because Jack had found out he also spent them with a copyist and worked tirelessly. Overnight he could bring in an orchestration that ran for fifteen or twenty minutes. And every chorus was different. He was clever, fast and admired by the composers Korngold and Steiner. Although he was young then, he was the patriarch of all the arrangers in town.

Forbstein was doing his job. He watched the money, the schedules and kept farther and farther away from making the music himself. But he knew talent when he heard it and old and new music men began to flow through the studio; lyricists Grant Clark, Sammy Fain and Irving Kahal, Allie Wurbel and Mort Dixon, Johnny Mercer and Dick Whiting . . . and com-

posers Adolph Deutsch (*The Maltese Falcon*), Heins Reimhold (*The Desert Song*), Franz Waxman (*Mr. Skeffington, Objective Burma*), Hugo Friedhofer, Frederick Hollander and others.

Erich Korngold paced himself, his contract allowed that, but on the job "he was a metronome," recalls Henry Blanke. "When I would show him the first cut of a film, he'd say, 'Blanke, this shot must be three feet longer, that one two feet shorter, etc., etc., so I can compose correctly.' He was a genius. I'd give him a script and he'd write the music without seeing a shot, all the main themes, then we'd recut the film so the music fit. I think even Steiner knew Korngold was special."

Korngold wrote sixteen original scores for Warner Bros., among which were *The Adventures of Robin Hood, Juarez, The Sea Hawk, Deception, King's Row, Anthony Adverse,* and *The Private Lives of Elizabeth and Essex.*

Steiner was the workhorse. During his career he composed scores for one hundred and fifty-five films. He also wrote the bombastic fanfare that announced a Warner Bros. film was about to appear up there on the silver screen. In one year, 1939, he scored as many as twelve films. That was the year he was loaned out to Selznick for *Gone With the Wind.* Jack preferred he only work at Warner Bros., but his original contract provided he could work for Selznick. It didn't break his rhythm at Warners, however. He still produced.

He worked at home at his piano and would often show up at the studio at night with a scene that was due to be recorded at seven the next morning. Friedhofer would meet him at the gate, go over the music with him, then go to his office and begin orchestrating so that Art Grier and the other copyists could begin their work and finish it before the session. Steiner would drive back home and begin again.

"Sleeping! That was my problem, trying to get some rest. A lot of times we used to start about eight o'clock at night and work until seven in the morning." Steiner took each assignment.

"What difference did it make, so it's a long picture, so it's a long score. Short pictures, a short score. It's like buying an automobile. A picture's a picture.

"I had stretches of work for fifty-six consecutive hours without sleep in order to complete a picture for the booking date. If the film's final editing had been delayed through some unforeseen happening, the music and rerecording departments had to pitch in and make up for lost time."

There were times when Leo Forbstein got worried about Steiner's health and hesitated, but Jack was always excited about Steiner's possible contribution, "Put Maxie on this one. It's an important picture." Or, "This picture needs a lot of help, give it to Maxie." And Forbstein did. "Max can begin his music with the opening fanfare and keep it going until the end title is over," was Warner's considered opinion.

"I know I had to have a doctor come in every night at midnight to give me Benzedrine injections to keep me awake," recalled Steiner. "Every night for months. Finally my doctor told me I had to stop, it was gonna affect my heart. I used to work sixteen, eighteen hours a day."

God, how Warner must have loved him.

But somehow public recognition never came to the musicians, not then. The movies were considered just vulgar picture shows in the thirties and forties. Korngold's father often asked his talented son to get out of the movie business and go into a field that deserved his talents. The Vienna Opera House crowd shook their heads with dismay and looked away. And when Steiner was at his best in *Dark Victory* or *Now Voyager*, Bette Davis was the one the audience cried for.

The songwriters got even less attention. Hollywood was the Other End of Broadway . . . the dirty end . . . oblivion, vulgarity and contempt. No one entered Harry Warren's or Al Dubin's names along with those of Irving Berlin, Ira Gershwin, Cole Porter or Oscar Hammerstein when they spoke of songwriters. Busby Berkeley and his dancing girls got all the credit. Their credit and their applause.

And once the film had had its run, it was buried in a cement vault, its music with it. The sleazy lyrics, good-natured rhythms and romantic songs quickly faded from fashion. There were no records and only a few song sheets. And the factory bosses figured that once it was used, the music could be forgotten . . . just like the films.

"There was a picture premiered at Sid Grauman's Chinese Theater," recalls Warren. "We rented a car, and of course there were crowds on the sidewalk and crowds in the lobby, crowds out in front of the theater . . . they had cops lined up everywhere. And as we came rolling along Hollywood Boulevard, a lot of kids would run over and look. And they said, 'Oh, that's nobody!' That's all we got, all the way to the theater entrance. Kids looking, saying, 'That's nobody.'"

Below. Ruby Keeler, James Cagney, Bill Koenig, Jack Warner, Busby Berkeley and Dick Powell on the set of Footlight Parade, *1933*
Facing. Erich Wolfgang Korngold

By mid 1938, Hollywood figured that the musical film was finished, and Harry Warren, along with Busby Berkeley and his dancing girls, left. "I felt kind of sad about it. It was like home. I'd been there many years. And every day in the week, sometimes plenty of nights. I felt sad about it even though it was a factory, as I recall it. But there was nothing I could do about it. Nobody said good-bye or, 'How've you been?' Or anything."

Al Dubin had already been forced out. Hal Wallis insisted that Dubin write with lyricist Johnny Mercer on *Garden of the Moon.* They were both under contract and they were both going to work. "Both their names are on as lyric writers," recalls Warren. "Al and Johnny, and that's when Al quit the studio. They paid him off. He wanted to be paid off . . . wanted to quit.

"I didn't blame him . . . he didn't want to write with another lyric writer." He couldn't. "But Hal Wallis, the Hitler of the studio, insisted they write together. They were on salary."

For a while Dubin went back to Broadway, continued to write, then they found him on February 11, 1945, in the Taft Hotel in New York, dead. He'd been there two days. He had lived too hard, and his heart couldn't take it.

"There is no ro-mance with-out a song,
And tho' it's such a lit-tle thing to do, dear,
I'll sing to you, dear,
My whole life long:
I'll sing you a thousand love songs,
And still they'll seem so few,
For I need a thousand voices,
To tell you how I love you,
I've only one heart to give you, one voice to listen to,
So, I'll bring a thou-sand love songs and I'll sing
Ev-ry one, dear, for you."

He died alone.

For Jack Warner, despite his past as a tenor, music remained a mystery. Composing, even songwriting, may have been an art form, and it may be a fact that music had to be imbued with the vision of a single individual in order to make it great and make it sell, imbued with the art of a man who works alone. But the movies surely weren't an art form, not the picture show. A film maker certainly can't work alone. The picture show is a business dependent on working with a crowd of people . . .

on communicating with, commanding and controlling a mixture of craftsmen and talents. The mouth is the medium in the movies, like a pencil is to a writer, a brush to a painter, a brass horn to a musician or a tassel to a stripper.

The composers could work alone, but in order to make films, Jack needed talkers, persuasive men to make the films . . . to watch it and force it out of the Writers' Building, into production, editing, scoring and finally into the theaters. Men who could control writers, directors, stars and keep them on schedule. He didn't even need stylish producers like the other studios used, not in his factory. He needed supervisors, men who talked the fastest and shouted the loudest. At Warner Bros. yelling was the medium.

If he could get away with it, Jack wouldn't even give his supervisors credit. But Jack had a gift and if the supervisors could make films like Warren, Steiner, Korngold and Dubin made music, well . . . with Jack L. Warner, anything was possible.

Left. Ruby Keeler and Al Jolson in Go into Your Dance, *1935*
Center. Ricardo Cortez, Dolores Del Rio, Al Jolson, Kay Francis
and Dick Powell in Wonder Bar, *1934*
Right. Rosemary Lane and Rudy Vallee in Gold Diggers in
Paris, *1938*

Facing. The girls are wired with neon violins for "The Shadow Waltz," from Gold Diggers of 1933.
Right. Gold Diggers of 1933
Below. "By a Waterfall," from Footlight Parade, *1933*

Top. Buck & Bubbles, Ted Healy and Dick Powell in Varsity Show, *1937*
Center. Lionel Hampton, Teddy Wilson, Benny Goodman and Gene Krupa in Hollywood Hotel, *1938*
Bottom. The Golden Gate Quartet in Hollywood Canteen, *1944*
Facing. James Cagney and Joan Leslie in Yankee Doodle Dandy, *1943*

Below. Jeanne Cagney, James Cagney as George M. Cohan, Joan Leslie, Walter Huston and Rosemary De Camp in Yankee Doodle Dandy, *1943*

THE MOUTH
IS THE MEDIUM

Producers

"How extravagant you are, throwing away
women like that. Someday they may be scarce."

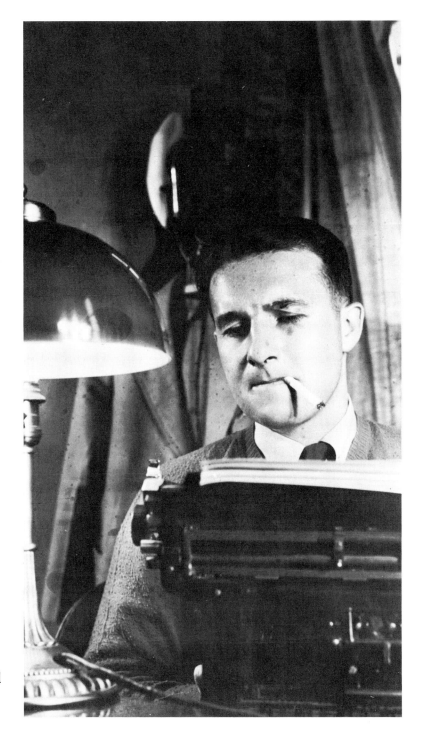

Everyone knows what a producer wants.

Ask any starlet, even one with only two to three weeks of
Hollywood interviews on her list of credits, and she'll be able
to tell you. If prostitution was indeed the first profession, then
the first procurer was a producer. And the first customer.

Screenwriter Ben Hecht precisely judged both what the
Hollywood producers wanted and selected, then pronounced
them "men with no taste to be violated or distorted."

When novelist S. J. Perelman visited the Chamber of
Horrors in London, he found that the wax heads of criminals
executed at Newgate Prison evoked the images of studio
bosses and producers he had hobnobbed with during
the 1930's.

Producers have been credited with inventing the casting
couch, debasing children and successfully spreading the cultural
wasteland. Whatever their desires, artistic or personal, they
are known to pursue them with the artistic integrity and the
manners of a dog in heat.

"The army of the inept," states a director. "If a producer
understands what you're talking about, he thinks he thought
of it himself."

And musicians are sure they all have "tin ears," the worst
crime of all.

Director John Huston remembers the joke that typified the
film producer when he was working on the Warner lot. "They
weren't liked much, you know. There was a joke about them,
you know it, everyone knows it, it's old hat now. About the
two producers lost out in a desert. They were dying of thirst,
starving, and when they finally see this oasis, they crawl to it
on their hands and knees. They're near death. And when they
finally get there, there's this cold tin of fresh pineapple juice
sitting there under the palm trees. They can't believe their
good fortune, it's just what they're dying for. They drag themselves over to the tin and one of them lifts it to his parched
mouth. But just as he is about to drink, the other one stops
him and says, 'Wait, let's piss in it first.'"

Hollywood producers are defined as those who take credit
for the films that the writers, directors, performers and
musicians make for them. "They touch nothing, not the script,
the camera, nothing, and when they do, they spoil it," recalls
a director. "One way or another they use you up." Get rich and
famous by making an art out of buying and selling talent.

The producers didn't arrive on the Super Chief, on foot or

in any normal fashion. At Warner Bros. they emerged from behind rocks, the bowels of Cadillacs, from German society and from Harvard. Suddenly they were there, in control, and only Jack Warner and his executives knew how they got there.

They had come either to be writers, actors or creators of mammoth picture shows, to get rich, or simply to get next to the beautiful people and by one means or another, through their weaknesses or strengths, they discovered the way to do it was to become a producer. And all they had to do to reach that goal was to convince Jack Warner that they could do things others couldn't do. And, more importantly, that they would do things no one else *would* do.

They took to the job like ants to candy. They had an ancient gift inside them. They filled a role in life that predated history. Back amid man's dark origins the producers had been called medicine men, witch doctors, magicians and eventually priests. Men with a gift for knowing what the people wanted to hear, for knowing how to sell it to them and for convincing others to build it, steal it, imagine it. Men who would allow themselves to believe most anything in order to bring others under their control. Men who could build lies the size of cathedrals or movie palaces because they believed in the results . . . the message, the power or the money.

In the thirties and forties you went to a place like the "T & D" theater in Oakland, California, the "tough and dirty," and made your offering of thirty-five cents. It was perfectly made for a Warner Bros. producer, with torn carpets, popcorn and girls with short skirts in the balcony.

To the intellectual skeptic of the thirties, however, the Hollywood producer cluttered his temples with doubtful attractions. Fleshy sensations and ideas built with junk. But both the dreaming talent and the studio bosses couldn't afford to be critical. For those men and women whose work was building man's popular attractions, producers were necessities. They did the persuading. They were the medium by which a film got made. They knew all the four-letter words that would put the talent together with the money.

Whatever the nature of the job, the producers at Warner Bros. were sure they could do it. They had egos so big they bounced them off the walls of offices, sound stages and toilets. They advertised them in the daily trade papers, *Variety* and *The Reporter;* they adorned them with fancy cars and clothes

and just in case you hadn't already noticed, they had their names and titles engraved in gold and nailed to their doors. A few producers had egos so big they didn't have to show them. They wore working clothes, drove Fords, didn't bother with a name plate and ate by themselves with total confidence. They knew they had the power.

Consciously or unconsciously, the producers also accepted their role as the traditional one. They were the middlemen between the gods and the common people. Between the dream and the audience.

It was a critical role. The picture shows at Warner Bros. would pass through a producer and come out as cardboard or silver depending on what his soul or glands were made of. On whether he was simply trying to provide himself with a steady flow of virgins or had grand plans for becoming a mogul himself, of becoming the power and glory of dreamland and stealing *all* the money. On whether he wanted social prominence or an awakened social conscience. On whether he was just trying to get his way or was honestly searching for a dream, a goddess. On whether the producers were simply attempting to get rich on cardboard and Celluloid or attempting to wake a genuine sleeping beauty.

Jack Warner, however, had definite plans for what would flow through and out of his factory. Dreams, cathedrals, goddesses and saving the world were not ideas, or even words, he used. He didn't want producers, he wanted supervisors. The word "producer" implied too much independence, and a sense of authority that might lead them to want the credit he and Hal Wallis were taking. And if they were called supervisors, they would be part of management and couldn't rebel. Couldn't strike.

Jack got his way. He didn't give his supervisors credit until 1932, and in 1974 they would still be unknown.

They had started, however, as contenders, young men convinced of their invincibility and eager to do battle with the impossible, with Jack Warner.

Lucien Hubbard was the first to be given credit, on *So Big* in April of 1932. "One of the finest, straightest, squarest men who ever existed," recalls Robert Lord. "A model human being. Dark, six feet tall, handsome. About a quarter Indian. He became a confidant of Zanuck because everyone had to have someone to trust in those days. He was a competent

Left. Henry Blanke in the thirties
Facing. Harry Warner (center) sees his son, Louis, and Henry Blanke off as they sail for Germany in 1929

screenwriter and Darryl wanted him near him. Lucien was his guru. He was the kind of guy you can write a check to for everything you own, then take a ten-year trip around the world, even get lost, and the check will be there when you get back.

"Lucien was both a supervisor and Darryl's executive officer. He was involved in practically all story conferences. He worked very hard indeed." *The Mouthpiece, Winner Take All, Week-end Marriage, Blondie Johnson, Ex-Lady* and many others.

"Zanuck started the polo team on Lucien's initiation, on the Warner Bros. property where the Forest Lawn Cemetery is now. Built a primitive clubhouse. Mike Curtiz, Lucien, Darryl and Ray Griffith were on the team." Lord refused. "I told Zanuck, 'I don't think I have to play, you just took up my option for two years.'"

Hubbard had come to Hollywood from Fort Thomas, Kentucky . . . to be a writer.

Ray Griffith arrived to perform. In 1914 he worked in Vitagraph and Kalem productions then moved to Hollywood and was a Paramount comic star from 1923 to 1927. A little man, about five feet three, he was stocky, endurable and a society man. A dresser. Griffith's first credit was also in 1932, with *The Rich Are Always with Us*. He also did *Blessed Event, Tiger Shark, The Crash, Central Park, Ladies They Talk About, The Picture Snatcher, Baby Face, Voltaire, Hard to Handle, Twenty Thousand Years in Sing Sing,* and *Frisco Jenny* . . . and he did them with lovelies like Zita Johann, Lois Wilson, Helen Vinson, Loretta Young, Sheila Terry, Joan Blondell, Ginger Rogers, Mary Brian and Claire Dodd.

Robert Lord received his first credit with *The Gold Diggers of 1935*. He had been with the studio as a writer and unofficial supervisor since 1927. As a graduate of Harvard's English 47 Dramatic Workshop, he went directly into Broadway theater and had been writing successful plays when Hollywood asked him to come to work . . . and even paid his train fare.

"I was invited to Hollywood to elevate the tone of the motion picture business by William Fox. They wanted classier scripts." Fox, at that time, was one of the city's most powerful moguls and had a plush complex of studios at Western Avenue and Sunset Boulevard.

"I got fired from Fox by producer Sol Wurtzel, who hated me because, in the first place, he was from a ghetto and I was from Harvard." In the twenties that was a good reason. Lord didn't belong in "tinsel town." He had been raised in Chicago,

Below. Another view of the underworld by Warner Bros.: Mickey Rooney and friends in A Midsummer Night's Dream, *1936*
Facing, left. Jerry Wald and Conrad Veidt on the set of All Through the Night, *1942*
Facing, right. Sam Bischoff

near the Dearborn Street Pumping Station. "We were always upper, upper middle class, always living above our income. My background was the antithesis of that of most everyone in the movie business."

By the time Lord left the University of Chicago's Experimental High School, he had had four years of Latin, four years of French and three of Greek. He had read the classics: "Shakespeare, the English Lake Poets, Shelley, Keats, Wordsworth, the elder Dumas and Dumas *fils* . . . in French. I read Dickens, Wilde, Thackeray and loved them all. I read Horace in Latin.

"I was really quite a serious kid, too serious."

A five-foot tightwire of a man, he had gone to Harvard on an athletic scholarship. "I was the best hundred-and-thirty-five-pound lightweight who fought in college. And still am." There is a small scar over his left eye that is still visible. "A guy from Yale did that, but I won." That they could understand at Warner Bros.

Jack hired Lord for $323 a week and after he swept out First National for Zanuck and had written a good thirty or forty scripts, he became a supervisor at $2,500 a week.

Jack was making choices.

Lord supervised *The World Changes, Havana Widows, As the Earth Turns, The Merry Wives of Reno, The Man with Two Faces, Dames, Bordertown, Gold Diggers of 1933, Black Fury, Footlight Parade* and *Black Legion* in the early thirties with a thin social conscience and half-grown goddesses.

Henry Blanke didn't receive credit until 1933, *The Mystery of the Wax Museum,* even though he had been with the studio since 1923. There was a distance between Blanke and Warner. It wasn't youth, even though in 1933 Warner was forty-one and Blanke was thirty-two. Jack liked youth, but Blanke dressed better than the vice-president in charge of production, dressed with what others called "excellent taste." And Blanke openly liked art, spoke with a refined foreign accent and had impeccable manners. Style. Class. And he was a careful man, indirect, yet determined. The studio called him "Heinz." Jack liked him, but he would pay him only $1,500 a week. He didn't trust class.

Blanke was born in Berlin, Steglitz, Germany, in 1901, attended the Oberreal School and studied music. His father was the painter Wilhelm Blanke, an accepted member of cultural society. People from the theater, opera and art

gathered in the Blanke home, people whom young Henry would meet again in Hollywood: Max Reinhardt, Erich Wolfgang Korngold, Salka Viertel, Nina Foch. It was an energetic, lively home and Blanke was raised on a mix of ideas and dreams, on Germanic legends and expressionistic visions. "I hated Wagner, but adored Bach, my God, such a genius." An accomplished musician, Blanke performed on the lute, but not at the studio.

Warner used Blanke's familiarity with the "arty" world and loaned him out as Lubitsch's assistant to Paramount; then, from 1929 to 1930, he sent him to Germany as the production head of Warner Bros. First National studios there. Blanke, on his return, headed the studio's production of foreign-language versions as an uncredited supervisor. Blanke had to be brought along slowly until his artistic notions went away. Henry had even been the production manager on Fritz Lang's "art film" *Metropolis* and Jack didn't want him making that kind of bomb for him.

Harry Warner was more trusting. When Blanke left to head the Warner studios in Germany in late 1929, he took Harry's son Louis with him. "Harry asked me to show him the best whorehouses, show him the cleanest women in the world. We went to the best International Houses, the girls were at least a hundred dollars. But I never asked Harry for the money." Blanke had taste. On the return trip, Louis Warner developed a toothache and flew off to Cuba in a plane that didn't have a pressurized cabin. The infection was forced into his system and he died. "The stuff seemed to go out of Harry after that, and he left Jack on his own." The music publishing business was turned over to Buddy Norris.

Blanke's early films as a supervisor were *Girl Missing, The Silk Express, She Had to Say Yes, I Loved a Woman, Convention City, Fashions of 1934, Madame Du Barry,* and *The Case of the Lucky Legs.* By 1936, however, Blanke's vision was clearing: *The Story of Louis Pasteur, The Petrified Forest, Anthony Adverse, A Midsummer Night's Dream, The Green Pastures, The Life of Emile Zola,* and by 1938, *Jezebel* and *The Adventures of Robin Hood,* the most expensive film, two million dollars, the studio had made.

Jack was taking chances but not with Blanke's salary. He was still only paying him $1,750 a week while giving Sam Bischoff $2,250 to do *Frisco Kid* and *Stars over Broadway.*

Bischoff had arrived in 1934 to do *The Merry Wives of*

Reno. A Boston University graduate, he had been in films since the early twenties. He had run his own company and worked for Columbia Pictures as head of production. He liked street pictures, *Angels with Dirty Faces, Roaring Twenties, Castle on the Hudson,* and when you made films starring James Cagney and John Garfield, you made money.

In the later thirties Jack took some more chances, mostly with men from the Writers' Building, where they were cheap. Robert Presnell, Mark Hellinger, Robert Buckner, Harry Joe Brown, Seton I. Miller, William Jacobs and Laird Doyle. Lou Edelman came from Harvard and from a career as a writer. Benjamin Glazer was a lawyer, playwright and had produced at MGM. He cost $3,000 a week in 1937. Jack was edgy about that, he preferred the $750 a week Edelman was getting and the $600 he was paying David Lewis, who also came from MGM.

Jerry Wald also arrived from the Writers' Building, in 1941. He had been waiting a long time and would add new curves to the life style of supervisors. "He used to follow everybody around," recalls Harry Warren. "He was sort of a *What Makes Sammy Run!* He was trying to get in . . . and he did. He was like all guys trying to get ahead. Busy all the time. I think Jerry latched himself onto anybody he could."

"Once a picture was started," recalls director Vincent Sherman, "Jerry was already interested in six pictures after that. He was a very prolific guy in that sense. My argument with him used to be that he lost interest in the picture once it started." *All Through the Night, Across the Pacific, The Hard Way, Action in the North Atlantic, Destination Tokyo, In Our Time, Objective Burma.*

"Jerry had a peculiar kind of talent. To be as honest as I can about it, he was a very sweet human being. Very soft. He could be very generous. But Jerry's weakness, in my opinion, and the thing that finally caused us to split up, was Jerry's ambition and desire for success was so strong that very frequently he would become very opportunistic in his decisions. He wouldn't always back up his director."

In 1935 Brynie Foy had come back to Warner Bros. to handle the production of the "B" films. Literally born in a trunk, he was one of comedian Eddie Foy's Seven Little Foys. He had grown up backstage. He had seen the vaudeville splendors of Lois Fuller doing her "Serpentine" and "Fire" dances, seen Will Ferry's "Frog Man" and Gertrude Hoffman in

Salome's "Dance of the Seven Veils." He had grown up watching fantasies being built with rusty nails and old sign boards, watching the lovely princess on stage as she was seduced by a stagedoor Johnie backstage . . . and saw she loved it. He had grown up in the backyard of the land called illusion, and making films for Foy was dollars, false fronts and two-week schedules cut down to eleven days of work. Even nine. And he would work for $1,250 a week. It was no nonsense and gray paint for silver. An ideal factory supervisor.

Jack had picked well, but the supervisors wanted their way and they wanted credit. Slowly he gave it to them, in small pieces. They were called associate producers by 1938 and finally producers in 1942, what they had been all along.

When Robert Lord made the transition from writer to supervisor, his job had been made unmistakably clear. "Director Edmund Goulding told me, 'Your job is being the liaison between the deficiencies of administration and the deficiencies of creation.'

"My responsibilities were to keep Warner and Wallis off the necks of the director. When anything was wrong with the dailies, they'd call me and I'd go to the director, who would say, 'Tell them to go *%&%#%¢ themselves.' And then I'd try to talk to them and to Warner or Wallis.

"Warner's was a spinal cord studio then; we all acted according to our instincts.

"I was primarily, I was always, a writer. I wrote the first outlines, then put a writer on it, then made copious corrections. During shooting I made more corrections. I was also the doctor of many other supervisors' scripts. I never got very far away from being a writer."

Lord's job, the supervisor's job, was also to keep the director from losing his way, from having too much fun. "The moment a director began deviating from the script, everybody mobilized to find out what was happening. A working supervisor had to be on the set as much as the director to anticipate trouble and stop it before the pipe burst. By the time a film got on a set, it was to be a fairly mechanical process.

"Part of my job was to suggest material. I'd tell Walter MacEwen or Bill Collier, or whoever was in the Story Department. It was immensely informal. Immensely. There was a tremendous amount of luck in our success, or God, or whatever

you want to call it. A lot of bunk and bullshit that people took artistic credit for."

But the supervisors were the ones making decisions. "We checked everything, sets, costumes, extras, actors, makeup, even Bette's brassiere. That was the only time Bette Davis and I had a quarrel, on *Housewife.* We had a costume test and I questioned her bustline. I told her she looked like she was smuggling two balloons in, which I should not have said. She screamed, got angry and I apologized. I told her, 'I'll worry about the story, you worry about the brassieres.'"

They also "cast all the character players, but we didn't have any readings, never looked at eight-by-ten glossies. We knew everyone. While a picture was shooting, the bit players that Casting figured were going to work next week came on the set, and the director and supervisor would say, 'You're fine, check out with Casting.' We always had to pass on them, but we never knew how much they cost and never cared. Personally, I don't think I ever discovered any new talent."

The money arguments with the stars were not the supervisor's problem. "Roy Obringer was the head of the Contract Department; he was the one you went to about money. My standard line was, 'I'm an artist and know nothing about money.'"

The directors, however, were a primary concern. "Jack, Hal and I sat down and said, 'Who could do this, Bacon, Curtiz, LeRoy? Someone under contract, or someone outside?' We were always in conference about this if we were in disagreement. And lots of the time we were."

The supervisors also followed each film through its editing, dubbing, scoring, preview and into its final print stage. "After the preview, and we went to previews at least once a week, we analyzed and recut the picture on the sidewalk. Then the next day we forgot it all and started over. Somehow Jack loved those sidewalk conferences, but it was a complete waste of time.

"We worked from 7 A.M. to 10 P.M., we all worked a twelve- to fourteen-hour day." Each facet, each conversation, phone call, fight and cup of coffee went into the film, for better and for worse. But the primary artistic control was the first decision a supervisor made. He chose the subject.

The brothers Warner had built their factory in order to make a product that would fill theaters with people, at fifteen cents a head, and then thirty-five cents and, during the war years, fifty

and sixty cents. The question was how to make that product, and the answer, obviously, was to make what the public wanted to see. But there were no computers, no motivational research companies, no universities to produce a statistical analysis of the public need for fantasy. No polls. Only the box office. It could clearly determine what was successful after a film was released and it did inform Warner of just who was making the hits, of whom to keep and to fire. And he followed its advice religiously.

In addition, the box office determined the genres that were successful: crime, melodrama, adventure, detective stories, biographies, racing pictures, musicals. And it determined when those genres became boring and should be discarded. But the box office couldn't determine what stories to tell within those genres. And you could retell the same old stories only so many times. In order to fill the theaters, Jack needed new stories, new subjects to exploit.

He didn't want the writers making the decisions. They could do the writing, but the supervisors were to tell them what to write about. If there was some hidden political meaning, some purpose, passion, or, God forbid, "art," then the supervisors were to remove it and get on with the action. Or defy him, fight him and convince him it belonged . . . if they could.

The supervisors got it from both ends. The writers produced reams of what they were certain were incredible film scripts, stories that were sure to turn to silver, even gold, when they reached the screen and touched the heart of the audience. And the performers were insatiable. An actress like Bette Davis would peddle scripts for months to a supervisor. A hard woman to turn down, particularly when you needed her for your own purposes. But the supervisors had to stay in the in the middle.

"I was never honest in those days," recalls Henry Blanke. "We all had to lie for our own purposes." The business of pretending, of creating the real with the unreal, creating lies with the fabric of life, often takes a personal toll on the integrity of those who take the business seriously. Blanke allowed himself to be misunderstood and used his accent for a multitude of double meanings. He regularly told Jack Warner John Huston was on medication when he was on the "laughing water," because in a way it was all too true. Personally, there would be decay, but there were moments at Warner Bros. when the story being told on the screen was about lying for

your own purposes, about chasing a black bird when what you really wanted, like Sam Spade, was to catch the person who killed your partner. Moments when the lying was honest.

With John Huston on *The Maltese Falcon,* Blanke bought two copies of Dashiell Hammett's novel, tore them apart and then pasted up the pages into script form so they could go over it story point by story point before Huston lifted his pencil.

"They trusted me completely. I was the conductor and I held the baton in my hand." Blanke knew what lies to tell and how to tell them. And when to say nothing. He knew precisely what and who he was up against.

"Jack was a wonderful executive. I'd tell him a story in three words and he'd say yes or no. As much as I mislike what I'm saying now, Jack Warner was a genius. And his philosophy kept our egos down and made Warner Bros. rich.

"It was the whole philosophy of the studio to never give anyone credit, or a percentage of stocks, and it was a good philosophy, I must say. The reason they became a big studio was not the invention of sound, but because of this philosophy.

"Jack was tough and we were tough as a studio. And we knew it. That was 'our' philosophy. If the other studios were tough, we'd be tougher, more realistic. The only theory we followed was that the characters had to talk like real people. That's the way we got away with it. Nobody else, except for Leslie Howard and Bette Davis in *Of Human Bondage,* did that, and only once. We were the only realistic studio at that time. And we never thought of appeasing or appealing to Warner's or Wallis' taste. I only wanted to make an honest picture."

Robert Lord recalls: "The only thing I cared about was the weekly check.

"My trouble was I couldn't lie. Blanke was conciliatory . . . or appeared to be . . . he never seemed to get into the toe-to-toe slugging contests with Jack like I did." Lord used the methods he learned as a lightweight.

Brynie Foy had still another method; he moved fast and straight, like his story lines, *Submarine D-1, Alcatraz Island, Racket Busters.* He knew precisely what he wanted. "I never looked at sets, hair or costumes, only the script," recalls Foy. "I saw a lot of phonies worrying about costumes and sets. A lot of guys who got rich making failures. Not me. Maybe my wife knew something about hair, but not me, and she didn't interfere."

Foy produced an average of thirty pictures a year between 1935 and 1940. "I never had to go to Warner or Wallis with ideas for 'B' films. Never had to ask anybody anything. Nobody approved the scripts but me. Some of the films were 'A's', then Jack would say yes or no. Boom! Just like that. No man could run a studio better than Jack. Every part of it. I'll tell you this about him, he could direct and photograph if he had to. I saw him. He knew it all."

"Foy and Warner talked the same language," recalls Blanke. "He was a big favorite of Jack's. He got the shit thrown at him and he made it into pictures."

But not without problems. Foy's annoyance with Jack is still active. "He won't stand up in a pinch. He'll shake your hand on Friday and tell you you're set for two years, then go to New York, call on Monday and fire you. I know him well and I like him, don't get me wrong, but he has no guts. Warner would fire anybody. I was in and out seven times, but he was fearless about calling you up three months later and insisting you come back."

Foy had no illusions about making dreams, he simply made picture shows. "It's not an art. Just take a look at any picture made twenty years ago, then look at Michelangelo . . . now *he* seems to hold up. People forget this business started when it cost five cents to get in. It's a nickel-and-dime audience.

"They made *The Glass Menagerie* at Warner Bros. Once! Mistake number forty-eight."

Foy recalls: "Oh, we had some decent writers. Waldo Salt couldn't do it then, but Dick Breen was a good writer. We had some secondary writers and class writers . . . but it took them a year to finish. I didn't have many of them. Everything they write is God.

"When Warner's had bought a good picture, we would take the good script and 'switch' it around. The background, etc. We made *Tiger Shark* five times. I took a Sheridan novel, and he wrote two hundred years ago, and 'switched' it. As long as we were stealing, let's say adopting, we stole the best.

"I remember Howard Hawks when I told him I was 'switching' his *Tiger Shark.* He said, 'That's okay, I stole it from *They Knew What They Wanted,*' a Sidney Howard play that had been the hit of Broadway's 1924 season and had won a Pulitzer Prize.

"We tried to keep the same fellows working all the time so we got to know each other. As soon as someone finished, I'd

Top left. Orry-Kelly's idea of what a "dame" should look like: Manpower, 1941. Marlene Dietrich, Lucia Carroll and Joyce Compton are at right
Top right. Olivia de Havilland and Milo Anderson
Below. Orry-Kelly with unidentified woman

put the writer with a producer and director and start again. We often had eight films shooting at one time . . . had thirty reels of dailies to look at each day."

On a rare occasion Jack Warner would attempt to infiltrate Foy's assembly line. "They'd hire writers like Erskine Caldwell and others with fancy names. Hire them, then fire them after nine months. And with three months to go on their contracts, they'd be sent to me. I'd give them *Mandalay* to work on. They all loved that title, it inspired them.

"Then one day Jack called and asked, 'Do you have a script down there called *Mandalay?*' I said, 'I sure do,' and he blew up and said, 'Well, you've got three hundred thousand dollars in it.' I said, 'That's right. I sure do. That's for all those fancy writers you fired. They've all done one. I've got five hundred scripts on *Mandalay*. No sense letting them ruin something I might use.'" Jack didn't interfere often.

Foy also had a way with actors and actresses. "The goddamned actors showed up and got parts, that's all. They contributed nothing. They could play, don't get me wrong, but they didn't make the business.

"Actors are all alike. A selfish group of people. They'll do anything for you up until they make it, then they're writer, producer, director, everything. Look at Cagney, as soon as he left Warner Bros., he was a bomb.

"Actors give you the impression they're the only ones who want to make a good picture . . . but they won't even put up the money to make that 'one great picture' they always talk about.

"I never had trouble with character actors and as a rule they're the best. British actors were usually no problem and most fellows from the stage, who came up the hard way, they were no problem. But the greatest actors I worked with were Rin Tin Tin and Smokey. And I know Lassie would be okay, too."

An assistant casting director remembers Foy's style with starlets. "I remember him 'blue-paging' girls once in a while in those days. He'd have a scene written for a young actress after the script had been completed. A scene that would call for a new character, a young, pretty waitress, or nurse, or gun moll, or something. The new pages would come out of the Script Department on blue mimeo paper. That's where the 'blue-paging' term came from."

Foy recalls: "I never let a girl come into my office that I didn't leave the door open. That doesn't mean I didn't have a girl. Sure I did. In fact there was one I kept working all the time, but I didn't chase these girls around. Some did and there were agents who would come in and offer you their clients. And many of the girls would offer, but I didn't go for that.

"There were guys who used to say, 'If a girl doesn't lay somebody over there, they can't work.' I said, 'Well, then, how the hell did Bogart and Cagney get work? Who did they lay?'"

There wasn't a female executive on the lot.

"In the good old days," recalls Lord, "there was very little monkeying around. We were just too damn busy. At Metro it was just the opposite, every producer had his stable of girls. But I never in my career laid a glove on an actress. My unique distinction as a producer."

"Never an actress," says Blanke. "Never, no, no, no, never an actress. I never went near an actress, that is the secret of my success as a producer."

Foy still looks like the typical producer. Like a spoiler. He has a head like a shot put, a mouth that fires instead of speaks and he wears expensive silk robes and slippers in the middle of the day. And the cigar is in place. You expect to find a hundred-dollar blond in his upstairs bedroom, maybe a three-dollar blond. But his daughter lives there, she has been with her father since his wife died. Foy married only once, to a woman from San Francisco who wasn't an actress. She died twenty-four years ago, but he's still a family man.

Blanke married twice; his first wife left him because he lived ninety percent of his life at the studio. He is still married to the second. Neither were actresses.

Lord married Martha Bliss, a Radcliffe girl he met in the Harvard 47 Dramatic Workshop, in June of 1926. She died in 1973 after forty-seven years of marriage and a painful eighteen months of cancer. In May of 1974, Lord married a woman his wife had introduced him to. "She was a great matchmaker, all great women are."

But on the screen the supervisors were supposed to supply the kind of women, heros, villains and love stories Jack wanted. And regardless of their methods, ambitions or hidden dreams, Jack intended to see they did.

Tenny Wright ran the Production Office and was responsible for the physical production of each film. The Camera, Art, Construction, Wardrobe, Makeup, Special Effects, Transportation, Communications and Postproduction departments

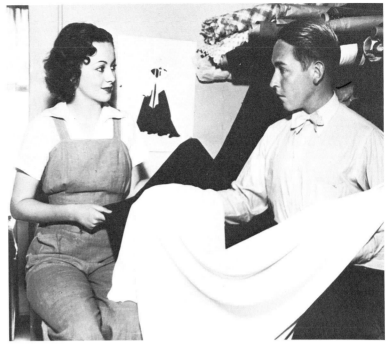

reported to him. There were a total of eight sound stages working at all times, and Wright knew what was happening on each one.

His assistant, James Vaughn, knew what was happening everywhere else. What couldn't be found on the lot, he found off the lot. "Whatever was required. The best sketch artist, stuntman, powderman, everyone," recalls Lord.

An immaculate man, Wright arrived early each morning in a limousine, with a freshly cut carnation in his lapel. He became a member of the polite Pigeons Club, but at the studio his background showed. An ex-circus hand, he had no difficulty with a language consisting of four-letter words and used it eloquently. "He'd call up for no apparent reason," recalls an art director, "and say, 'Remember, I'm running this #$%@¢&* studio,' then hang up. Just in case you forgot, he let you know who was in charge."

John Huston recalls, "In those days you sat around a horseshoe table and the heads of the departments would throw questions at you. 'What kind of pictures do you want on the wall?' 'How many extras in this scene?' And you'd ask for a hundred and fifty and Tenny would make it a hundred and seventy-five so you couldn't come back later and say you didn't have enough. They always went up on you, never down, unless you were completely unreasonable. When it came to the picture, that's where they spent the money."

Warner checked himself, however, to make sure it was spent correctly. "He always worried about the sets," recalls Blanke. "Mostly the hours of painting, etc. He arrived each morning in those days, early, and went to each set. He was a real boss."

The sets were normally small, dark, and little attention was given to the detail that "wouldn't be missed in long shots," as Warner put it. Shadows would be used to cover areas that were unfinished. It suited the Warner look.

For the grand romances, however, a certain splendor was required. "I had Stage 9 built for *The Sea Hawk*," recalls Blanke. "It was called Blanke's Folly then." A term coined by Warner. Stage 9 was a tank stage and was large enough to have fifty-foot scale models of English and Spanish galleons fight on it. The tank was thirty feet deep and there were tracks on the bottom to guide the ships into combat. Blanke had taste; he liked expensive cardboard.

The Wardrobe Department was the supervisor's easiest make.

George Orry Kelly, who ran the department, seemed hand-made for the films they produced, for costuming gun molls, waitresses, dames and actresses like Ida Lupino, Barbara Stanwyck, Ann Sheridan and that rough, rising ingenue of the thirties, Bette Davis. Warner also recognized his talent and when he arrived in 1932 gave him a long-term contract, had the Publicity Department change his name to Orry-Kelly and let him loose among the threads. He fit.

The costume designers at MGM and Paramount, Adrian and Banton, relied heavily on brilliant white satins, gold lamé and buckets of sequins to provide the glitter and glamour that were needed to color the limited attraction of black and white film. But Orry-Kelly worked in neutral grays and with dull finishes that had a reality, a street look. "When I first came here," Kelly recalls, "I found Hollywood to be a layer of tinsel over tinsel. I have dedicated myself to stripping off the surplus. 'Never a spangle' was my motto."

When the supervisors needed a few sequins, some cellophane or the uniforms for the Spanish Armada, they went to designer Milo Anderson.

Anderson arrived from the Goldwyn Studios in 1933 with Busby Berkeley. At Warner Bros. he continued to drape the Berkeley girls in sequins, Celluloid and ostrich feathers, but as few as possible. He specialized in historical costume, lace and brocade, and if there was an actress on the lot so beautiful it hurt, he could make it hurt more. If a supervisor had a script that required ornate buckles and a cape that swashed, he supplied it.

Howard Shoup arrived in 1935 to supply Brynie Foy with his needs. The policy of "switching" immediately spread to the Wardrobe Department. Shoup reworked costume after costume, skirt after skirt, blouse after blouse and suit after suit into new wardrobes. It was appropriate, men in the streets, in prison, in alleys and women on the make often wear hand-me-downs. Particularly in the thirties, at least at Warner Bros.

Whether an actress wore asphalt gray or silver lace, or whether her leading man had a face like an old rock or perfect marble, the supervisors always cast the actresses in the traditional image of the heroine. The romantic image. They were all beautifully made specimens of female flesh . . . and used as if that flesh were to serve as a compelling mask of some inner perfection, an inner morality or mystery.

Facing. Three ideas of what Henry Blanke thought the female should look like. Olivia de Havilland, Anita Louise and Verree Teasdale in Milo Anderson's costumes for A Midsummer Night's Dream, *1936*
Below. Errol Flynn tests Milo Anderson's costume for cameraman Tony Gaudio in preparation for The Adventures of Robin Hood, *1938*

"It was important they looked good," insists Blanke. "The leading man or lady must look as good as possible. For the story they had to look attractive to each other. But the theory was they had to look beautiful. It was understood."

Lord: "We never thought about it then, it just happened that way. The business is based on a belief in beauty, in heroes. I started writing for Tom Mix. Nobody was more heroic than that. He could do anything, he and his horse."

Foy: "Who wants to look at an ugly dame?" Vaudeville had its own required reading, the same as Jack Warner's—the box office receipts. On occasion, no less a guide to the human need for the reaffirmation of the human spirit than the Lake Poets, than a Bach cantata.

The concept of beauty also had to be captured, projected on the screen, and the supervisors had a choice of cinematographers: "Sol Polito . . . he just worked like a dog," recalls Lord. "And did his best. Very quiet. Photographed women a 'tick' on the hard side. Tony Gaudio, much more a traditional Italian. Under pressure he would scream, yell and curse in two languages. Really good with women stars. Tony used a few more filters and gauzes and made them softer. Ernie Haller was wonderful with women and James Wong Howe made Bette Davis into an extraordinary beauty in *The Letter*."

"We usually chose the cinematographer in concert with the performer," recalls Blanke. "Bette loved Ernie Haller, Bogart took anyone, Muni liked Tony Gaudio or Sol Polito. Flynn, he had no choice, no preferences, because he was so young and beautiful any camera made him look good."

Foy: "I used whoever was available."

But regardless of how wisely, stupidly or crassly the supervisors picked their cameramen, wardrobe, stars, stories or subjects, their choices had to be approved by Hal Wallis and Jack Warner. Wallis was their first obstacle. Jack L. Warner the last. Most of the supervisors were wary pushovers, but a few weren't and met Wallis and Warner head on, sideways and from the back. The reactions varied.

"If Hal respects you," recalls Lord, "there's no problem. If he doesn't, he'll cut you to pieces. He was easy for me to communicate with. He and I were similar, kind of square, no bullshit and not, I repeat, not part of Hollywood society.

"To Jack I was a pain in the ass because he would make statements with a thousand things on his mind, European

Top. Hal Wallis and Henry Blanke in a studio projection room
Bottom. Humphrey Bogart, Henry Blanke and John Huston
on the set of The Treasure of the Sierra Madre, 1948

trips, cars, his steam room, a trip to the White House . . . drastic statements like, 'We're going to change the convict to the warden.' And I would say, 'Of course you're kidding, we'll have to rewrite the whole story,' which would enrage him.

"I'd argue, 'Do you want us to wing this picture, to write as we go along?' And he'd say, 'Of course not,' and then change his mind.

"But when I left the office, he hated me.

"This went on often. I must confess I didn't know what he was talking about and he didn't know what I was saying." But Warner didn't fire him. "I had a very good contract there, but I could have had a better one at Fox or MGM, so he was in the unenviable position of having an employee he couldn't discipline."

Lord had another advantage. "These men, these belligerent men who come from the bottom of society respect physical strength . . . and there was a gym at Warner Bros., and I worked out there every day, went through a complete fighter's workout, had a sparring partner, everything. Lewis Hippe ran the gym.

"It made Jack mad, and every time he heard the bag popping, he'd tell his secretary to 'call Lord up here.' Hippe would take the call and tell me, but I'd say tell him to say I'd be there at one o'clock when I finished. And Jack would be furious . . . and he had a right to be.

"But he knew if our screaming matches ever became physical, I wasn't someone he could hit. And he did throw a punch at someone, but I don't want to get into that."

Lord found ways around the obstacles. "Neither Jack or Hal Wallis, who was pretty crude at that time, had much idea of what they were doing, but the thing that gave them a kind of social conscience was the rise of the Nazis in Germany. The management was Jewish, immensely Jewish, naturally, and it looked like the Nazis weren't going to be stopped . . . and it frightened them. It was the spark. They were sorry for the Jews, the poor, criminals, blacks and so on.

"Two of their big stars, Muni and Robinson, also influenced things. It was very hard to get Muni into some film that didn't have a message. If he wasn't, he would scream and yell and fuss and drive everyone crazy. This was catching. Cagney caught it and said, 'I just don't want to make ordinary pictures any more, I want to make pictures that mean something.' They became, including Davis, thinking actors, which to us were a pain in the ass, but it made for a high-quality product."

Henry Blanke recalls: "Jack had his attitudes which he would never change.

"He bought The African Queen from C. S. Forester for fifty thousand dollars. I worked on it with James Collier and Huston for thirty weeks, but when he read the script, he said, 'I will not make a picture in which the leading man gets bitten by a mosquito. Then he sold it for less than he'd paid. Huston, Collier and their agent made a fortune on that script. I can't understand it to this day.

"With The Life of Emile Zola, the word 'Jew' is cut out, by Jack Warner. It's in there, but you can't hear it . . . it's less than three feet. With Come Fill the Cup, he said, 'I won't make a picture in which, practically, the lead is a colored man.' With The Treasure of the Sierra Madre, Jack cut out the shot of Bogart's head rolling into the water. The most magnificent scene. He said the audience wouldn't stand for it. With The Sea Wolf, he cut out Barry Fitzgerald's role, and his character motivated every character. And Gene Lockhart, the scene where he jumps off the mast, you see him lying on the deck, but the falling was cut out.

"The stories are all the same, somehow. Jack had his ways."

And Blanke had his. When screenwriter Robert Rosson took twenty-nine weeks to write the script for The Sea Wolf and Warner discovered it took Jack London only eight days to write the novel, he was wild. But the work was already done; Blanke had planned carefully.

When John Huston finished the script for The Maltese Falcon in four weeks and wanted to show it to Wallis and Warner immediately, Blanke made him wait another four weeks. "Because I know they don't believe it can be good writing in three or four weeks."

Blanke also recalls the losses. "Jack obeyed the censorship of the Hays, Breen and Sherlock office. We had a code and we had to obey it. Every script had to go there . . . and I had objections to being forced to change the best plots for forty years, stories and plots by the best writers. It was the filthy lucre, that's the question. What does that mean, integrity versus filthy lucre?

"I was never honest in those days. I would have liked the test, more freedom to be more honest."

Jack Warner also confronted Blanke head on. Blanke hired Ali Hubert, a German who had worked for Lubitsch and costumed The Adventures of Robin Hood for the studio, to

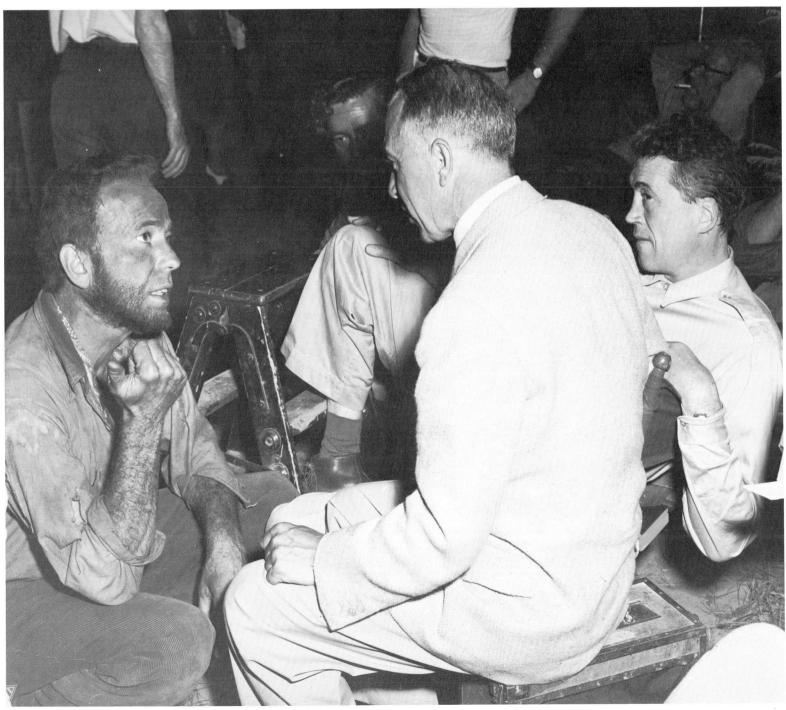

Right. William Jacobs
Far right. Lou Edelman
Facing, left. Hal Wallis, William Dieterle, Paul Muni and Henry Blanke in Mexico for Juarez, 1939
Facing, right. Henry Blanke signs his fifteen-year contract with the studio on May 2, 1945, as Jack Warner watches. The photo inscription reads, "Dear Henry, one of the happiest days of my life—Jack"

design the costumes for The Life of Emile Zola. "In the middle of the film, Jack came into my office and locked the door. He said, 'We don't need this man, we have our own Wardrobe Department.' I said, 'I'll quit right now and you can continue without me if this man doesn't stay on.' He never said another word. That was the only real argument I had with Jack."

Jack had his ways, mysterious, crude, unexplained because he didn't have to explain them, to anyone. And sometimes he was right.

When Blanke and Huston started to make Dashiell Hammett's The Maltese Falcon, it had already been made twice at the studio, once by Blanke with the title Satan Met a Lady. "I didn't know what Huston wanted, but when I saw the script and he told me, I understood. So did Hal Wallis, give credit where credit is due. Jack didn't understand, but approved it because Wallis did.

"When we finished and screened it at Jack Warner's house, he said, 'Well, I asked for it and I got it.' But Jack added what made the picture a success. Number one, Jack told us to add a gloved hand that shoots someone in the beginning of the film and, number two, he made us write the foreword. That made it a hit. We had previewed it several times and people hadn't understood it up to then.

"It comes out that despite the fact Jack Warner never had anything to do with some of the greatest hits ever made at the studio, he was a genius. We used to call it the Warner luck. Somehow he always came out on top . . . even when we had to lie to gain our intentions."

"Jack's track record is phenomenal," recalls Lord. "And it can't all be a misprint. He was brighter than I thought then; I often thought he was stupid and I was wrong."

Jack never let up the pressure; even when he dismissed a factory employee, there was a profit to be made. Lord was called into Roy Obringer's office three weeks before he was to leave the studio and report to the US Army. It was 1941 and there was a sizable war to be fought. "Obringer told me that Jack wanted to know if I wanted to settle my contract, to buy my way out. I told him to tell Jack to stick it up his ass, 'I have another job. I am through with motion pictures, I don't need a contract.'

"That was a facet of Jack's character I couldn't understand. When I thought about it later, I got really mad. It was a lousy thing to do."

Jack's first consideration always appeared to be money. Brynie Foy was getting expensive, at $3,500 a week, and his option was dropped on June 5, 1940, with four years to go on his contract. And on December 1, 1939, Henry Blanke was still making only $1,750 despite the fact that nearly all of the studio's most prestigious films were now being produced by him.

Orry-Kelly was also dropped, called up to Warner's office one day and told to pack up and be off the lot by the end of the day. The excuse was that producer Mark Hellinger didn't like the skirts for The Doughgirls. The rumors were that Kelly was too influential with Jack's wife, Ann.

William Jacobs picked up where Foy left off and made fifty-six films during the forties, most forgettable. Hellinger made They Drive by Night, High Sierra; Robert Fellows made They Died with Their Boots On; David Lewis King's Row; Howard Hawks produced and directed The Big Sleep and To Have and Have Not; and Louis Edelman did White Heat.

In the mid-forties several independent producers came onto the lot. They shared in the profits of their films, were in complete command and had a sizable share of the power and the glory. The contract producers were envious of the independent, but only a studio boss at Warner Bros. could successfully make a safe transition.

Hal Wallis left his studio job in the early forties and became an independent producer on the Warner lot. His first films were Air Force, Now Voyager, Saratoga Trunk and Casablanca. "He took Casablanca from Jerry Wald," recalls Blanke, "and Saratoga Trunk from me, then two others, and put the scripts in his drawer. Then he quit and became an independent producer. He took all the scripts from us and became a ten-million-dollar man."

Shortly after Wallis' departure from the studio in 1944, Warner approached Blanke and asked him to head production. "I said, 'Jack, I work here long enough, from seven to eight, ten, eleven. I have no married life, my first wife left me for that same reason.' I told him no."

Louis B. Mayer was also interested in Blanke and wanted to buy up his contract, but, "Harry Warner called and told Mayer, 'If you take Blanke away from us, we won't run an MGM picture in our theaters.' Mayer told him to just forget they ever talked about it.

"Warner Bros. wanted me, but they wouldn't give me a

percentage or stocks. They said, however, that they'd give me a fifteen-year contract for five thousand dollars a week, but no more. Without options. Jack wouldn't pay me more than he was being paid, or couldn't. He said something about the Wage Stabilization Board, who were running those things during the war. I signed on May 2, 1945. It was called the 'Sir Henry Blanke' contract in those days. I had a clause that said they couldn't talk to me about money from then on. That made Harry mad."

Blanke produced *Juarez, The Old Maid, The Sea Wolf, The Great Lie, The Maltese Falcon, The Constant Nymph, Old Acquaintance, The Mask of Dimitrios, Deception, The Treasure of the Sierra Madre, The Fountainhead, Beyond the Forest, Bright Leaf, Come Fill the Cup, The Nun's Story* and seventy-eight others.

Blanke: "What does it mean, integrity versus filthy lucre? The films that weren't honest, I'd do over tomorrow. But I guess the main thing was, we had something to fight against." His speech is still fast, but occasionally slows down. "Youth also played a part, I was young then. I haven't the guts now to lie for my own purposes."

Foy: "I remember all the hits, I can't remember the flops." *Alcatraz Island, Crime School, Girls on Probation, Hell's Kitchen, Devil's Island* and countless others.

Lord: "Now I look back at it, it's the principle of going up to bat. If you don't swing at it, you'll never get a hit and we swung and swung and swung." Lord produced *The Prince and the Pauper, Tovarich, The Amazing Dr. Clitterhouse, Brother Rat, The Letter, Confessions of a Nazi Spy, The Private Lives of Elizabeth and Essex, Dive Bomber, One Foot in Heaven* and forty others.

Most of the supervisor/producers got exactly what they wanted, cardboard and tinsel, but the few who wanted, needed, silver found they couldn't make it alone no matter how they shouted or lied, not at Warner Bros. If they wanted to build a complex, moving second act into their picture shows, then someone else would have to do it for them.

At that critical moment—the script finished, the performers perfectly cast, the sets and costumes built—when the dream was ready to take life, the supervisor had to give control to another man, a man who was likely to be a creative whore or a simple factory foreman that Jack Warner had honored with the title of director. Regardless, a few supervisors would eagerly turn the medium over to the directors and then protect and support them as they did the yelling and lying in the fragile belief that the impossible just might be made possible.

But the supervisor's chances were slim. "I knew the director was the most important thing," recalls Blanke. "It just depended on who it was. Give me a hundred names and I'll pick the three or four good ones for you.

"Yes, I remember the directors. They got well paid, got credits . . . they got everything."

Below. Charles Boyer and Claudette Colbert serve dinner in Tovarich, *1937*
Facing, top. Charles Boyer, Joan Fontaine, Peter Lorre and Alexis Smith in The Constant Nymph, *1943*
Facing, bottom. George Raft and Marlene Dietrich in Manpower, *1941*

Below. Charles Boyer and Claudette Colbert serve dinner in Tovarich, 1937
Facing, top. Charles Boyer, Joan Fontaine, Peter Lorre and Alexis Smith in The Constant Nymph, 1943
Facing, bottom. George Raft and Marlene Dietrich in Manpower, 1941

Facing. Marlene Dietrich and Richard Todd in Stage Fright, *1950*
Top. Paul Henreid and Bette Davis in Now Voyager, *1942*
Center. Bette Davis does it to Claude Rains in Deception, *1946*
Bottom. Irene Dunne and William Powell in Life with Father, *1947*

Top. Stephen McNally and Jane Wyman in Johnny Belinda, *1948*
Center. Bette Davis and Errol Flynn in The Sisters, *1938*
Bottom. Joan Crawford in Possessed, *1947*
Facing. Bette Davis and Humphrey Bogart in Dark Victory, *1939*

Facing, top left. Mary Astor and Bette Davis in The Great
Lie, *1941*
*Facing, bottom left. Doris Day, Lauren Bacall and Kirk Douglas
in* Young Man with a Horn, *1950*
Facing, right. Barbara Stanwyck in Meet John Doe, *1941*
*Top. Zachary Scott, Joan Crawford and Sydney Greenstreet
in* Mildred Pierce, *1945*
*Bottom. Barbara Stanwyck, Eve Arden, John Ridgely and
George Brent in* My Reputation, *1946*
Right. Barbara Stanwyck and Gary Cooper in Meet John
Doe, *1941*

Patricia Neal and Gary Cooper in The Fountainhead, *1949*

Below. Bette Davis is right where she belongs in
Mr. Skeffington, *1944*

SCOTCH
AND CELLULOID

Directors

"I'd like to think you killed a man, it's the romantic in me."

The directors preferred refried beans, roasted venison and
scotch with sand in it to the pleasures of illusion. They wanted
work they could bite into. And a lot of peppers.

One or two of the Warner Bros. directors liked flowers or
Celluloid patterns, but most preferred carhops to sleeping
beauties and barroom brawls to politics. If they were going
to work in the picture business, their films were going to have
hips on them, wrinkles made with laughter, and be able to take
a punch. So were the crew and the actors.

Warner Bros. was a director's neighborhood, rough and
willing to get rougher. A great place to play.

During the shooting of a film, the director had absolute
control over all of the studio's toys: the lovely actresses, the
stunt men, horses, castles, forts, streets, tommy guns, gangsters,
tear gas, smoke bombs, bandits, beggars and heros. It was a
"perfect" neighborhood and during the thirties and forties the
directors strenuously refused to grow up.

Jack had other plans for them. He wanted them to act like
foremen, not directors, men who took the assignment, the
materials, the employees and the cameras the supervisor gave
them, then drove them all in one direction, hard, until the
product was squeezed out. On schedule, within the budget and
profitably. Both theatrical and motion picture tradition kept
Warner from calling them foremen, but it didn't stop him from
using them that way.

In the early thirties he broke whatever spirit many of them
had, Ralph Staub, Archie Mayo, Alfred E. Green, William
McGann, John G. Adolfi and others. They fit neatly into the
factory, like a main gear, and ground out films for both the
tuxedo and underwear sets. Well-paid men who were forced
to grow up and do as they were told. When their salaries got
too high, Warner fired them and brought in a new batch from
the Writers' Building or the Editing Department. Anyone who
looked like he could shout loud and push people around. The
idea of hiring a woman never occurred to him.

A few directors apparently deserved to be fired, but weren't.
They were the most childish, the wildest and roughest inmates
in Jack's prison, but their films made money. And somehow
they controlled the belligerent stars. Whatever their faults, that
made them good foremen.

Where the rough ones came from wasn't certain—they lied
like drunken marines—but it was certain they had all left home
at an early age, or were thrown out. And they had no training.

The only dramatic school was the theater and few film directors went near it. It was indoors.

Before they stepped onto the lot, the directors had spent their years wandering in and out of the world's great cities, harbors and brothels. They had worked on the *New York Times,* backstage at the St. James Theater, traveled with the Ringling Brothers Circus, sold newspapers and Shanghai coke on San Francisco streets and flown with the Lafayette Flying Corps in World War I. They were nomads, adventurers, hunters and bandits tight with the last draft of the American spirit, womanizers, boozers, liars and bare-knuckle fighters who would tell stories only if they had to. But they had been born too late, at the turn of the century, and by the time they were half grown all the frontiers had been crossed, except dreamland, Hollywood.

When most of the directors arrived, in the silent era, they took her . . . in as many ways as man has devised and several new ones. Hollywood couldn't have been more delighted; she simply rolled over and cheered. She needed men who wore polished boots, carried whips and gave commands from horseback. All the posturing pretties and prettier men had to have someone to tell them what to do. They wanted it, needed it. And directors crammed with their own need for violence and action made the moving pictures move, fast, if they shouted loud enough.

Directing silent films was a good job and on more than one occasion Jack Warner came on the set and started shouting himself. The directors liked him, he was one of them.

But when the sound men with their microphones and all the efficient young department heads arrived in 1929 and 1930 with their schedules, costumes, makeup and sets, the directors' status dropped. Then Jack, their friend, gave the writers top billing, and put a species called supervisors in charge of them. The directors were sure it was just a fad, like writers, but when the trend persisted, the Screen Directors Guild published a report showing that it took only 39 producers in 1927 to make 743 pictures and 220 producers in 1937 to make 484 pictures. To the directors, those were alarming figures, but no one else cared.

But the directors weren't going to give up all the toys easily and if it was necessary to show that they were the pros, it was easily proved. They already drove Pierce Arrows, had houses in Malibu and were members of the Beach Club in Santa Monica. Some even ate lunch with Jack in his private dining

room. One way or another they'd stay in charge, and did. You could tell just by looking. They were the generals and they found appropriate uniforms.

Lloyd Bacon had played "heavies" in early silent films, sailed with the navy during World War I and directed silent films at Warner Bros. Sunset Studios. "He was a flamboyant guy," recalls Harry Warren. "He wore the loudest clothes you ever saw; big houndstooth jackets, loud, colored hats." Bacon was Jack's favorite. He directed the studio's biggest star, James Cagney, in fourteen films and during the thirties was the highest paid director, at $4,225 a week.

Mike Curtiz carried a bottle of codeine cough medicine in one hand and a megaphone in the other. He wore gray sweatshirts, jodhpurs and McClellan boots. "He never sat down," recalls Lord. "He was in perpetual motion. He loved it." He could afford to at $3,500 a week.

Busby Berkeley worked in loose white pants, white shirt, often a white woolen sweater, plaid socks and white sneakers. For $1,750.

William Keighly was a cutout of a Lord and Taylor ad. English and perfect at $1,750 a week.

Roy Del Ruth was a fat little man who wore stiff collars and smelled of cologne at twenty feet.

Mervyn LeRoy wore whatever was current, fashionable; silk suits, scarves, tennis sweaters and a pipe or cigar. He had been a newsboy on San Francisco streets, a gagman, a director of silent films and had married Harry Warner's daughter in 1932, instead of Ginger Rogers.

William Wellman wore a French beret, rolled jeans, Western boots and bits of khaki and plaid. He also had a limp that he would exaggerate whenever he met a pretty girl. "The prettier the girl, the larger the limp," he recalls. Wellman had flown a Nieuport fighter plane in the Chat-Noir, the Black Cat Group of the Lafayette Flying Corps, when he was nineteen. He killed a man over Germany, one-on-one in the air. A neat little tin can of Murad cigarettes was generally stashed in his breast pocket. He started in films doing whatever they let him. Director Bernie Durning taught him about directing. "I did stunts, walked on wings for him, airplane wings." Wellman was born on February 29, 1896, leap year, which made him nine years old in 1932. The average age for a director.

Others even more colorful would follow: Howard Hawks, suntanned, white-haired and bent like the hawk. William

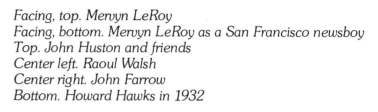

Facing, top. Mervyn LeRoy
Facing, bottom. Mervyn LeRoy as a San Francisco newsboy
Top. John Huston and friends
Center left. Raoul Walsh
Center right. John Farrow
Bottom. Howard Hawks in 1932

Wyler in his beige Stetson and faking a deaf ear. Raoul Walsh with his black leather eye patch. John Huston in white flannels, safari jacket and a monkey on his back.

There would be alligator shoes, Western bandannas knotted against graying temples, swagger sticks and immaculate creations from Durango, the French Riviera and the Levant. And at one time or another they all would smoke large, expensive cigars. Havanas. From the middle of their mouths, like a giant whistle.

The egos, however, had more brass than the uniforms.

When Michael Curtiz arrived in New York from his native Hungary in 1927, the streets were crowded with cheering, screaming crowds, thousands of flags and exploding firecrackers. It took the best efforts of a studio representative, several large slugs of whiskey and a very patient translator to convince Curtiz that the city had not turned out to welcome the celebrated film director, but was in the streets to celebrate the Fourth of July.

Director John Farrow had someone fire a cannon every time he boarded his yacht in Newport Harbor.

The directors were no doubt convinced that they were the chosen ones, that if a single personality could dominate the cinematic art form, then it was theirs.

After all, it is the camera that narrates the story, it is the single eye with which the audience sees the story and it is the director who selects the shot, the position of the camera and what it will see. It didn't matter that the directors hadn't conceived or written the story; they were the ones who would tell it. And they could tell it any way they chose. Just as the minstrels in the Middle Ages told the story of Roland a thousand different ways. It wasn't the story that counted, it was who told it.

Getting a story told on film the way a director wanted it told, however, required total control over the pompous, overpaid actors and actresses from the decadent world of the theater, Broadway. A director had to fight to get the studio to give him stars and then fight to make them behave. And Cagney, Davis, Robinson, Flynn, and Bogart made a good fight, but Jack Warner made a good war.

"The resistance of the studio was good for you," recalls John Huston. "Not only for the writers and the directors, but for all the talent. They were the establishment, you might say, and we were the criminals. It gave you something to fight.

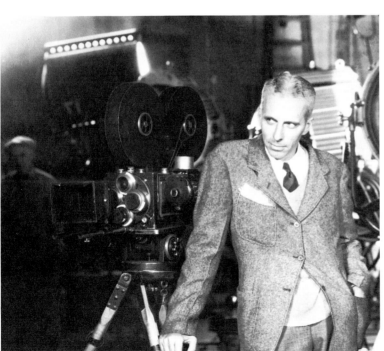

"When I went to MGM later, it was a completely different atmosphere, a different ambience. There was a sense of leisure at MGM, almost a luxury of time. People talked a lot about everything and there were those Cedric Gibbons sets. I'm not saying they were bad, mind you, but they were different. At Warner Bros., the pressure was always on.

"The departments were totally prepared, everything was made and done for you. In the Art Department there would be model sets of every scene, even the little rooms, and there were these small cutout figures so you could move them around and set up your shots with them. Look down a tele-scope lens device they had and select each shot. I didn't use it, I made my own drawings instead, but they made them anyway."

Henry Blanke spent considerable time convincing Jack Warner not to fire John Huston because he was consistently late for work. "When I first met him," recalls Blanke, "he was just a drunken boy, hopelessly immature, without an ounce of discipline inside him. He'd attend every party, wear a monkey on his shoulder and get sincerely drunk."

Vincent Sherman was hired to write for Brynie Foy at the studio, but on a condition. "Foy told Sherman, 'Well, I talked to Mr. Warner and he says that if you are willing to sign a seven-year contract to act, write or direct, then we'll start you with two hundred dollars a week.'" Warner liked to cover his bets. Sherman wrote, worked like a foreman and directed, *The Hard Way, Mr. Skeffington* and *Adventures of Don Juan* among others.

"None of us thought of ourselves working in an art form at that time," recalls Sherman.

Raoul Walsh started his career as an actor in D. W. Griffith's *Birth of a Nation* in 1916. "I was terrible. Just terrible. It's a wonder I wasn't shot. I shot Lincoln, they should've shot me." He played John Wilkes Booth and when he gave up performing he took to direction like a hammer to a nail.

He arrived at the studio in 1930 to make *The Roaring Twenties.* "In those days at Warner's, we used to work until three or four o'clock in the morning. And when I'd get home, at daybreak, there'd be a script on my lawn, like a newspaper . . . somebody threw it there. We went back and started the new work at nine o'clock. You see, we got into the training of 'take everything.' Just do it and get started and get out of here. Once in a while, you'd get a nice one, a gem, but the rank and file of them were not too hot."

"The only concern in those days was to do it right," recalls Huston. "The goal was excellence. You wanted the script perfect and when it was finished and approved, it didn't change. You shot it the way it was written. Your hope was for a good cast, everything."

Busby Berkeley had his own sense of excellence. "I had sixteen magnificent girls under contract and I engaged others for each film. They would ask me, why did you pick that one, she isn't good-looking. But they didn't know how I was going to have her dressed, they didn't know how I was going to have her made up, they didn't know what kind of costume I was going to put on her so she would become a new personality. I talked to every girl before I chose her and I looked into her eyes. And her eyes really mirrored herself. I found out more about her character and all the ingredients just by looking into her eyes." The youngest, nicest and most beautiful were picked as "close-up girls," others as "dancers" and some as "fakers," large show girls whose talent consisted of clapping and stepping to a time step.

"One day I had seven hundred and fourteen girls show up for one call. I picked three girls out of the seven hundred and fourteen and put them aside with my sixteen."

The privileged sixteen were to be always available, even when no picture was being shot. "We'd knit, play cards," recalls Lois Lindsey, "we'd play every kind of game we could dream up. We sat around for days, but Buzz would always tell the front office that he couldn't do anything without the girls. 'I get my ideas from the girls,' he would tell them. But on a picture we'd earn our money, we'd really work hard."

Berkeley drank consistently, the best scotch, married nine women, mostly dancers, but left all but one to go back to his mother. Always an overgrown kid, he had a soft spot inside him when it came to the girls. "No matter what, he'd hire the girls with the hard luck stories," recalls Lindsey. "Particularly if they had come from New York. If they had worked with Buzz there, he'd hire them and see they ate. We worked with girls and guys over fifty. They'd work the back line."

Off the set, Berkeley also liked the "close-up" girls around. "He called me one day at home," recalls Lindsey. "He was at the Biltmore and wanted me to come have a drink with him. I was scared to death, so I didn't go. He was the big director and I was only a kid. Nothing. But he was with some other people so Virginia Grey said, 'Let's go together.' So we did.

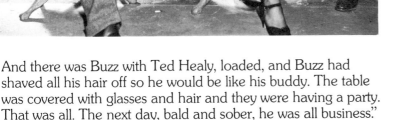

And there was Buzz with Ted Healy, loaded, and Buzz had shaved all his hair off so he would be like his buddy. The table was covered with glasses and hair and they were having a party. That was all. The next day, bald and sober, he was all business."

On occasion, the Depression bothered Berkeley, but he handled it differently than the writers. His piano player, Malcolm Beelby remembers: "When word went out about a Busby Berkeley call, the whole town would come alive. Everyone wanted to audition, they needed the money, and he always hired more dancers than we needed. And a lot of extras worked, too; he'd put ten extra men on a boom that required six. He was rough, but he put a lot of people to work."

Berkeley also had ways of handling Tenny Wright and his tight budgets.

"We were doing this picture," recalls Lindsey, "that was supposed to take place in Mexico and Buzz wanted to do something special with Dolores Del Rio. Something with white horses that they didn't want him to have. So he told us, 'I'm going to get them, do you want to see how? I've got a great idea.'

"We all sat and listened as he phoned the front office and said, 'I'm gonna need some pigs, chickens and cows . . . and maybe a few white horses.' We could hear them scream over the phone that they'd dirty up the place, the sets, the cast, everything. Then, little by little, Buzz would withdraw the pigs, chickens, etc., but he stuck with the white horses. And got them. And when he got them, they messed up the whole lot."

Berkeley's offstage dramatics were as colorful, but on occasion tragic. Following a party in the Pacific Palisades home of studio manager Bill Koenig, Berkeley left in his car late at night and on his way home killed five people in an auto accident. Henry Blanke and several others who had attended the party refused to testify at the trial that Berkeley wasn't drunk, but many others did and after considerable effort by attorney Jerry Geisler and Warner money, Berkeley was acquitted.

A short time later, when Warner and most of the Hollywood moguls figured that the musical genre was used up, Berkeley left for Fox and MGM. His best efforts, however, remained at Warner Bros.: *Footlight Parade, Dames, 42nd Street, Gold Diggers of 1933, Gold Diggers of 1935, Gold Diggers of 1937, Wonder Bar* and *Hollywood Hotel.*

Director William Wellman preferred working with men "because they don't have to bother about being made up and putting that goddamned hair in curls. The people that I couldn't get along with in this business were the hairdressers. 'Oh, those time killers. They ought to line up every hairdresser and pluck them bald.'"

Wellman made films with balled fists. "You make this picture for someone, and whoever he is sleeping with at the time has something to do with it. More wives, in the middle of the night, have ruined something that a director has gone out and belted himself goofy to make, than you can possibly imagine. Or the agent. Oh, the agents are wonderful!"

Nothing intimidated him, not even the press. After three days shooting on *Public Enemy,* he saw that screenwriters Bright and Glasmon had been right about the casting, that Cagney should be playing the lead instead of Eddie Woods. He went directly to Zanuck. "'Look, there is a horrible mistake. We have the wrong guy in here. Cagney should be the lead!' Zanuck said, 'Well, you know who Eddie Woods is, don't you?' And I said, 'No, I don't. Who is he?' 'He's engaged to marry Louella Parson's daughter.' I said, 'Well, for Christ's sake, are you going to let some newspaperwoman run your business?' He said, 'Change them!'"

Wellman liked things to go his way. He hit a labor union representative in the face when he wouldn't move out of a scene after he had been asked. He leveled a pistol at an assistant director who wasn't working fast enough, and fired. The bullet tore up the wood at his feet and the work sped up.

He had many nicknames, but the one that stuck was "Wild Bill." It fit. "That is the one thing that I have done. I have had a wonderful life. I really have. I ran away and went into the air corps in 1916 and I've been married many times to beautiful women. One of them was a big star at the time. And I've had my ups and downs. Mentally and physically, and every way. And a tremendous respect and great hatred for talent. A lot of them that have it are such horses' asses. Jesus, they burn you up.

"Goddamn, I have had companies where we would go out and make a picture and fight for that picture. Fight with our fists for Christ's sake."

Other Men's Women, Public Enemy, Night Nurse, The Hatchet Man, So Big, Frisco Jenny, Wild Boys of the Road, Island in the Sky, The High and the Mighty, Track of the Cat.

"He was all over the place," a powderman recalls. "If he

liked a scene, he'd let out a yell and tell you how marvelous it was. When he didn't like a scene, he'd roar and curse and tell everybody how lousy it was."

"A rough guy, a real bully," recalls a publicist. "Old Hollywood stuff, always yelling at his actors, rude, loud. Those kind of guys were monsters."

When Wellman was shooting, he flatly refused to read the memos Jack Warner sent to his set. On more than one occasion, he advised the messenger boy to read it himself and give Warner his own answer.

Actresses were his special delight. "They hated to work for me as much as I hated to work with them. Women! Always fussing about their makeup, lighting, their poses! Let 'em get tough with me and I let 'em have it. And believe me, I can outcuss anybody in this *#$%¢&*# town!"

Ida Lupino was just sixteen when she met Wellman at Paramount on *The Light That Failed.* "He said, 'Who's that? I want her over here! I want to meet her.' And I'll never forget my first meeting; I walked in absolutely terrified of him. He said, 'Well now, goddamn it, can you act? I saw you in a small role and I don't want you to test.' I said, 'I want to read it for you.' He said, 'All right, but goddamn it, if you're no good I'll take a twenty-two pistol and shoot your head off.'

"I read and he said, 'Okay! You're Bessy, but if you let me down, I'll shoot out every light on this #*%¢&$% stage.' I said, 'Mr. Wellman, I'll be Bessy.'

"He got me a star dressing room and a parking spot. He made me feel like something, like I was somebody.

"They were rough, tough men at Warner Brothers. 'Go and get your fanny out there and do it.' These were the kind of men I understand. They used to chew my——— out. 'Don't do Nell of old Drury.' 'What do you mean, darling?' 'I mean don't overact.'

"Walsh, Wellman, Curtiz . . . men who you loved.

"Curtiz would come over when we were doing *The Sea Wolf* and say, 'Lupe, Lupe, Lupe, listen to me, you do a little . . .' and then he'd explain it forever. Afterwards, Julie [John Garfield] would say, 'I don't understand a goddamned thing he was saying, but I think he was right.'"

Mike Curtiz had trouble with the English language. "When you smile," he once told an actor, "you should brighten your teeth." He also told Jack Warner, on various occasions, that the film he had just finished was the *pinochle* of his career.

During *This is the Army,* he hollered at the lighting gaffers to remove the black silk screens, whose slang name was "niggers," from the arcs so he could get more light on the set. He nearly started a riot as over two hundred Negro soldiers who were participating in the film, courtesy of the army, came down out of the chorus to make a few things clear. Curtiz didn't blanch and after it was explained to him he simply hollered to the gaffers, "Okay, okay, get the *Negros* down."

"Curtiz had more energy, more drive than anybody," recalls Lord. "And Mike always had struggled with the language, but he had a language that was better than English, more expressive, even clearer in dramatic points. Mike had a very excellent story sense. He would say something stank and I'd ask, 'Why?'

"'I don't know,' holding his stomach, 'he just, he act like a shit to her.'

"'In what way? Torture her?'

"'No, he, it would be better if he hit her, he act like goddamn faggot.'

"And after a while you would realize something *was* wrong with it.

"On the set, if he was unhappy, he'd say, 'Get Bob.' And then he'd say, 'I rehearse for you.' And if I thought he was wrong, I'd say so and he'd say, 'I don't know.' And I'd say, 'I don't know what to do if you can't be more explicit.' And he'd say, 'Okay, I do it your way . . . when you see the dailies, you be very unhappy.'"

Lord, however, was seldom unhappy. Neither was Jack Warner. *Captain Blood, Casablanca, Yankee Doodle Dandy, The Sea Hawk, The Adventures of Robin Hood, The Sea Wolf, Breaking Point, The Charge of the Light Brigade, Angels with Dirty Faces, Dodge City, The Private Lives of Elizabeth and Essex, Mildred Pierce,* and seventy-four others. One of the two highest paid contract directors, his weekly salary would rise to $5,000 in the forties.

He earned it. He bullied actors into performances. Olivia de Havilland recalls working on *Captain Blood* with Errol Flynn, his first film and their first together. "Errol was terribly ambitious. He wanted to be a success so badly and when we sat in that screening room to look at the first dailies, Mike ridiculed the footage unmercifully. And Errol did nothing, there was nothing he could do, not then when he was just starting, but I could feel the hurt for him on the other side of the room."

Facing. William Wellman
Below. Humphrey Bogart, Ingrid Bergman and Michael Curtiz
on the set of Casablanca, *1943*

Below. Harvey Perry decks James Cagney in The Irish in Us, 1935. Perry played small parts as well as performing Cagney's stunts and being the studio's director of Special Action Effects
Right. Writer Norman Reilly Raine and Michael Curtiz on the set of The Private Lives of Elizabeth and Essex, 1939
Facing, left. Erich Wolfgang Korngold and director William Dieterle, in his white-gloved uniform, go over the score for Juarez, 1939
Facing, right. Edmund Goulding, Joan Fontaine and Joyce Reynolds on the set of The Constant Nymph, 1943

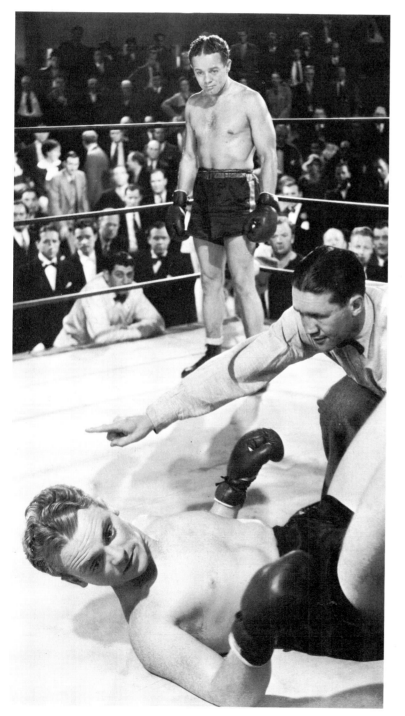

Curtiz walked off the film in protest at Flynn's acting, but Jack Warner personally convinced him to stay. Both Flynn and Curtiz were eventually grateful—it made both their careers—but on the set Curtiz's direction got even rougher. In a scene that required Flynn to withstand a volley of prop rocks thrown by an angry mob, Curtiz was unable to get the proper reaction from his young actor. When he shot the scene again, he personally began throwing real rocks. Flynn was bruised and angry, but Curtiz got his scene.

Curtiz also believed lunch slowed people down and told Bette Davis when they were about to begin The Private Lives of Elizabeth and Essex, "When you work with me, you don't need lunch. You just take aspirin." Before he arrived on a set at 8 A.M., he had already eaten his normal four eggs, steak, potatoes and coffee, with both hands. He knew he wouldn't eat again until nine or ten that night, but he didn't bother to inform the performers.

Curtiz pushed everyone. The Special Effects Department knew that when they staged a battle scene for Curtiz, the normal smoke pots and flash powder weren't going to provide the wind, thunder and smoke he demanded. During the filming of The Charge of the Light Brigade, Curtiz became loudly and profanely dissatisfied with their efforts and began to get behind schedule until a fast-thinking technician came up with the idea of detonating a charge of dynamite from a nearby location. Curtiz was more than pleased; he liked the real thing. And when he was pleased, Harry Warren recalls, "he used to kiss everybody. And he had arms like rails, he used to be an acrobat or something."

The rumors were that he just couldn't stay away from the lovely young actresses, but his wife, screenwriter Bess Meredyth, chose to ignore the rumors. Her influence on the story of each film Curtiz directed was always evident and since Warner wasn't paying her, greatly appreciated. She stayed away from the set when Curtiz was shooting, too wise to try and cork a volcano.

During the shooting of The Private Lives of Elizabeth and Essex, the cast believed that Curtiz was having an affair with the redheaded stand-in for Bette Davis, who was playing the role of Elizabeth the Queen. Flynn told his director that he had slept with the young beauty and caught the "most incredible" social disease from her. Curtiz promptly left for the doctor.

There was life, excitement on a Curtiz set. "And there wasn't

a man or woman at the studio who didn't want to work for him," recalls a veteran special effects technician who had worked a dozen Curtiz films. Curtiz built a family of workers around him and they worked each film. He always had "Sailor" Vinson with him. An all-navy welterweight champ, Vinson was a great morale builder and, "the hardest man in the world to jibe into a fight," according to Harvey Perry, who was the studio's director of special action effects, or "director of spills, chills and thrills." "Sailor" was a stunt man and in those early days would do most anything for a dollar. Warner liked the the price.

"A good stunt man was like a good actor," recalls Perry. "You're always trying to improve your part, do something extra." And on *The Charge of the Light Brigade*, Curtiz gave them their greatest opportunity. "There were a lot of pitfalls on *Charge*, sometimes five horses at a time. And in those days the 'running-w' was legal. Leather socks hobbled the front legs of the horse and were attached to a ring. Then there was a belt around the belly with a hanging ring and we ran cables through the belly ring to the horse's feet. The other end of the cable was tied to a 'dead man' buried in the ground, or to a group of men. It could be rigged to make the left or right foot go first so the horse would fall left or right.

"The rider had to sit way back in the saddle so the rear of the saddle wouldn't knock him forwards when the galloping horse was suddenly yanked to a stop. Instead of stirrups, we had 'steps,' a solid piece of metal which L'd out. The rider tried to jump away from the horse." The riders usually made it safely, but they killed a lot of horses.

The directors at Warner Bros. suited the stunt men's style of life. They weren't much on acting out adventures, but they were good at the real thing. Perry started his career by running away from home to join a circus, to do a "free act," a high dive into a tank of water for twenty-five dollars a week. His start in films came in the mid-twenties when they asked him to do a hundred-and-sixteen-foot dive off a castle wall built on Point Lobos near Carmel, California. For seventy-five dollars. He took it and then found he also had to clear sixteen feet of cliff and do the jump in women's clothing. He still took it, made the dive, cleared the cliff, landed in the water of the Pacific Ocean, but he hit a piece of wood the size of a pencil and broke three ribs. William Wellman, who was just edging into his own career then, came in after him, stark naked, and pulled him out.

Director William Dieterle liked a different style of life on his set. A tall, remote, scholarly man, he loved flowers and always had an abundance on his sound stage. His uniform was small white gloves, which he wore on all occasions. Astrology ran his life. His wife prepared astrological charts for him each day, and production schedules were sometimes changed because the planets were not in favorable positions. But when things were right and his supervisor and friend Henry Blanke got him in gear, flowers and all, he directed *Juarez, The Life of Emile Zola, The Story of Dr. Ehrlich's Magic Bullet,* and *The Story of Louis Pasteur* for $3,000 a week.

Edmund Goulding also didn't appear to fit the lot. He wore gentlemanly gray tailored suits and moved without noise and attending sycophants. He provided Warner Bros. with women's pictures, with four-handerkerchief melodramas that were scorned by the intellectuals and critics of the thirties and forties who were so fond of the seamy, bitter, brutal side of human nature. *That Certain Woman, Dark Victory, The Old Maid, We Are Not Alone, Till We Meet Again, The Great Lie, The Constant Nymph.* Goulding ignored the critics and his agent had made it possible to avoid Warner's prison when he tired of it.

He wasn't a contract director; he was a visitor for one year at a time. His June 11, 1937, contract called for him to direct two films for $50,000 each in twelve week's time and $4,166.67 a week thereafter. His mutual option came up on May 11, 1938.

Henry Blanke, Goulding's supervisor, had to handle him as a guest, but he was one of Blanke's favorites. "He was the most sensitive to the feelings of the performers, he could feel everything. He could tell how they were feeling before they got on the set. He went to Davis one day and said, 'You'll only work two hours today.' She got furious. 'What's wrong, how the hell can you tell? Do you smell me or something?' He simply nodded. 'No, but I can feel it.' She only worked two hours; he could control anybody."

Of all the directors on the Warner lot, Mervyn LeRoy knew his way around best. Even after he divorced Harry Warner's daughter, he still maintained Jack's personal friendship. He had the boss on his side and he either understood, imitated or was naturally gifted with the studio's style. He made telephone calls to most anyone at 2, 3 and 4 A.M. to get answers that could wait until tomorrow, even until next week. And he picked

fights with alacrity, almost without caring, as if it were the thing to do. He would order someone to his office, then when they arrived start yelling at them and asking them what the hell they were doing there. But it never seemed to mean much. The opinions are many about LeRoy. Some shake their heads without understanding, others simply laugh: "He's a *shmuck* who never had a bad script."

Edward G. Robinson had another opinion: "Mervyn was so likable that I distrusted him instantly. I have fears of professionals who make jokes of everything.

"But I soon learned something about Mervyn that makes him special.

"More than any director I know, Mervyn *is* the audience. He is the man who goes to the box office and plunks down his thirty-five cents (now three dollars or more) and loves or hates a picture through his own emotions. He is morally indignant about injustice, but the injustices must be large and blatant. He loves love; he loves children; he loves mothers; he feels deeply that in the end justice must be triumphant. I must say it again: He is the audience."

LeRoy understood politics. He made phone calls daily to whoever he thought could help him. He'd call messenger boys, hacks in publicity, a legman for a columnist in New York, and ask them all to get his name in the paper. It had nothing to do with making a movie, but a lot to do with getting the opportunity to make good ones. He would call from anyplace, once from a ship halfway across the Atlantic to tell Warner to read the novel *Anthony Adverse* and to buy it for him to direct. Jack replied, "Read it, hell, I can't even lift it." But he did buy it and LeRoy directed it.

"I read everything I could get my hands on," recalls LeRoy. "You can't make a good picture without a great story, without a writer. And I never forgot it. It's the story that counts, without it you have nothing." *Little Caesar, Five Star Final, I Was a Fugitive from a Chain Gang, Three on a Match, Hard to Handle, Gold Diggers of 1933, The King and the Chorus Girl, Anthony Adverse, The Great Garrick* and many others.

Often during the early years the directors appeared to enjoy the toys more than what those playthings produced on the screen, but the fun was about to thin out. As the thirties began to bump into the forties, some of their films began to play for six, seven and ten weeks instead of the regulation two and Warner Bros. began to build a dangerous backlog. At first Jack

Warner was bothered by the change in audience behavior, as it disrupted his factory, but their money was always acceptable no matter how it came to him.

In 1938 Warner Bros. reduced production to fifty-two films, then to forty-five in 1940 and then thirty-five in 1942 as the war years began and supplies were scarce. With the continuing reduction, Warner found he had to assign his toys to directors with greater care. But the audience had proved at the box office that a director who was simply an obedient, careful foreman was not to be trusted. The wild, undisciplined boys were the ones bringing in the money, so they were the ones to be trusted with the most expensive toys. He also gave them more money as well as their choice of stories and stars, providing the stars agreed. In addition Jack Warner had to go off the lot for more and more directorial talent. Warner's control began to slip and his chances of finding young, inexpensive talent was reduced.

William Wyler visited the lot to direct *The Letter* with Robert Lord producing and *Jezebel* with Henry Blanke. Bette Davis starred in both and found Wyler a match for her. "We had some snow scenes to shoot with fake snow," recalls Blanke, "and Bette was going to the mailbox to put a letter in and Wyler said, 'Bette, don't wiggle your ass so much, the big scenes are coming later.' And she was completely obedient. They were in love, of course, and how!"

Howard Hawks, a frequent visitor to the studio, arrived in the forties to direct *Sergeant York* and *Air Force* and then to team Lauren Bacall and Bogart in *To Have and Have Not* and *The Big Sleep.* Sam Wood directed *Saratoga Trunk* and *King's Row;* Frank Capra *Meet John Doe* and *Arsenic and Old Lace;* Fritz Lang *Cloak and Dagger* and King Vidor *The Fountainhead* and *Beyond the Forest.*

When the studio wasn't worried about her, Bette Davis worried about herself. Irving Rapper is credited with directing *Now Voyager, The Corn Is Green* and *Deception,* but a young actress who appeared in the films recalls: "Bette directed all her own scenes, she moved us around, told the cameramen where she was going to enter and how to shoot her. The only time Rapper got mad was when she showed up on the set for a scene she wasn't in. He told her to get off, and she did, but she came back and did her scenes. She could do it all."

Lloyd Bacon would back down when confronted by Cagney's energy and desires and other "foremen" gave in to various pressures, but the "directors" spent each minute finding ways to whip the overpaid egos called stars. The easiest way was to steal the show from them entirely. With the camera.

It was simple for a director to make the camera dance, lift and sweep, and draw attention to itself and away from the stars. They could also pull the camera back and reduce the performers to mere specks of humanity struggling through vast landscapes. They could fill the sets with dark, covert shadows, with glimmering shafts of white light, and make picture shows where the performers were merely props, use them as just another part of their Celluloid designs as Busby Berkeley used his dancers. They could use the camera in the same manner as the expressionist painters used their brushes and put their personal vision of the world on the screen, and do it with such elegance and splendor that the audiences would know it was the director who thrilled them, not the performer.

The directors, however, preferred to win their fights with the actors on the sound stage rather than on the screen. They had no time for aesthetic questions and if they thought about them, they didn't mention it. A second act wasn't something you talked about, it was something you did. And if art and life were in constant and irrevocable conflict, as the intellectuals claimed, then they picked life over art every time. Hands down.

Scotch over Celluloid. They'd followed a distant drum to dreamland, but once on a sound stage, they began to beat it. As loud as they could. It was the doing of it, the trip of the film that counted . . . that trip on which you must get totally lost or you will never find your way up onto the screen . . . find your way through the darkness.

On a sound stage Raoul Walsh was uncomfortable around strangers and staffed each of his production units with the same technicians, stunt men and often the same performers. The result was a team of loyal friends who stuck together from the days of The Roaring Twenties until Walsh retired in the mid-sixties. They didn't pretend to understand him, but they wouldn't forget him.

"Life was always a ball on Raoul's locations," recalls a powderman. "Everybody pitched in and helped each other no matter what union affiliation they had. We did our work, but we had our share of fun, too. When we were making Battle Cry on a marine base, we formed our own team of commandos and spent our free time raiding the Marine Corps supply depot. The marines did the same thing, but we always won because one of their boys was working with us. And the great part of it was that Raoul was right there with us."

Walsh preferred shooting away from the studio, away from the sound stages and bosses. On They Died with Their Boots On he took his crew into a wide, sweeping valley near Lone Pine, California. "They gave the schedule to you in those days by the day instead of the week," recalls Walsh. "For a short picture you got thirty-two days and for an extra-long picture they gave you forty-two, maybe forty-three. They would tell you you had five days on location. You'd go on location and it would rain for five days. They'd put the five days back again and we'd struggle through it.

"It was a kind of rough picture to make with all those riders and stuff. The Screen Actors' Guild has passed a ruling that there were to be no 'requests.' Now, in the early days of pictures, I knew of forty cowboys and good riders that I would request, but they finally stopped the 'requests' and the Extras' Guild office supplied the riders. Well, half of them couldn't ride and there were about two hundred people hurt in the picture. I'd go down and watch them getting on the horse from the wrong side. Well, they didn't last long, they were off on the right side.

"There was one fatal accident in the picture. There was a young fellow there, a young actor, playing the part of a lieutenant. When we took a long shot where they have swords, we supply them with wooden swords with a silver tint to them so that it looks like the real blade. Well, this chap, when the property man went to take his sword away from him and give him the phony sword, he said, 'No, I'm going to use this one.' Well, the property boy argued with him awhile and couldn't get anywhere, so he let him keep the sword. So, we took the scene and there were a couple of explosions on either side and he was thrown off his horse. The sword was thrown into the air and he came down on top of it. So, I saw the whole thing, I wasn't very far away from him, and I ran down and pulled the sword out of him, called a limousine and sent him to a hospital. Unfortunately, his mother wouldn't sign to let them operate and find out what happened and in three days, the boy died.

"Another cowboy who was pretty drunk fell off a horse and broke his neck. Another fellow was watching the scene and evidently it didn't look good because he had a heart attack and died.

Top. Dolores Del Rio and Lloyd Bacon
Bottom. Bette Davis makes a point to Irving Rapper on the set
of Now Voyager, 1942

"We had about seven hundred horses in it and when they broke loose that time when Custer and his men dismount just before they die, well, there were a lot of drunken cowboys about three miles away down the road where they loaded horses. Well, when those drunks saw the horses coming at them, that was the end of them. We haven't seem them since."

A smile pokes at Walsh's mouth like an old wound worn with pride as he tells stories of the old days. "We had about four or five doctors going along with the troop and when we left the studio in the morning, four or five buses, limousines and everything, like a traveling circus, and finally two ambulances. Well, some of these extras would look out the bus and see these ambulances and that was all they wanted. The bus stopped and they were out and gone. So someday, somebody played a joke and there was a hearse following us one morning and they damn near went crazy." It's not hard to guess who the "somebody" was.

Asked why there was so much drinking in those early days: "Well, I own stock in the Schenley company." Or, "Oh, sure, I know Flynn and the bottle too." Why was he so good at directing large crowds? "I come from a large family."

Women didn't know how to approach him. "The curious thing about young actresses that come for an important part, or something, the first thing they ask is 'How many changes of wardrobe, Mr. Walsh?'" But the men often knew. "Some actors would say, 'How many guys do I knock down, pardner?'"

On directing cinematographers: "Play this in shadow, this gal can't act very well. But this guy is a dog, don't light him at all."

Why did it take so long for Cagney to die at the end of *Roaring Twenties?* "Well, it's pretty hard to kill an actor. And, because you see, in those days, Cagney and Bogart were the only two stars you could kill in a picture. You couldn't kill Flynn, you couldn't kill Gable, you couldn't kill Cooper or any of those fellows. The exhibitor wouldn't even play the picture. But, with Cagney they accepted it, and with Bogart. So, I thought as long as they accepted it, we'd give them a good load of it."

In *They Died with Their Boots On,* he did kill off Flynn in the role of General George Custer. "You couldn't change history. He didn't mind dying, as long as he got paid." Walsh understood Flynn. "Toward the end, you know, Flynn used to imitate Barrymore, when he'd have a couple of charges of

Schenley in him. I'd say, 'Listen, Errol, you're yourself, not Barrymore. Come on.' So, he finally got out of it."

Walsh also helped on scenes in about twenty films for which he wasn't credited. "If a fellow was sick, or if he'd had too much of the 'laughing water,' then we'd go in and help him, you know. Of course, there was a lot of 'laughing water' in those days."

He also physically fought for his films: "Oh, they're too rough to talk about."

And he even handled Bette Davis: "Warner called me in and said, 'Raoul, this is a tough dame and I think you can handle her.' That was the way he approached it. So, he said, 'Will you go over to Pasadena and make this ending so we can get this thing done and get this dame out of the studio.'" John Huston was directing Davis in *In This Our Life* and they had a fight about how the picture was going to end. "Nice girl, but really tough, she'd demand this, that and the other thing. But she was all right. Bette was all right.

"I finally talked her into it after a couple of shots of 'laughing water.'"

If it had drama in it or a great joke, Walsh couldn't resist it. Not Bette Davis, the 'laughing water,' Flynn or even the death of a friend, a fellow entertainer. After the great John Barrymore died on May 28, 1942, his friends met at The Cock and Bull to fill their sadness with spirits. But Walsh left early, feeling bad. Walsh and two friends then proceeded to the Pierce Brothers Mortuary on Sunset Boulevard, convinced the caretaker there that they were acting on the part of the deceased's relatives, removed Barrymore's body, took it to Flynn's home and propped it up in a chair to greet the movie star when he returned late that night.

When Flynn entered he nearly dropped in place; the body hadn't been embalmed yet, was white and the flesh loose, but it was unmistakably John Barrymore. Flynn screamed and ran.

Later he forgave Walsh, but he didn't care for what he did: "It was no way to remember the passing of John Barrymore." But perhaps Walsh knew something Flynn didn't, that Barrymore would have loved it. It would have beat anything you might see in a Raoul Walsh picture show: *Roaring Twenties, They Drive by Night, High Sierra, The Strawberry Blonde, Manpower, They Died with Their Boots On, Gentleman Jim, Objective Burma, San Antonio, Pursued, Silver River,*

Fighter Squadron, Colorado Territory, White Heat. Perhaps!

Few producers could keep up with Walsh. Mark Hellinger made four films with him, then Bischoff, Bill Cagney, Fellows, Buckner, Edelman, Arnold, Crump, Miller and Wald took their turns. Most tried only once.

When the shooting was over, Walsh moved on to his next project and left the editing, looping, dubbing and scoring to the factory. Life inside a small cement room with nothing to amuse you except a white-skinned editor and a Moviola were not for him. If Jack Warner wanted to recut his picture, and he recut many of them at the studio, then he wasn't going to worry about it. He had done his part, put everything he had to give on the Celluloid with his cameras and crew.

John Huston stopped work on two films at Warner Bros. even before the shooting was finished, but he had good reasons . . . a fight with Bette Davis and World War II. When his films were produced by Henry Blanke, however, he completed shooting, editing, sound mixing and scoring.

Huston had written seven scripts for the studio, *Jezebel, The Amazing Dr. Clitterhouse, Juarez, Dr. Ehrlich's Magic Bullet, High Sierra, Sergeant York* and *Three Strangers,* before he was allowed to direct.

On *Juarez* he had written for a year and, after watching Dieterle direct a scene one day, he told Blanke, "I've never seen a scene so misinterpreted. That's the last time I will only write, from now on I'll only write and direct."

Huston recalls, "I had the idea of being a director in the back of my mind when I came and eventually had it put in my contract that when the option came up, I could direct a picture. I even got to choose the film. They didn't care much for the idea, but they let me."

One day Huston showed Dashiell Hammett's novel *The Maltese Falcon* to Allen Rivkin, the screenwriter with whom he shared an office and secretary. They both realized that Hammett's writing style was practically in screenplay form, all action and dialogue with a minimum of description and comment by the writer. Huston handed the book to the secretary and she typed it into the studio's screenplay format. Weeks later, Huston got a note to go ahead with it. Warner's spies had gathered up the script during their usual routine of going over everything the writers put on paper and sent the script to him.

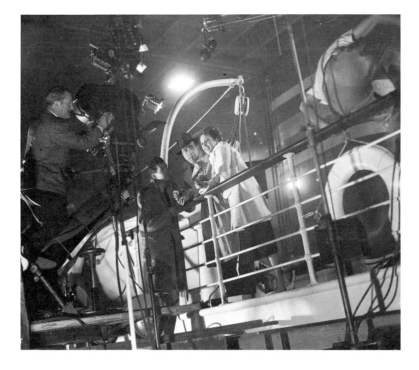

Facing. Errol Flynn and Raoul Walsh on the set of Objective Burma, *1945*
Top. Arthur Edeson, John Huston, Humphrey Bogart and Mary Astor on the set of Across the Pacific, *1942*
Center. John Huston, Mary Astor and Humphrey Bogart on the same set
Bottom. Humphrey Bogart, Vincent Sherman, Sydney Greenstreet, John Huston and Mary Astor on the set of Across the Pacific, *1942, as Huston turns the directing over to Sherman and leaves to serve in the army*

In the middle somewhere was Henry Blanke, convincing Wallis then Jack Warner to let Huston direct this one. He would be the associate producer and guarantee its completion on schedule. The story had already been made twice, but "there was something in the *Falcon* that attracted me," recalls Huston. "That hadn't been done in the two other versions. That is, of course, why I wanted to do it. No, I don't suppose they cared about that or would have understood it. They had different reasons for making the picture and I didn't attempt to explain it. It wasn't their business."

"He is complex," recalls Blanke, "that is why he understood *The Maltese Falcon.* The only one to understand it to start with . . . later I understood . . . when the first pages came in.

"He came to me on my ranch in Tarzana and said, 'Henry, I want to make it a different motion picture.'" Together they sat down and Blanke went through his fundamentals of camera direction, the ones he had worked out with Lubitsch. "The fundamentals of the religion I follow. John understood everything. He came to me for eight lessons at my house. I was the only person he could trust."

Together they put together a script and camera style that would test the best of performers. A script with only one gunshot (put in by Jack Warner), two punches, and reams of subtle dialogue about lying, cheating, love, honor, death and the hard ways of violence. It also had a violent woman, a woman with more weapons inside her than the hero. Not exactly an actor-proof script.

David Lewis produced Huston's next, *In This Our Life,* with Davis and Olivia de Havilland, Huston's love at that time. "They kept telling me that the way Bette was performing was awful, but I argued it was what I wanted and Bette backed me up. Wallis even had Warner look at the rushes and Jack agreed that Bette's acting style was all wrong, but I wouldn't change it. Then they started complaining about Olivia's performance and when I looked at the rushes with them, I had to agree they were right and changed it. Did what they wanted. They never could figure that out."

Huston left the picture after the squabble with Davis about the ending and Walsh finished it. Bette, however, received an Oscar nomination for her performance.

During the shooting of *Across the Pacific,* Huston was commissioned in the US Army Signal Corps as a lieutenant. He was given twenty-four hours' notice to report to Washington,

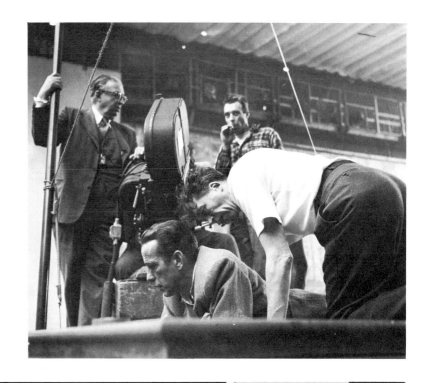

D.C., so as a joke on the studio he altered the script. He wrote a scene where Bogart is trapped in Panama, held prisoner by a roomful of Japanese soldiers with his hands tied behind his back and machine guns surrounding him. He shot the film up to that point, then left.

"I knew there was no way in God's green world he could logically have escaped. I also knew Warner's would never reshoot the whole ending. I had them. So I waved good-bye to Bogie . . . and was in Washington the next morning."

Producer Jerry Wald called in director Vincent Sherman to save him and they worked for two days with a squad of writers, then gave up, decided a Japanese soldier would suddenly go mad, start shooting and that somehow Bogart would come out of it alive with a gun in his hand. And he did, boasting, "I'm not easily trapped." Sherman laughs as he recalls the hours trying to write Bogart a believable escape. "Listen, if you'd have asked me back then, I'd say we were lucky to get the bastard out at all!"

Jack Warner was pleased Huston was gone, the director was breaking his toys.

"John's somewhere irresponsible inside." Blanke's eyes wander as he goes over those old days. "Despite how I love him, something doesn't tick quite right.

"Bogart, Bacall, Huston and I used to go bowling in Tarzana. After a few rounds and drinks, he'd put his foot out, out of love I'm telling you, and make me fall down. Later some hookers would come around and he would say he had to go home, that some girls were waiting and then leave us standing there.

"These are stories I can't explain, nobody can.

"He used to live next to me on Van Alden, two blocks away, and he'd come over and visit. I had horses then and he would only ride the toughest stallions, the toughest horses in the world. I used to call him when we had a stallion that was so wild that no one could get near him. John would go to the stable, lie down on the straw and eventually the stallion would lie down next to him. On the straw. And John could pet him, quiet him . . . the stallion understood something we couldn't."

On the set, Blanke didn't attempt to understand or control Huston. He left him alone on the set of The Maltese Falcon and spent his time making sure he had whatever he needed. He would do the same when Huston returned after the war, if Jack would allow him back.

At the beginning of the war Huston was stationed in the basement of the Knickerbocker Hotel in Hollywood and Olivia de Havilland would come visit him there. Olivia was doing Princess O'Rourke on the Warner lot at that time. At first she wasn't going to do the film. "It seemed to be nothing but tricks, but John convinced me that they were all good tricks and well put together so I took the role. I'd get lost with the character and I'd call John at the Knickerbocker. He'd meet me and we'd have lunch and he'd act the princess for me and then I'd rush back and do it.

"John was brilliant, brilliant, brilliant. He did bewildering, self-destructive things, but brilliant things of such beauty. You could talk all night long with that man, unending interest.

"But he destroys lives, it's too bad, but he does." He almost destroyed Olivia's! "No, he didn't. But he was the only man I knew, the only man whose life I thought I could fulfill, but he would have been a full-time job. He could have given me what I sought in films and I could have done it. It would have been just as rewarding, just as important. Fortunately I had the alternative, the work . . . I had the work. It only took me twenty-seven years to get over it.

"But the breaking up only increased my drive to do work that he would damn well have to respect, because he could be arrogant. Oh, he was affectionate, but not loving. I think he could love, but not sustain it . . . maybe!"

Blanke stayed at the studio during the war while Huston went to the island of Adak. There, as he made the documentary film Report from the Aleutians, a waist gunner was shot to death at his side. "That kid died and I lived . . . and who knows why?" He then went to Italy and made The Battle of San Pietro, the story of a Texas infantry regiment, the 143rd of the 36th Division. Eleven hundred replacements were fed into the bloodbath and Huston's cameras photographed every foot of death. They also covered the children of the village emerging from the caves and basements after the battle. It was a film about both the living and the dead, many claim the best anti-war film made. Back at the studio, Henry Blanke was holding a novel for Huston to make when he returned, a story about life, The Treasure of the Sierra Madre.

After the war Huston wanted to do an O'Neill play on Broadway, but the studio made him return to direct Key Largo with Wald producing. The future of the motion picture business was growing dimmer and Jack needed talent more than ever regardless of their life style. "I was pissed," recalls Huston,

Top. Howard Hawks, John Wayne and Angie Dickinson on the set of Rio Bravo, 1959
Center. Director Al Green instructs Marjorie Rambeau on how to slap John Garfield on the set of East of the River, 1942
Bottom. Joan Crawford, director Robert Aldrich and Bette Davis on the set of Whatever Happened to Baby Jane?, 1962
Facing, left. Elia Kazan and Stashis Giallelis on the set of America, America, 1964
Facing, right. Alfred Hitchcock and Henry Fonda on the set of The Wrong Man, 1957

"for personal reasons I wanted to do it very much, but the studio made me stick to my contract."

Back in Hollywood, he immediately returned to his old style, but harder. In April of 1945, in producer David O. Selznick's home in Beverly Hills, he fought Errol Flynn and Flynn decked him ten times. After the tenth knockdown, Flynn, now in a friendly mood, was ready to quit. Still on the ground, Huston was quoted as saying, "That's when I knew I had him."

In a burst of emotion, he flew to Las Vegas in stunt pilot Paul Mantz's plane and married Evelyn Keyes, his third marriage.

"Hollywood had changed after the war," recalls Huston, "it was different. But I suppose . . . I'm certain . . . we all changed. We had never seen anything like that."

At the studio, Key Largo was put aside for a rewrite and Blanke went ahead with The Treasure of the Sierra Madre. He also convinced Warner to let Huston shoot for two months on location in Mexico, around the small village of Jungapeo near San José de Purua.

Blanke stayed in Hollywood. "I never went near them. I knew they were drunk, brawling all the time, but that didn't matter. The footage was marvelous."

Warner wasn't as delighted, and as the shooting continued and continued, he told Blanke, "If that son of a bitch doesn't find gold soon, I'll go broke." On several occasions, Blanke almost lost. He nearly had to replace Huston and change the ending to keep Bogart's character alive. But he didn't. He was in the right place.

When Huston returned to the studio to shoot several scenes, the tricks continued. He glued character actor Alfonso Bedoya, who played Gold Hat, to a plaster rocking horse, then turned it on and went to lunch.

The film won several Oscars and when Huston picked up his he held it up to the audience and said, "If this were hollow and had a drink in it, I'd toast Henry Blanke."

"I was blessed with fine producers," recalls Huston. "Hal Wallis, who I never saw for six months after I arrived, Robert Lord was one of the best there and the finest was Henry Blanke. He did it all, story, casting, of course organization. I never worked with a producer who did so many things well. I owe everything to Blanke."

In 1948 Huston needed a personal loan of fifty thousand dollars, but Jack Warner wouldn't loan it to him, not even on

a picture commitment. Huston left Warner Bros. and went to producer Sam Spiegel to form Horizon Pictures. Blanke stayed behind.

With the close of the forties, the directors were on the ascent to total power. There were fewer and fewer contract directors, and many were receiving credit as both producer and director. Some even as writer, producer, director. They were doing it all, just as they thought they could.

They could see television coming and with it the decline and fall of the studio system. When that happened they could be their own bosses, in total control, and hire or fire the actors as they pleased. They could have their names above the title and at last receive the applause they had always deserved.

Even those directors who had been only obedient foremen would share in the coming credit, power and money. All they had to do was wait, just stay alive. The best was still to come. Art. Recognition.

During those good years, those classic years of the thirties and forties, however, the directors had made the right choice. They had commanded their cameras by sheer instinct and put them in exactly the right place. The place that would make it the most difficult for the performer and cause the most tension on the set. The place that would force the actor or actress to succeed or fail, come alive or die on the spot, in front of the crew and eventually the audience.

Instinctively the Warner directors had rejected all the stylish forms of shooting that would call attention to the camera, to themselves. They had unconsciously mastered their medium, the camera, so that it became second nature to them . . . and their natures naturally chose to use it to provoke as much life on the set as possible. Then they focused on that life, on the actor or actress trying his or her best to overcome bad stories, rotten dialogue or a complex second act and left them on their own, didn't help with revealing camera moves, artful lighting or shadows. The single eye simply watched, carefully, closely, challenging the performer never to drop character, never to let the tension of the story ease, and moved only when the story was moved forward by a performer.

At Warner Bros. the cameras obeyed the performers, they rose one beat after the actor rose, sat down as the actor sat down, and moved, ran, drifted as the actor did. The cameras moved in closer when the tension within the actor heightened,

moved to another performer when his or her reaction demanded it. Performance was the one drum the directors couldn't beat, but they followed it.

Thinking back on the way in which he had proceeded with his choice of camera style, Huston recalls: "It's as though I am there . . . the camera is me and I am there and watching. What fascinates me, fascinates the camera and if it is sufficiently fascinating, I move up to it.

"I didn't start out with these ideas, but they occurred to me as I went about making motion pictures. We touched on this . . the camera follows the mental processes. Film does. I think even more than that, more than many realize, it also follows physical processes." Life.

Walsh, Wellman, Hawks, Curtiz, Wyler, Huston . . . men made for scotch and sound stages, men who made Warner Bros. the toughest neighborhood in dreamland.

But if the writers, musicians, producers, directors and Jack L. Warner were going to get any part of what they wanted on the screen . . . if Warner Bros. was going to have anything to say to the audience . . . if it was going to collect its share of tears and laughter . . . and more than its share of money . . . it was up to the performers to fight their way through that neighborhood and touch and capture the audience. In the theaters they were what would be seen amid the darkness.

Whatever it was going to be, *schmaltz*, cardboard, silver or tinsel, melodrama or art, comedy or foolishness, profits or losses, it was up to the faces on the screen, the Warner players. The actors, of course, had no doubt they could handle it. They were certain their faces could move mountains, make alligators laugh and even make Jack Warner cry. They were the best, the toughest, and they knew it.

Facing. Errol Flynn as Major Geoffrey Vickers in The Charge
of the Light Brigade, *1936*
Below. The Sea Hawk, *1940*
Below right. Errol Flynn as Captain Geoffrey Thorpe in The
Sea Hawk, *1940*

Facing, top. Errol Flynn in The Adventures of Robin Hood, *1938*
Facing, left. Flynn and Olivia de Havilland in the same film
Below. Errol Flynn, Olivia de Havilland, Alan Hale and Basil
Rathbone in another scene from Robin Hood
Right. Errol Flynn as Robin Hood

Below. Basil Rathbone, Olivia de Havilland and Henry
Stephenson in Captain Blood, *1935*
Facing. Bette Davis *in* The Private Lives of Elizabeth and
Essex, *1939*

Top left. Edmund Breon and Neil Hamilton in the first version of The Dawn Patrol, *1930*
Bottom left. Errol Flynn as Captain Courtney in The Dawn Patrol, *1938*
Below. Richard Barthelmess, Douglas Fairbanks, Jr., and Neil Hamilton in The Dawn Patrol, *1930*
Facing, top. John Garfield in Air Force, *1943*
Facing, bottom. Cary Grant and John Garfield in Destination Tokyo, *1944*

Below. James Cagney in The Fighting 69th, *1940*
Facing, left. Sydney Greenstreet and Humphrey Bogart in
Passage to Marseilles, *1944*
Facing, right. Tony Caruso, Dane Clark and John Garfield in
Pride of the Marines, *1945*
Facing, below. Errol Flynn in Objective Burma, *1945*

Top left. Humphrey Bogart and Tim Holt in The Treasure of the Sierra Madre, *1948*
Bottom left. "Do you believe what that old man who was doin' all the talkin' at the Oso Negro said the other night about gold changin' a man's soul so's he ain't the same kind of guy as he was before findin' it?" Tim Holt and Humphrey Bogart
Below. "Fred C. Dobbs don't say nothin' he don't mean."
Facing. "Out for gold, always at your service." Tim Holt, Walter Huston and Humphrey Bogart in The Treasure of the Sierra Madre, *1948*

Below. Joy Paige, Helmut Dantine and Sydney Greenstreet in front of the Blue Parrot in Casablanca, *1943*
Facing, top. "I stick my neck out for nobody." Peter Lorre as Ugarte and Humphrey Bogart as Rick in Casablanca, *1943*
Facing, below. "I remember every detail. The Germans wore gray, you wore blue." Humphrey Bogart, Claude Rains, Paul Henreid and Ingrid Bergman in Casablanca, *1943*

Above. "I bet they're asleep in New York. I'll bet they're asleep all over America." Dooley Wilson and Humphrey Bogart in Casablanca, *1943*
Below. "Round up the usual suspects." Claude Rains, Humphrey Bogart and Conrad Veidt (on the ground) in Casablanca, *1943*

The Smart Screen Magazine

SCREENLAND

November

15¢ NOW

20¢ in Canada

NRA MEMBER
WE DO OUR PART

Joan Blondell

Garbo–Gilbert Together Again!

Joan Crawford's Intimate Diary
In The "Grand Hotel" of Hollywood By Vicki Baum

MOTION PICTURE

N.S.C.

COMBINED WITH

Movie CLASSIC

APRIL

10¢

"IF I WERE QUEEN—" MYRNA LOY

OLIVIA DE HAVILLAND

JEANETTE MacDONALD GIVES ADVICE TO GIRLS IN LOVE

movie MIRROR

Combined with Shadoplay

10¢

MACFADDEN PUBLICATION

SEPTEMBER

RUBY KEELER

WHY ANN HARDING SAID GOODBYE TO LOVE
—
HOLLYWOOD'S COMPANIONATE DIVORCE

PHOTOPLAY

25 CENTS
20 Cents in Canada

NRA

FEBRUARY

KAY FRANCIS

UNDRAPING HOLLYWOOD

HUNDREDS OF INTIMATE PICTURES!

Modern Screen

AUGUST
10
CENTS

THE LARGEST
CIRCULATION
OF ANY SCREEN
MAGAZINE

BETTE
DAVIS

JACKIE COOGAN'S
OWN STORY
"I WANT MY MONEY!"

MODERN SCREEN

May
10
Cents

ANN SHERIDAN

Inside Story of the PAYNE-SHIRLEY DIVORCE!

PHOTOPLAY

SEPTEMBER   25 CENTS

BARBARA
STANWYCK

THE MAN
WHO TRIED TO ELOPE
WITH GRETA GARBO

A HOLLYWOOD
STAR WHO IS
GRANDDAUGHTER
OF AN EMPRESS

$1500.00 Prize Winners in this Issue

PHOTOPLAY

25 CENTS
30 Cents in Canada

JANUARY

JOAN
CRAWFORD

Phantom
Daddies of the Screen

Facing. Barbara Stanwyck
Top. Ann Sheridan
Right. Joan Crawford

Top, left. Jane Wyman
Bottom, left. Ida Lupino
Facing. Lauren Bacall

Facing. Errol Flynn as Don Juan in Adventures of Don Juan, *1949*
Top. Joan Crawford and John Garfield on the set of Humoresque, *1947*
Center. Humphrey Bogart and John Huston on the set of Across the Pacific, *1942*
Bottom. Director Delmer Daves, Agnes Moorehead and Humphrey Bogart on the set of Dark Passage, *1947*

Facing, left. Virginia Mayo
Facing, right. Doris Day
Right. Ingrid Bergman in Indiscreet, *1958*

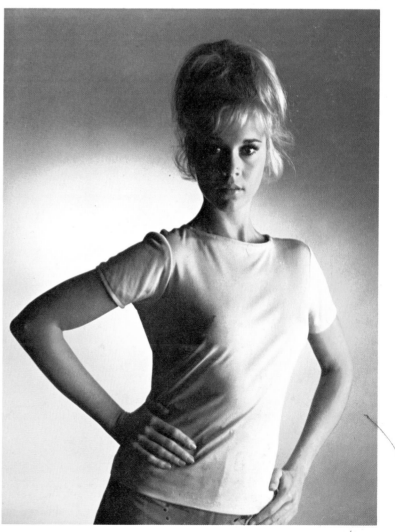

Facing. Natalie Wood
Top. Paul Newman and Lita Milan in Left-Handed Gun, *1958*
Right. Jane Fonda

Below. Rock Hudson and Elizabeth Taylor as the Bick Benedicts in George Stevens' Giant, 1956

STREET KIDS

Actors

"Oh, I don't know what's right any longer. You'll have to think for both of us, for all of us."

"All right, I will. Here's looking at you, kid."

Chapter opening. Lucille LeSueur
Overleaf. The Dodge City Special carried most of the studio's talent to Kansas City for the film's premiere: Standing left to right are Lya Lys, Gilbert Roland, Frank McHugh, Chief Santa Fe (in headdress), Maxie Rosenbloom, Priscilla Lane, Errol Flynn, John Garfield, Jack Warner, Humphrey Bogart (kneeling), Rosemary Lane, Wayne Morris, John Payne and Alan Hale. Squatting are Leon Turrou, Hoot Gibson, Lee Lyles, Buck Jones, Guinn Williams, Jean Parker and Frances Robinson
Top. Humphrey DeForest Bogart with his mother, Maude Humphrey, in New York
Bottom. James Cagney at one
Facing. Rin-Tin-Tin

From childhood the actors had been in training for life at the Burbank studios.

"On New York's East Side, kids grew up scrapping," recalled James Cagney. "Street fighting was an everyday occurrence. Years later, I went with a sandlot ball team to Sing Sing to play the prison club. I met a lot of my boyhood cronies from the old neighborhood on the other team."

John Garfield told Louella Parsons: "Public School 45 in the Bronx was where the school authorities sent juvenile delinquents. That's where I was sent and I was as tough as the worst of them."

"Growing up in Hell's Kitchen, New York, it was a rare day that I wasn't bruised or bloodied in some alley brawl," recalled George Raft. "After I was old enough, I went into the ring. I fought seventeen fights for five dollars a fight. The money looked good. I won ten bouts. I was knocked cold seven times."

Pat O'Brien wrote: "Somewhere past the middle of the nineteenth century ... the native American Know-Nothings had a slogan ... 'Hit 'em again, he's Irish!' We fought bloody battles in the schoolyards to survive. Sometimes Irish confetti was used. Irish confetti is the Gaelic term for a flung brick."

Edward G. Robinson had his own kind of fighting childhood. He arrived in steerage on the ship La Louraine, amid the manure and dank foul breath of other immigrants fleeing persecution of the Jews in his native land, Rumania. He went to school at New York's P.S. 137 speaking Rumanian, Yiddish, German and reading Hebrew, but not a word of English.

Recalling his days at sea on the Maski, Sirocco and Empress of Asia, the days he spent fighting his way through the brothels of Macao and Shanghai's Street of Happiness, Errol Flynn wrote: "I fought dirty, without the English sense of fair play. If I got into a quarrel, I was out to win, not negotiate.... I swore then that I might get beaten up in life, but the joker will know he's been in a fight."

Humphrey Bogart's family was in Dau's New York Blue Book every year. Bogart had money, culture, but a street disposition. He started riots in his classrooms. "I always like stirring things up." He also went to war as a sailor in World War I and a German U-boat torpedoed the ship he was standing on. The myth is that a splinter from the explosion drove through his upper lip, severed the nerve and left him with a lisp. Regardless of the fact or fiction, he talked like a street kid.

Warner Bros. was a tough neighborhood, but when the actors

arrived and signed up as Stock Talent: *male,* it looked familiar and they knew they could handle it without pretending, without behaving like actors.

All Jack Warner wanted was one more John Barrymore and eight or nine Rin Tin Tins, but the actors came eagerly expecting all the great parts and that "one great role." They had no idea of just how hard it would be to upstage a dog, to be more believable than Rin Tin Tin.

Most of them didn't even look like movie stars. Except for Flynn, who was designed by Michelangelo and had the deep, sad, laughing eyes of a wandering sailor who had traveled forbidden waters, they were an ugly bunch. Cagney was made like a hammer, Robinson's cigar was the best-looking part of him and Bogart had a face, even at thirty, that looked like it had been used to break rocks. Given Flynn's minimal talent and the others' appearances, it didn't appear likely they could perform on 8″ x 10″ glossies, on magazine covers or on sound stages and go charging across the nation as thirty-five-cent heros.

The actors, however, weren't interested in their appearance or in playing cheap heros. They had nobler ambitions.

"I wanted to create something important," wrote Flynn.

Cagney came to dance.

Paul Muni came to save the world.

Edward G. Robinson had a variety of mixed goals . . . playing parts that elevate the human heart . . . the excitement of putting on a putty nose, a set of whiskers, false eyebrows and a French accent . . . money being the overriding consideration, "not art." But when he wasn't thinking about it, he revealed what all the actors came to Hollywood for, "and then I heard that noise that makes an actor a thousand feet tall: aplause! Bravos!"

Bogart would have probably said, "Cut the crap," all he wanted was to know where the hell the icebox was.

Regardless of their ambitions, they had signed away their right of decision. Only Paul Muni, who was already a movie star, got paid in four figures and had script approval. In 1931 the vice-president in charge of production was still making some mistakes, but not many.

The actors had agents to represent their needs, but in those days, Robinson recalls, "It was difficult, in my case, certainly, to tell whose side some of them were on . . . the client's or the studio's."

The actors never had a chance. It was only fitting that the Wardrobe Department would put so many of them in prison stripes.

At the studio, Warner, Zanuck and Wallis immediately put them into the factory process. The supervisors handed them scripts, led them though Wardrobe, Makeup, and then pointed them in the direction of the sound stage, where the directors told them where to stand, whom to kiss, whom to shoot and where they should fall down and die. The cameras ran from 9 A.M. until 10 and 11 at night and photographed their best moments badly and their bad moments endlessly. When one film was finished, the actors were issued bicycles, another script and pointed in the direction of another sound stage.

When Robinson saw his first rushes he was not only appalled at the script, but at himself. "Was I really that short, stocky, ugly creature up there? And the voice! Did I speak with such affectation, such rolling r's, such low bass sounds?"

Bogart had his problems too. He managed to get a part in Wellman's *Grand Central Airport,* but his lisp was bothering him and he was considering having it corrected by surgery. Wellman advised him: "You just keep right on lisping. Nobody lisps the way you do. You keep it."

Bogart kept his lisp, but no one liked it in 1934. He got a part in *Three on a Match* directed by LeRoy, but got sixth billing, had his option dropped and got back on the Sante Fe to return to New York, almost whipped.

The next year Errol Flynn got his first break in *The Case of the Curious Bride.* He played a dead body on a slab in a morgue. His performance lasted thirteen seconds.

Cagney's first role came in 1930 with *Sinner's Holiday,* he got third billing. Joan Blondell played opposite him and was impressed by his natural makeup. "His hair was a Van Gogh, Renoir, Titan red, with blobs of gold weaving through. His eyes were delft blue, fringed with the longest, thickest lashes I had ever seen. He blinked his eyes at me, and since I had never seen a blink like that before, I instantaneously fell in love. The jolt was so horrendous, I kept my eyes floorward."

Despite young Miss Blondell's impression, Cagney was bad. They all were.

The camera saw through all their stage tricks. It recorded each small gesture, all the acrobatic facial gestures that had pleased the galleries on Broadway, even those the actors hadn't planned, then enlarged them. On the screen, their faces were

Facing. Humphrey Bogart's first feature film, A Devil with Women, *1930, was made by Fox Pictures. Mona Maris and Victor McLaglen are at the left.*
Right. Humphrey Bogart doing utility work in The Return of Dr. X, *1939*

twenty feet high, their mouths five feet wide. And the directors seemed to enjoy it. They kept moving the Mitchell cameras in closer and closer and the actors found out that Rin Tin Tin was not an actor to laugh at. The dog never had a false moment, never even thought about the camera and simply did his stuff without pretending. The dog was a pure actor, totally believable no matter what he did. But the actors were very aware of the camera and worried that they might never be believable. There was no place to hide.

"The truth is you have to be more honest in films than on stage," wrote Robinson as he recalled his early performances on Celluloid. "You cannot afford the slightest hint of mugging."

The actors began to reappraise their craft, reexamine the sources and motivations for their performances and look for new ones.

A few stuck to their stage methods. When Paul Muni arrived in 1932 he went right into a socially conscious film of his choice, *I Am a Fugitive from a Chain Gang.* His acting style had already proved successful at RKO with *Scarface,* and he was not concerned with how close the camera was. He was a complete professional, in character "twenty-four hours a day" as he put it.

Mary Astor, who had risen to a female leading lady in the thirties, was reappraising her own talents and the direction her lovely face and figure were forcing her into. She studied Muni's style: "I didn't approve of his way of working; his total attention to externals, makeup, hair, clothing, manner of walking, gesturing. Every word of the script memorized and actually recorded and rerecorded before he ever went on the set. And the theory that if your eyes twinkled you conveyed humor, if you shook your fist and shouted and allowed spittle to form on your lips, presto! You were an angry man."

In addition to competing with the camera, there was competition with other actors. George Arliss and Richard Barthelmess were still the studio's stars and were getting all the good parts. Monte Blue, Jack Mulhall, Frank Fay and Alexander Gray were playing leads regularly and new faces would be contracted every month right into the forties: Charles King, Jack Whiting, Dick Powell, Eddie Woods, Warren William in the early years and youngsters like Ronald Reagan for $200 a week and Dick Foran for $750 later. It was apparent that only a few would make it, those that could dominate the prying camera.

"On all sides there were the handsome and talented," recalled Flynn. "And they might be as good as you if they had the break you had." Dreamland was crawling with actors. Across town in Culver City, MGM had the glamorous, sophisticated male types who spoke eloquently and maintained that magic distance from the audience: Bob Montgomery, Robert Young, Franchot Tone and Robert Taylor. Metro would also pick up both Clark Gable and Spencer Tracy, who could play it tough in the thirties.

Paramount had the bright, wacky, nutty types: Bing Crosby, the Marx Brothers, Bob Hope, George Burns, Fred MacMurray, Ray Milland, W. C. Fields and the eloquent gentleman William Powell. They also had the most American of them all, Gary Cooper, who was then trying his best to be sophisticated. RKO was surviving on Fred Astaire and young Cary Grant. Fox had the pretty people: Tyrone Power, John Payne, George Montgomery and Don Ameche, men who had the kind of beauty the silent stars became rich and famous with. Universal had the lurch and crawl group, Boris Karloff and Bela Lugosi.

Columbia rented whomever they could while working Jack Holt to death.

In 1931, Warner was still unsure his male talent could handle what was coming. He kept hunting, and with the aid of agent Myron Selznick made the first talent raid on another studio. He came away with Paramount's William Powell and actresses Kay Francis and Ruth Chatterton, all established stars at that time. All Selznick clients. It was the gutsy, audacious move of a street fighter and Paramount, the other studios and particularly Louis B. Mayer, Hollywood's king, were outraged. But it was only the beginning. They were all street fighters and Jack was simply the first to reveal it. The raid almost worked, but Jack gave the performers contracts without options and with script approval.

Clark Gable came on the lot for Wellman's *Night Nurse,* but Warner didn't care for his large ears and dropped him.

Spencer Tracy and Mickey Rooney also passed through without much attention from Jack, as did John Wayne, who made a series of "B" Westerns at the studio in the thirties. "That big lunk," recalls Blanke, "we really missed that one."

Warner's preferences in talent would remain a mystery. Near the end of the forties his personal talent scout, Solly Baiano, brought him a young actor. "This guy's an animal. He's got bad

teeth, his hair is wild, but the women will go mad for him."
Jack, however, wanted no part of him. "I don't want any
acrobats." Burt Lancaster went elsewhere.

But in 1931, Warner discovered his choices were paying off.
Edward G. Robinson appeared in *Little Caesar,* James Cagney
in *Public Enemy,* and the money began to flow. Warner counted
it and began making decisions. With more of the same, he
could get the studio out of the red.

His preferences in stories changed drastically. In 1931 the
studio had made thirty-five films that featured male stars in
male stories as opposed to thirty-one featuring female stars in
women's stories. In 1932 the ratio changed from twenty-six
male stories to fourteen female. By 1938 it was thirty-eight
male stories and stars to fourteen female stories and
starring parts.

The neighborhood was getting even rougher for the actresses,
but it was taking a turn the actors liked. More and more
stories were coming out of the Writers' Building featuring heros
and badmen who had control of their own destinies, who ran
the world with sheer guts, a gun in their hand, or with the will
and brilliance of their incredible minds. If they were at all written
well, the actors would have great roles to play.

But they weren't. Instead, the factory was put into high gear
and ground out more and more of the same. Robinson made
five consecutive pictures in 1932 and Cagney did the same in
1933. All with the same character, just different wardrobe,
and with the actors playing themselves, reacting not acting.
Warner had found where the money was.

The studio was finding its face, one the audience recognized.
The folks in Kansas, downtown Dallas or in Boston no doubt
didn't know any criminals like Caesar Enrico Bandello or Tom
Powers, but they knew men like Cagney and Robinson. They
lived on the same streets with them, talked with the same
dialects and drank and fought in the same kind of bars and
gutters. They were good faces with both good and bad in them,
faces as believable as Rin Tin Tin.

Cagney and Robinson had worn makeup on the screen,
their eyebrows had been darkened, their eyelids painted to
heighten the whites of their eyes and their lips rouged as was
the custom in those days. Makeup was that last vestige of the
classical Greek theatrical masks, which were intended to invest
the actor with the sacred personality of a god, a hero, a dream
figure out of reach of the common man or woman. Makeup

had aided the silent stars as they postured and posed, made their already beautiful faces perfect. Masked their true identity. But on the screen, Cagney and Robinson had broken out of their makeup and brought their characters down to earth, within easy reach of people who were fighting a depression and who could afford only thirty-five cents to see them. They smashed whatever was left of the theatrical mask with their own raw individuality, smashed it clean with a grin and snarl right from the streets. And if that individuality wasn't beautiful and was sometimes even ugly, it was no less compelling, alive and vital.

In order to compete, Hollywood was going to have to change its acting style to look like Warner Bros. and theatrical makeup began to disappear. But Jack was on the run, way ahead.

In 1933 Pat O'Brien came on the lot from a series of films for other studios. And his fast-talking Irish temper mixed easily with the fighting. His first film was *Bureau of Missing Persons* with a busty young lovely named Bette Davis.

Tenor Dick Powell was contracted to sing the Warren and Dubin songs and George Brent to play the handsome, debonair gentleman in the women's pictures. He seemed to fit the studio. Before he arrived he had been an Irish freedom fighter, a member of the IRA. A hunted man.

Warner, however, needed another Barrymore, or at least a reasonable facsimile. An actor who would satisfy those super-visors who were certain the studio could profit by selling high adventure and romance in addition to street fighting.

Errol Flynn was ready! He was too alive to play dead bodies. His past was filled with sailing, gold prospecting, smuggling and slave trading and he was already stirring the hearts and bodies of the soft, nubile creatures in Hollywood. Between affairs he married the exotic star Lili Damita and even though he had not made a film he was an attraction in tinsel town.

When Robert Donat canceled out of the role of *Captain Blood*, a story that the studio's highest priced writer, Casey Robinson, had been developing, Warner plunged. He put Flynn in the role, set Curtiz to direct, Olivia de Havilland to costar and surrounded the young performers with Lionel Atwell, Basil Rathbone, Guy Kibbee, Donald Meek, J. Carroll Naish and twenty other fine character performers. It was almost like Jack L. Warner could see things coming.

Flynn put up with Curtiz's abuse, took every punch the camera threw and stayed off the "laughing water." He was

within reach of success. "The sea raged inside me."

The same year, 1935, Humphrey Bogart returned to Warner Bros. to play Duke Mantee in *The Petrified Forest*, the role he had created on Broadway. On arrival, he discovered Robinson had been set for the role. He instantly wired Leslie Howard in Scotland, who was to star in the film as he had in the theater, and Howard wired Jack Warner that either Bogart did the picture or he would withdraw. Bogart got the part, then the same part in another picture, then another and another.

"In my first thirty-four pictures," Bogart recalled, "I was shot in twelve, electrocuted or hanged in eight and was a jailbird in nine. I played more scenes writhing around on the floor than I did standing up."

"Nobody likes me on sight, I suppose that's why I'm a heavy," he once said. "There must be something about the tone of my voice, or this arrogant face . . . something that antagonizes everybody. I can't even get in a mild discussion that doesn't turn into an argument."

Bogart was the "B" film utility actor. Brynie Foy figured: "He didn't have the confidence in those days, he wasn't sure of himself. Something seemed to always be bothering him."

The studio tried to turn him into a romantic lead even though Warner thought no movie star could have a ridiculous name like Humphrey. On the casting of *Crime School*, director Vincent Sherman recalls, "When I finally saw Mr. Warner, he said, 'I'm giving you this guy, Bogart, and see if you can get him to do something besides Duke Mantee.' For many, many years on the Warner Bros. lot, Bogart was considered to be nothing more than a heavy. Nobody paid much attention to Bogie. As I say, he was the utility man."

Bogart, however, was trying. He was older than the others, thirty-seven in 1936, and took to wearing "wedgies" for added height and a hairpiece that he jokingly called "curls."

But as of December 1, 1939, Bogart was still being paid only $1,250 a week to say "Drop it!" "Get over against the wall," and "No, no, no, don't shoot!"

James Cagney was making $12,500 a week. Edward G. Robinson $8,500. Claude Rains $6,000. George Raft $5,500. Errol Flynn $5,000. Pat O'Brien $4,000. George Brent $2,000. Frank McHugh $1,600. Donald Crisp $1,500. John Garfield $1,500.

By 1939 Jack Warner's thirty-five-cent heroes were costing him a lot of money but making him much more, and he wasn't

Left. Lili Damita, Flynn's first wife
Below. Humphrey Bogart
Top right. As the "utility actor," Bogart wore pinstripe suits
and a hairpiece in half a dozen films
Below, right. Humphrey Bogart as the bad guy in black in
Oklahoma Kid, *1939*

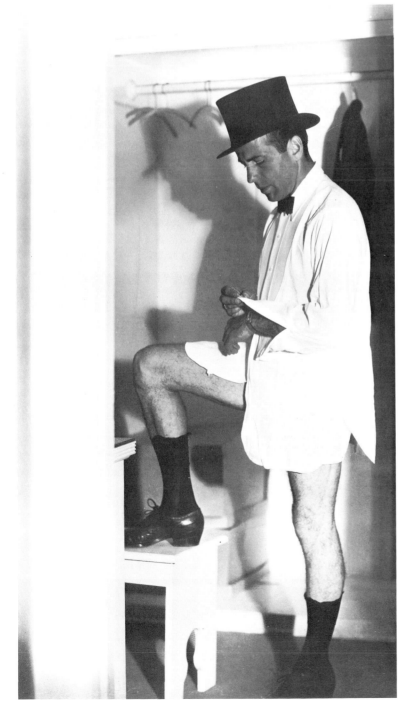

going to let them escape the factory. The streets were paved with gold. But his Stock Talent: *male* was unhappy.

They were doing most of the work, carrying the writers' stories, the musicians' songs, the directors' pictures and the junk ideas and cardboard dreams of the supervisors to the audience. They were delivering Jack Warner's vulgar picture shows to the whole world, making it believe the impossible and making the studio rich. But they had no say in the choice of scripts, the subjects or the budgets of the films they made. They had no control over the destiny of their own careers and they wanted it.

The actors wanted to play all the great roles of theater and literature, but were expected "by our very presence or box-office appeal, somehow to put flesh on bare bones," recalled Robinson, "add motivation where none existed, and bring self-inflicted characterization to the cardboard characters we were to play.

"It was not against the writer that we were making the fuss; it was against the system that had produced a hundred and twenty pages of mimeographed inconsistency." Robinson knew that sometimes up to twenty writers had worked on a script. "If so, the script was in a number of styles and thus did not represent one man's vision."

Flynn became embarrassed about his roles, about his ruffled shirts and cardboard castles, and avoided the writers' table in the Greenroom, which was sure to grin and snicker as he passed. "He was always trying to get away from doing costume drama," recalls Vincent Sherman, "and action films and Westerns. He wanted to be an actor. He wanted to prove that he was an actor."

"I became labeled a swashbuckler," recalled Flynn bitterly in his book. "You have to have the roles. You have to have the chance to grow ... I felt used. Used by the studio. Used to make money. Used by the press for fun. Used by society as a piece of chalk provides the world with a dab of colour. ... Don't experiment, don't pander to an actor's whim that he might like to do something special, different. Keep the sword shiny, shoe the horse and turn Flynn loose on a new one."

And Jack Warner wanted him just as he was. Sherman went to Warner about a Flynn script he had received. "'The writer says that this is like a piece of Venetian glass.' Warner said, 'What in hell is that?' I said, 'He means that it is very delicate.' I told him that I thought it was a little too delicate for Errol.

Warner said, 'You're right. He's either got to be fighting or *¢%$ a girl, or something. You've got to keep him busy. None of this delicate stuff with him.'"

Bogart believed: "We actors are better judges than any studio as to what is good for us." But Warner wouldn't budge.

When, on November 6, 1939, James Cagney had his contract renegotiated he demanded script approval. Cagney and his agents argued, pushed the price up and up, and Warner gave a little, then a little more. When the contract was settled, Cagney was to receive $12,500 a week as opposed to $5,000, but without script approval. Cagney took the money and a guarantee of "12 consecutive weeks vacation or rest period during each year upon three weeks advance notice."

Other actors did the same, took the money and vacation time in lieu of script approval.

The actors needed a rest. The audience had stood up and cheered, but they wouldn't leave them alone. The Warner Publicity Department shipped their faces all over the world, on cardboard, pulp paper, newsprint, gum cards and wire services. An actor couldn't enter a nightclub, a bar or a beach without a crowd surrounding him. And the audience didn't understand, they liked the actors for all the wrong reasons. Not as people, as reasonable human beings who were just doing their job . . . and certainly not as inept, plodding employees who were painfully failing to do what they wanted to do most. The audience believed they could do anything, believed they were just what they saw on the screen. It was mad.

The actors had to find a place to hide, to escape, then they could go back and day by day fight with Warner. But Hollywood had few places to rest, no marvelous restaurants and less culture. When they came, however, "it never occurred to us to give up the apartment on Eleventh Street," back in New York, and Edward G. Robinson and others often returned to that land of the "theater." They had debated the Broadway versus Hollywood issue. "And we came to a sensible conclusion," recalled Robinson. "Take the money and run!

"You know, there wasn't a decent delicatessen in Hollywood until after World War II. . . . We were miserable . . . I said pain and I mean pain."

They missed the black-tie dining, the book reviews in the *New York Times,* the museums, the major league baseball games and concerts in the Metropolitan Opera House. The Burbank Burlesque house in downtown Los Angeles, the

Hollywood Bowl and Magnetic Hill, a road on the north side of the Sunset Strip where you could turn off the ignition in your Chrysler and coast uphill, were not the kind of amusement their soaring souls could accept as replacements:

Bogart went to sea on his yacht, the *Santana,* where he could fight with his wife, Mayo Methot, alone. "The noise was incredible," recalls Powell's son, Norman, who could hear them when the *Santana* was docked in Newport Harbor.

"I think he loved his yacht, the *Santana,* more than any woman," his wife would recall.

When he was struggling in New York, Bogart had done his drinking at Tony's on Fifty-second Street and speakeasies like the Dizzy Club, Chez Florence, the Hotsy Totsy and the Bandbox. When he returned a star, he went to the El Morocco and the Stork Club. But he still behaved as he had in the speakeasies, drank too much, started throwing punches, and the management reacted as it always had and threw him out.

"Everybody's three drinks behind," was his philosophy and he did his best to stay ahead. "I don't trust any bastard who doesn't drink. People who don't drink are afraid of revealing themselves." When he had something to hide, he headed for the *Santana* or back to work, to Burbank.

Cagney also had a yacht, *Martha,* but Cagney was nicknamed "The Captain Hates the Sea" because he got seasick everytime he sailed on it. He'd go over to Avalon on Catalina Island with his stand-in, Harvey Perry, and watch the White Sox work out in winter. He'd also meet with the Irish Legation—Regis Toomey, George Murphy, Bill Cagney, Pat O'Brien and Frank McHugh—and go to the boat races in Long Beach on Sunday. On one occasion a local boy sold them counterfeit tickets and they swept through the parking lots until they found him. The local was belligerent, recalls Perry. "He told Jimmy, 'Shut your mouth, you got your money back, didn't you?' And Jimmy decked him, then turned to us and said, 'I'm sorry, every now and then the gutter comes out.'"

Flynn had several yachts and they were usually crowded with young lovelies. They were his amusements, his escape. One of his best friends was also a woman. He called her Mad Ides and Lupe. "I only know one thing," recalls Ida Lupino, "he never raped anyone. They all raped him. He'd call and say, 'Lupe, come up here. There's a daughter and her mother and a deputy here, come help!' And I'd go up and throw them out. Can you imagine him having to rape anyone?"

One New Year's morning he brought Ida home at 7 A.M. just as her mother, Connie, showed up. "'Where's my daughter, Baron?' And he said, 'She's putting on her blue jeans, we're going to my house to have breakfast.' And Mum said, 'Well, see she eats something.' That's the kind of man he was. You never had to worry. He was my friend, my buddy. A gentleman. We never did anything that would hurt anyone in the world.

"He loved my mother. 'Ides,' he once said, 'I only want one thing from you. When I die, I want either you or Connie, I want you placed right next to me in Jamaica.'"

Flynn also found friendship in the bottle. "He was a great friend of the 'laughing water.'"

Back on the lot, away from their temporary hiding places, the actors continued to fight.

They tried to get help and understanding from the writers, but were often dissatisfied with the scripts and would use devious means to get them changed. They would claim they couldn't read such and such a line, then change it on the set. And when they were performing at their best, they would imbue the character with their own raw personality to such a degree that the writer would believe they had stolen it from them. Changed it, destroyed it, taken out all the subtlety and replaced it with vulgar specifics of their street gestures and speech patterns.

The directors and actors squared off with the camera between them, but the actors wanted it that way, wanted the challenge. One way or another the actors intended to whip the cameras, find the acting style that would keep the lenses from digging too deeply into their private personalities. A style that would let them pretend.

For the actors, the actresses were no contest, they were only actresses—women.

The character actors were tough, but that was fine. They provided the kind of problem an actor is supposed to have. Competition on the sound stage.

The supervisors were the stumbling block; they continued to select bad scripts. Bogart liked one of them, Mark Hellinger. "Mark introduced me to scotch." But he had little regard for the species. "In twenty years in Hollywood I've never been able to figure out what they do. I suppose they give the Green Light. After they flash it, they ought to go on a fishing trip until the picture is over."

Paul Muni didn't have to escape; he was getting his way: *Juarez, The Life of Emile Zola, The Story of Louis Pasteur, Bordertown, Black Fury* and others. He used the muscle of script approval to gain other controls. "Muni used to insist that all his scripts be written by his brother-in-law, Aben Finkel," recalls Blanke. "After Finkel wrote the first version of *We Are Not Alone* and Muni read it, he said, 'Heinz, why can't we get the original author, novelist James Hilton?' I hired Hilton and after Muni read his version, he said, 'Heinz, it's beautiful. That's the difference between chicken salad and chicken shit.'"

With his important roles and films, the Warner Classics, Muni won two Oscars and in 1940 renegotiated his contract so he would receive eight hundred thousand dollars a film with the understanding that the first would be the life of Beethoven. The film, however, never materialized into a satisfactory script. Finally, after Muni turned down *High Sierra,* he and Warner canceled the contract by mutual consent.

Muni's wife recalled that after eight years he was free of the Warner factory. "He did somersaults in the living room. Believe me. He jumped up and down yelling, 'No one owns me! I'm a free man!'"

Muni would make only six more films as a free man, forgotten films like *Hudson's Bay, Counter Attack, Angel on My Shoulder* and *Stranger on the Prowl* at other studios, then retire from the business. It was prophetic.

Gary Cooper came over from Paramount in 1941 to make *Meet John Doe.* He was already a movie star and worked on a per-picture basis. He came back fourteen times to make *Sergeant York, Saratoga Trunk, The Fountainhead, Task Force, Bright Leaf, Dallas, Springfield Rifle* and others.

Dennis Morgan and Jack Carson were signed in the forties to play leads along with Ronald Reagan in the program pictures, pictures considered "A" quality, but with limited budgets. Their contracts were without script approval. Morgan made thirty-nine films, Carson thirty and Reagan thirty-seven. All stable factory employees but no Rin Tin Tins.

If an actor wanted something better, contract time was the time to fight, the only time when the actor had any power. The time he could go over the heads of the supervisors. In 1940 Pat O'Brien's contract came due for negotiations and he was growing tired of playing priests and Jimmy Cagney's buddy who never got the girl. It had become so repetitious that O'Brien's wife, Eloise, would be asked by utter strangers,

Top. John Garfield works out in the studio gym
Bottom. James Cagney and George Raft on the set of Each Dawn I Die, 1939
Facing. Edward G. Robinson is visited by Ann Sheridan and Ann Sothern on the set of Brother Orchid, 1940

"Doesn't your husband ever get the girl?" On one occasion, Mrs. O'Brien exploded, "No! And if he doesn't get her pretty soon, people are going to think I won him on a punchboard!" O'Brien could usually put Warner off his guard with a funny story and some Irish blarney, but this time they couldn't come to terms. O'Brien left for Columbia Pictures to make Crack Up, Johnny One-Eye and others with less recognizable titles.

Taking a suspension was another way to get in a punch.

John Garfield arrived at the Warner Bros. neighborhood in 1938 from New York's Group Theater, where he was used to roles that made demands on his talent. Warner Bros., however, liked his dark good looks, put him in a sailor's uniform, tuxedo, and loaded him down with Celluloid glamour. Shortly after arrival, Garfield began refusing one film and taking a suspension for every film he agreed to make. "I wasn't carrying a chip on my shoulder. I appreciated the fact that Warner made me a star. But they didn't pick me up from a filling station. I had enough stage experience to know I was no Cary Grant or Robert Taylor and that I couldn't do their kind of pictures. So I just took the suspensions and waited for the parts I could do."

Garfield and Warner finally disagreed in 1946 and the actor left to free-lance. Film work became difficult for him to get in 1947, however, when his suspected left-wing sympathies were investigated by Congress. A friend later said, "The tragedy was that Garfield wasn't accused of anything. He was a street boy with a street boy's sense of honor and when they asked him to give the names of friends, he refused. They blacklisted him for that."

Edward G. Robinson and Warner got along well as the actor kept their differences private. "To Jack Warner I was the second coming."

Robinson attempted to explain to Warner that to share the wealth not only meant the money but the right to determine your own fate. He finally got Warner to allow him to cure syphilis in Dr. Ehrlich's Magic Bullet, but the audience wasn't impressed. Warner forced him back into a gangster part, Brother Orchid. Robinson was ready to quit after the film was released, but two new scripts arrived, A Dispatch from Reuter's and The Sea Wolf.

"No actor could ask for more . . . no actor nearing fifty, that is. I enjoyed them and perhaps it is not mere coincidence that the associate producer on both was a man named Henry Blanke."

James Cagney was a street fighter. He took hold and wouldn't quit until he'd won or lost. Four months after he completed *Public Enemy,* he decided he was worth more than the $450 a week he was being paid. The Academy Arbitration Board stepped in and Cagney returned at $1,000 a week

"Don't forget that when you're through," Cagney told one reporter, "don't forget that when you're washed up in pictures, you are really through. You can't even get a bit, let alone a decent part." Like all street kids, Cagney knew a good thing could end any time you turned a corner. The future didn't count, but today did.

Cagney's contract was for four pictures a year and top billing, but in 1935 he was working in five pictures and at the Hollywood Warner theater, where *Devil Dogs of the Air* was playing, Pat O'Brien got top billing on one side of the marquee. Warner happened to notice it, roared back to the studio to fix it, but Cagney's lawyers were already in action. The case went to court, where it stayed for two years. During that time Cagney made two forgettable films for Grand National, then returned to the factory to make *Angels with Dirty Faces, Each Dawn I Die, The Strawberry Blonde, The Fighting 69th, City for Conquest, The Roaring Twenties* and *Yankee Doodle Dandy* before he fought again.

He left in 1944 to form his own company, but its failure was spectacular, *Blood on the Sun, Johnny Come Lately.* His friends got him and Warner back together in 1948 and Cagney returned to the studio to make *White Heat, Kiss Tomorrow Goodbye* and *Come Fill the Cup.* In 1950 the split became permanent, the contract was torn up and Cagney would only return on special occasions, like *Mr. Roberts,* as a guest. The fighting was over, he was free, but his great films were behind him, not ahead.

George Raft arrived on the lot as a star, and his contract allowed him to refuse a script that was a remake. He had years of films behind him and a career as a celebrated adagio dancer prior to that. His first film for the studio was *Each Dawn I Die.* He became worried, however, about his star image and the fact that Warner liked him in gangster roles. He consequently turned down *High Sierra, The Maltese Falcon* and *Casablanca.* Like most of the actors, he was certain he knew what he was doing.

Raoul Walsh was set to direct *High Sierra* and Warner sent him to see why Raft turned it down. "So I went over to see

him. And George refused to play in it because he didn't want to die at the end. He refused. I said, 'Well, look George, the censors will demand, after you kill a couple of people, that you pay the penalty.' He said, 'I don't give a damn about the censors, I don't want to do it.'"

Walsh went back to Warner, who accepted the refusal. But he wanted to get started immediately with someone else. Paul Muni turned it down because it had been offered to Raft first. Cagney and Robinson also turned it down, because it was just another gangster role and Warner didn't figure the film was worth making them mad. Walsh said, "Well, you got a guy here under contract called Bogart. I'll take a chance with him."

When Bogart's agent called to tell him he had been offered the part, Bogart said, "Sure. Where the hell's the script and when do I start?"

Raft didn't have to make *The Maltese Falcon* because it was a remake and turned it down because he would not entrust his talent to an untried director named John Huston. He objected to *Casablanca* because he would lose the girl, Ilsa Lund, Ingrid Bergman, at the end of the picture. Raft eventually bought out his contract in 1943 for ten thousand dollars and left to make *Nob Hill, Mr. Ace, Christmas Eve* and others that have been forgotten.

By 1941, Bogart was about to get the kind of role he wanted, but it hadn't been accidental. *High Sierra*'s producer, David Lewis, insists that the wily Bogart was responsible for Raft's refusing the roles. "Bogart was devious," recalls Lewis. "Exciting, vital, but devious. Raft was insecure, and after being killed off in some eighty pictures, he was anxious to play the hero who lived, got the girl and won the audience's love and respect. Bogart knew this, and with devilish glee he would get Raft aside and tell him, 'Look, you're too big a star for this small-time stuff. You lose the girl. They bump you off at the end. That's not good for an established star, it's all right for a punk like me, but your fans won't go for this.' Raft would get steamed up, stalk into Jack Warner's office and refuse to play the role. The part would then go to Bogart, and *High Sierra, The Maltese Falcon* and *Casablanca* built Bogart into the biggest star on the Warner lot."

"*High Sierra* gave Bogart a chance to get out of those standard hero and gangster stereotype roles he had been playing," recalls Walsh. "They wanted him to be a matinee hero, but he didn't want that. He worked hard, a total profes-

sional. He would act cool, try to show he didn't care, much like he did in the films when he'd say he did it for the money, but you always knew better. He was cool, but he was always there on time and prided himself on it."

Working on *The Maltese Falcon,* "Bogart once arrived at nine-fifteen, fifteen minutes late," recalls Huston. "He was completely chagrined, embarrassed, ashamed. It really bothered him even though that was the morning that his wife, not Betty Bacall, but the other one, had stabbed him in the stomach with a knife."

"No matter how bad a hangover Bogie had," recalled Peter Lorre, "he'd always be on time, knowing his lines when it came to a shot on the set. One night we'd been out drinking all night and hadn't been in bed. For Bogie's puss that didn't matter and we went directly to the studio."

Warner didn't mind. "Bogie's face looked no worse on camera after an all-night binge than it normally did," he recalled.

Bogart and Warner found ways to get along. Bogart would always drop by his office after a drunken spree and apologize and once, after he and Lorre had told a New York reporter that Warner was a creep and the reporter printed it, he explained to an outraged and hurt Jack Warner, "Different word. We spell it 'kreep,' with a 'k.'"

Bogart fought for costars as well as roles. "Bogart refused to play in *The Treasure of the Sierra Madre* without the Old Howard character being a better actor than he was," recalls Henry Blanke. "We had to wait a year for Walter Huston, who was doing a play in New York, without him Bogart wouldn't work. He knew where the story was."

He would also worry about small things like props and bits of wardrobe, little things that added up to reveal the past of the characters he portrayed. Reveal the life the character had before he walked in front of the demanding, soul-stealing camera that saw everything with its large, prying eye. Over the years the props, wardrobe and acting style would come together to reveal the man. The "square" Western belt buckle he wore in film after film, the belted trench coat, or how he would lift a shot glass. Watching him smoke became special. Chesterfields. They were just small things on the screen, but telling. Like brushstrokes identify a painter.

Jack Warner had Bogart right where he wanted him, at work in his factory. A prisoner on his Celluloid. And the price was

right. In 1943 Bogart's agents renegotiated a new seven-year contract for $3,500 a week and forty weeks a year, but the studio had no options. As long as Bogart showed up for work, he would have to be paid.

In 1946 the contract was again renegotiated but Warner was still buying cheap. Bogart was to receive $5,000 a week, but for only one picture a year and he had the right to refuse two out of three stories submitted to him. He made *The Big Sleep, The Two Mrs. Carrolls, Dark Passage, The Treasure of the Sierra Madre, Key Largo* and *Chain Lightning.*

"Nobody can be a good actor without a sense of truth, of right and wrong," he once told a group of young actors. Not of what is right and wrong in the outside world, but what is right and wrong inside the actor, inside the man. The equal parts of right and wrong with which a second act in a story is made.

The directors liked Bogart because he would let both parts show, the ugliness and the beauty, and their cameras recorded it. Moved in close and watched him work. Watched him tear himself apart inside. With Bogart, a second act didn't have to be written, and when it was, he changed it, added something with his face. With the face that was three drinks ahead of the rest of the world.

Bogart could lose up there in the darkness and win by losing. He had revived the tragic heros of the old mythologies, but hidden them in "hard dicks," cardboard gangsters and cynical nightclub owners.

"He was no hero, he was no hero at all," recalls Mary Astor. "It is true his personality dominated the character he was playing—but the character gained by it. His technical skill was quite brilliant. His precision timing was no accident. He kept other actors on their toes because he listened to them, he watched, he looked at them. He never had that vague stare of a person who waits for you to finish talking, who hasn't heard a word you have said. And he was never 'upstage center' acting all by himself. He was there. With you.

"Bogie had his troubles, his longing for a good world, his need to trust and believe in something. Like the rest of us. But he couldn't dismiss it with a philosophy, or stick his head in sand. He was aware and he blew. Violently and often. And when he got drunk he was bitter and smilingly sarcastic and thoroughly unpleasant.

"There he is, right there on the screen, saying what everyone

is trying to say today, saying it loud and clear. 'I hate hypocrisy. I don't believe in words and labels or much of anything else. I'm not a hero. I'm a human being. I'm not very pretty. Like me or don't like me.' We who knew him well liked him. Bogie was for real."

Bogart knew what roles he wanted and somehow got them. The others seldom did, but the desire to gain control over their own destinies, to select their own roles, to do the thinking and even the writing, directing and producing, continued to grow with the actors' popularity. And given their talent, their energy and desires, the power began to shift from the studio to the stars as the forties raced for the fifties. The actors still had the largest egos and they would ride them hard, even into their own blazing destruction.

From inside Warner Bros., Jack's factory looked like prison to the actors and it was only natural for a street kid to want to "crash out." They had to even if oblivion was waiting outside. But while they were inside, fighting their way through the neighborhood, they had looked good in prison stripes, behind a Smith and Wesson and on mean streets . . . and there was a reason.

In 1974, when James Cagney received the American Film Institute's Life Achievement Award, he could see yesterday clearly, with the vision only a seventy-year-old song-and-dance man can have, and he saw "people doing things that are essentially themselves. And what they're doing should be of great interest to everybody, from an artistic point of view, because if we are looking at it in that way we are holding the wonder that we are born with."

He described how he had learned all the characteristic Cagney gestures, the hiking of the pants, the one-finger hello and the tucking of the chin from a fellow who hung out on the corner of Seventy-eighth Street and First Avenue. A fellow who, when Cagney was a boy of twelve, would stand there and make those gestures all day long. "Now, let's face it, we are all indebted to that fella."

And he talked about art: "Life plus . . . life plus caprice." Seventy-eighth Street and First Avenue plus Warner Bros.

Cagney knew where all those toughs, sailors, wanderers, fighters, slave traders and street boys that appeared up there in the darkness came from. And he thanked the sources of his performances. His wife, brother, sister, stunt man Harvey

Perry, and then all those who had been with him on the streets where it had started, taken life. "And the names . . . the names, the names of my youth. Loggerhead Quinlaven, Artie Kline, Pete Leeden, Jake Brodkin, Specster Forcer, Brother O'Meara, Picky Houlihan, who were all part of a very stimulating early environment which produced an unmistakable touch of the gutter without which this evening might never have happened at all. Bless them."

The actors had come to act, to pretend, but the cameras wouldn't let them hide and the world saw past the bad dialogue, past the makeup, past the movie stars. And saw what they were, thirty-five-cent heroes made from life. Both cardboard and silver, they *were* what you saw at the picture show.

The actors didn't work alone in front of the cameras, however, and if they found life intolerable in Jack's factory, the actresses found it impossible.

Left. Rin-Tin-Tin
Below. John Barrymore as Svengali
Facing. John Barrymore

213

Facing, left. Richard Barthelmess
Facing, above. George Arliss as Voltaire
Facing, below right. George Arliss as Disraeli
Left. Paul Muni
Below left. Paul Muni as Juarez
Below. Edward G. Robinson

Facing, left. James Cagney, twice as Cagney, once as Bottom
Below. Fredric March as Anthony Adverse
Top. Leslie Howard
Bottom. Douglas Fairbanks, Jr.

Facing, left. George Raft
Facing, top. Dick Powell
Facing, center. Pat O'Brien
Facing, bottom. George Brent
Below. Paul Henreid
Right. Gary Cooper

Left. Errol Flynn as Lord Essex
Top. Errol Flynn as Robin Hood
Bottom. John Garfield
Facing, left. John Garfield
Facing, right. Humphrey Bogart as Roy Earle

Below, left. Humphrey Bogart as Sam Spade
Below. James Dean

WAKING BEAUTIES

Actresses

"Who are you really? And what were you before? What did you do and what did you think? Huh?"

They should have stayed home. Stayed in their own neighborhood, trapped a man and made him feed, clothe and house them. Stayed and been good daughters, wives and mothers. But they saved their nickels, packed their mirrors and left home nervously looking at themselves.

They were mostly losers, starry-eyed kids who had been deluded into believing they were special or who simply had to get away to something better, anything better. There were tramps, hustlers, four-bit frails, simpleminded floozies, shopgirls, secretaries, teachers, a lot of decent kids and loud girls all marked with more than their share of beauty—at least with what the men in their hometown considered beauty. Amid the hordes there were also a few gutsy girls, one or two ladies laced with dynamite and a thundering dame.

They had two choices, to head east or west. In New York there was Broadway, the theater. "Art." If a girl was successful in the East she could write home about it. If she went west, to Hollywood, to the movies, she either became a star or didn't write home.

But even if they had headed east, they eventually ended in Hollywood, to be a shimmering, glowing star in the cinematic firmament . . . and make money. To be part of the picture shows.

When they got off the train at the Los Angeles station, all they had were their big smiles, good figures and their innocence, or a profound lack of it. Either one would do. Inside they knew that men are suckers for both and one way or another they were going to convince some movie mogul they could deliver what he wanted or needed.

You could tell the actresses. They had poodles under their arms or on silver leashes and they spoke with finely drawn English accents.

A girl named Ruth Elizabeth was left standing at the station in 1930. The studio representative either overlooked her or couldn't believe she was an actress. Even if she did have a dog, and her mother. She was such a plain little girl.

At the Burbank studios in 1930, Jack Warner wanted grand actresses. The great beauties of the silent film era had made other moguls rich and he'd find the same kind to make him rich. But his had to read dialogue and rather than trust his own male drives, he plunged ahead and stole two supposedly bonafide actresses from Paramount, Kay Francis and Ruth Chatterton.

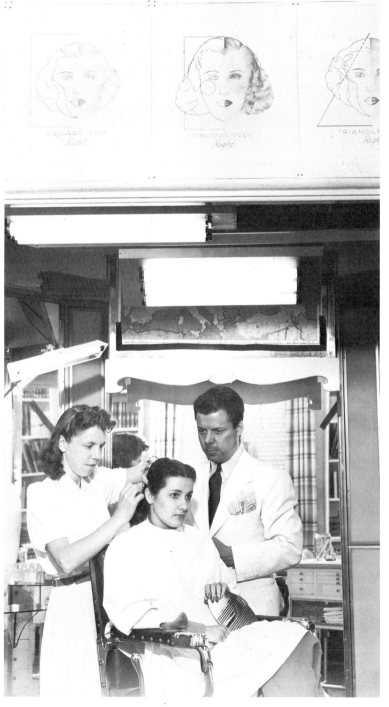

His disappointment was sudden, profound and extended. When the actresses' first films were released in 1932, *Man Wanted* and *The Rich Are Always with Us,* they weren't smash hits. And he was paying Francis $5,250 a week and Chatterton $8,000 while he was paying Cagney only $450 and Robinson $650 to make films that were turning to gold at the box office. And the actresses had script approval; they were telling him what kind of stories they wanted to make. Women were telling Jack Warner what to do. But he couldn't get rid of them until their options ran out. He would put up with them, use them unmercifully, but he was trapped for at least five years.

Warner contracted Barbara Stanwyck in 1931. She was an actress and had script approval, but she was also a knockout. She gave the boys in the audience what they wanted and her films sold, *Night Nurse, Illicit.* Warner decided on more of the same. He didn't need actresses, he needed dames.

His instincts knew what would sell, he'd seen it at the carnivals as a kid: hootch dancers, belly pushers, a lot of leg, lovely innocent faces with big sad eyes, beauty contest winners, a little bump-and-grind, lacy lingerie and swell curves. Fleshy decorations. Snake charmers. The male talent would handle the acting, the girls would be good to look at.

It was a timely decision. The Hays Office of the Motion Picture Producers' Association hadn't commanded the studios not to show the inside of a girl's thigh, too much cleavage or to show a woman in bed with a man only when she had one foot on the floor. Warner Bros. could make the kind of picture it wanted to and the Writers' Building was put to work to do just that.

Between 1930 and 1934 the studio's films would be populated with lovely fallen women, with silken creatures of beauty who would make you hurt, girls blushed with dark olive skin and those stained with a sinful touch of the Orient, with the deadly "yellow peril." And the Stock Talent: *female* was ordered to slip into the wardrobe and attitudes of a tough, crude, male world.

If they could read lines, it would help. If they couldn't, the studio would teach them. They'd change their names, dress them, redo their makeup, tell them where to stand, how to move their hips, what to say and who to go out with. And the actresses would work like everyone else, fourteen hours a day, six days a week and no overtime pay. There wasn't going to be any nonsense just because they were women. They were employees, and Jack wasn't waiting for them to arrive on the train. He sent his scouts throughout the nation.

They came back with Louise Beavers, Marie Wells, Claudia Dell, Laura Lee, Laura La Plante, Sheila Terry, Ginger Rogers, Claire Dodd, Collen Coleman, Mary Maguire and hundreds of others. They even found little Ann McKim at Hollywood High School and changed her name to Ann Dvorak so it sounded exotic. Myrna Williams from Helena, Montana, was dressed in beads and Oriental flowers, her skin was coated with dark oils and her name changed to Myrna Loy.

If a girl arrived on the lot a trifle plain, the studio made her a trifle exotic, offbeat, with a sense of the chaotic in her eyes.

Perc Westmore in the Makeup Department would handle nose problems. "Maybe a corrective in the nostril, maybe a Dietrich eyebrow or a Crawford mouth."

Jean Burt Reilly in the Hair Department would provide wigs, falls and dye more than one head of hair platinum blond.

Madison Lacy, Scotty Welborne, Buddy Longworth and Eddie Stone in the Publicity Department would then photograph the girls endlessly; do "handies," "cheesecake," "leg art," and seminudes for the publicists to send out to the press. Most went to the smaller, more wicked fan magazines like *Film Fun, Snappy* and *Screenies*. Once a girl fit Jack Warner's ideal, she seldom missed a day in the photo studio. Toby Wing became the Warner Bros. "stills girl" even though she seldom appeared in a film . . . and then only for seconds.

The still photographers were necessities and were paid up to $500 a week. The girls were expendable. They were signed to short-term, six-month contracts for $50 to $75 a week. Picture making at the studio was a business and if a girl, no matter how beautiful she was, didn't provide that something extra, that something a trifle mad for the audience, as well as for Jack Warner, she was promptly dropped.

Of the thousands of girls who arrived in Hollywood, less than one percent would get past a studio gate. But some got lucky, got work and it was enough to convince the others that they would too.

Those who weren't working were looking for work. Central Casting Agency in the early thirties was receiving between fifteen and twenty thousand calls a day from the young, the old, the ugly and the beautiful. A special switchboard had to be put in for the "weepers," for those girls who wanted to know why they hadn't been called, why the casting directors and producers were interested in them instead of their acting ability, why they were being abused, why they weren't wanted.

The "trouble desk" at Central lit up daily from 4 P.M. to 7 P.M. in the evening after the "calls" for tomorrow's work had all been placed by the studios, normally by 4 P.M. Those who called often had real problems, not just complaints.

They were the runaways, dreamers who had become pregnant without the dignity of a husband and without the means of supporting their child. "They would be down to putting all the money they had into buying their baby's clothes and food," recalls a switchboard operator. "That left nothing to dress themselves and anybody with sense knew you couldn't make it out here if you looked bad." Some of the girls who called would ask for "any work" they could get. "Some meant it and found it. They usually didn't call again and we knew." Central found some work for girls in department stores, even found homes for their babies and, for a few, they raised enough money to buy a bus ticket home. "Most of those girls, however, lied and called us again the next day." And the next until they ran out of nickels.

The dream was just too big to hold onto. Little Claudia Dell, whom Warner Bros. had found and whose lovely figure was used by Columbia Pictures as its signature for years, one day walked to the top of the hill where the huge white sign that spelled out Hollywood stood. She climbed to the top of the H, then jumped to her death. Others would follow her up and down the H in later years. Still more would find quicker ways to end their dreams without the benefit of publicity. The lucky ones would go home before tragedy hit, but most would stay on as secretaries, shop clerks, waitresses, assembly line workers and eventually accept the roles in life they had run away from, become wives and mothers.

A few girls, however, just wouldn't be thrown away. They had looked at themselves and realized they wouldn't be happy, wouldn't even know who they really were, until the audience was watching them do it, whatever it was.

Ruby Stevens started life skinny, redheaded and freckle-faced. As a child, she danced for pennies thrown at her by the ditchdiggers near Prospect Park, in Brooklyn. It was small applause, but contagious. Her story contains an orphan asylum, a job as a telephone operator from which she was fired at fourteen, a scar on her breast from a cigar burn placed there by a customer in a New York nightclub where she danced the

228

black bottom, a striptease behind a white screen in the Ziegfeld Follies, on-the-cuff meals at The Tavern on Forty-eighth Street and a trip to Hollywood on the Santa Fe.

By the time she went to work for Jack Warner in 1931, she had already made several successful picture shows, walked out on one movie mogul, Harry Cohn of Columbia Pictures, and changed her name to Barbara Stanwyck.

Ruth Elizabeth Davis grew up having to be first, win the cookie contest, win all the Girl Scout medals. As a teenager she dated the football star, posed for the Statue of Spring in Beacon Hill, hid under an elm to watch the Shawn dancers perform nude in the moonlight and played the role of the moth in a production designed by her dancing instructor, Roshanara. The effect was one mass of shimmering silk as she danced on a lighted, multicolored glass floor that turned from blinding white to amber and blue to the eventual orange flame in which she fluttered to her final self-destruction.

Jack Warner would never understand that arty nonsense nor the feisty young girl who did the artless dancing. But she was headed in his direction.

"I remember the excitement of performing that night in front of an audience—the audience thrilled me." Her mother Ruthie and her friends, however, weren't any more understanding than Warner would be. "I recall their looking at me afterwards as if they'd never seen me before." They, of course, hadn't.

Ruth Elizabeth kept on changing, kept on becoming some-thing never seen before. She had an engagement broken by a boy whose father didn't approve of actresses, lost a Vilma Banky look-alike contest, played the daughter in a play with the ridiculous title of *Broken Dishes* on Broadway, had her teeth straightened, stupidly did her own makeup for her screen test, then took the five-day ride on the Sante Fe and arrived in Hollywood on December 13, 1930, as Bette Davis.

She went to work at Universal Pictures, where they tried to change her adopted name to something more devastating. Bette was a secretary's name, not a star's. She resisted and no one cared enough to fight with her about it. She was a mess.

She had never been inside a beauty parlor, her eyebrows were thick and unplucked and her long hair was wound up and broken only to curls at her face. They dyed her hair platinum blond, took countless photos of her legs and even put her into a film, *Bad Sister,* with a young actor named Bogart. She got third billing, he got eighth.

On the lot, the comments about her weren't flattering. Director William Wyler thought she was trying to get ahead on the size of her breasts and she overheard a producer say, "She'll never get ahead; she has about as much sex appeal as Slim Summerville." They were paying her $350 a week, but dropped her option after two more films. She worked for three small studios, then the star George Arless at Warner Bros. asked her to read for him. He liked her and sent her to Wardrobe for costume fittings as Grace in *The Man Who Played God*.

The film was a success and Warner Bros. picked up her option for one year, She was just a curvy kid then with little idea of who she was, but Jack Warner sent her to Publicity for "leg art" and pinups . . . and the fighting started.

The year Bette Davis arrived, Olivia de Havilland ran away from home. "I had a wicked stepfather who forbade me to try out for school plays." She was sixteen, a junior in high school and a competitor who hadn't as yet come in first. She was second in a spelling bee that could have made her small town of Saratoga, California, famous, graduated only third in her class of 1934 and was often seen with her friend Margo Goodrich, the great beauty of Saratoga. After leaving home, she performed in many school plays, did the part of Puck from *A Midsummer Night's Dream*, and won herself a scholarship to Mills College.

Acting at that stage in her young life was something she thought about, but her goal was to make sure her scholarship at Mills was continued a second year. When she heard that the famous European director Max Reinhardt was going to present *A Midsummer Night's Dream* at the Hollywood Bowl, she believed that if she could in any way work for the celebrated Reinhardt Company, her second year at Mills would be secured. Through a friend she met Felix Weisberger, Reinhardt's assistant, and played Puck for him, then Hermia. Weisberger liked her and said she could go to Hollywood and understudy the part of Hermia.

"I knew I had a scholarship then; I was going to be queen of the campus."

In Hollywood, however, Weisberger kept her waiting in his outer office three days before she discovered he was avoiding her and leaving by a rear exit. She then intimidated a man she recognized from San Francisco and got him to take her to Weisberger. The trapped and apologetic Weisberger told the young Olivia he had cast another girl as the understudy. He hadn't thought Olivia would really come, but since she had, he let her understudy the understudy. And Olivia de Havilland went to work.

Gloria Stuart had the part of Hermia and Jean Rouverol was her understudy. Since Gloria was working in a film at Warner Bros., Jean took the rehearsals and Olivia spent much of her time allowing the child Mickey Rooney, who was playing Puck, to sleep in her lap.

A Midsummer Night's Dream was strictly a stage performance at that time, but Henry Blanke was interested in the property and spent some time watching rehearsals in the Hollywood Bowl. "I saw Olivia there, sitting by herself, even then she was so beautiful."

Then it happened like it happens only in the movies. Jean Rouverol got a job at Paramount and Olivia became the understudy. A short time later, Gloria Stuart left to do a film role. With five days before opening, Reinhardt told Olivia that she had to do the part. And she did. "Somehow the lines came out, but I couldn't hear them."

The first night's audience was filled with luminaries of the picture business: Gloria Swanson, Joan Crawford, Charlie Chaplin, Jean Harlow, Bette Davis and twenty-six thousand others. And Reinhardt had staged the presentation so the young lovers parade in a long walk past the audience after the first act. By that time Olivia knew where she was. "I heard the applause . . . oh, did I hear the applause."

With a performing commitment to the company, Mills College had to be put off until January. The eighteen-year-old college girl was now a working actress.

At Warner Bros., Blanke convinced Warner to contract Reinhardt to make a film of his production, then had Max Arnow, head of talent, have lunch with the agentless Olivia. Arnow offered her $150 a week and she got him up to $200. He asked her to come back at 5 P.M. to sign. She returned, but the contract was for seven years and she refused to sign.

As she left Arnow's office, she ran into the Warner German contingent, Henry Blanke, William Dieterle and Erich Wolfgang Korngold. She apologized to them for not being able to work with them on the film version. "They all went, 'Ach!' They backed me into Arnow's office and when he offered to cut the contract to five years, I finally said yes. I signed out of weakness and a sense of responsibility. I went home and cried

and cried and cried with the most ghastly feeling of depression. I was black with despair. I was sure I had made the wrong decision."

Blanke had what he wanted; Olivia not only could act, but she looked like a star was supposed to. "She was so beautiful it hurt."

Ann Sheridan and Ida Lupino also had their doubts about being movie stars. In the early thirties they roomed together with Ida's mother, Connie. They both had contracts at Paramount and had worked in Cecil B. DeMille's religion and flesh epics—as flesh. "Ann would say, 'I'm never going to make this scene. I can't stand it.' I agreed," recalls Lupino. "If you wanted to be an actress, forget it. And neither of us did. We didn't know what we wanted to be. Ann would say, 'I was brought out here for a beauty contest,' and I would say, 'I was brought out here for *Alice in Wonderland* and neither of us made it.'"

Ida Lupino had been pushed into show business by her father. "I used to tell him, 'Dad, don't you understand. I don't want to be an actress.'

"'No, I don't understand. Now go put your makeup on, you little coward.'

"'But Dad, I want to write lyrics.'

"'You'll go out and perform tonight.'"

And she did.

In London, Ida attended "the Royal Academy of Dramatic Arts, or rather tarts, and the first thing I played in was by Shaw. And every night I went to work absolutely terrified. They told my father, 'She'll never make it.' And I did hope he would believe them. I thought, 'I really am a flop' as far as the family was concerned. But Dad said, 'She'll make it.'"

Did her father put her in the wrong direction, did she regret it? "Let me say, I never said he was wrong."

Ida Lupino came in 1940 for *They Drive by Night.* Director Raoul Walsh convinced Hal Wallis and Jack Warner she could play a great "dame" with a lengthy screen test.

Ann Sheridan was contracted on July 1, 1936, for $75 a week, and her contract ran until December 18, 1943, with a maximum salary of $750 a week. Warner had his beauty contest winner and other qualifications he wouldn't expect.

Lucille Le Sueur started life as a "slavey" in a private school in Kansas City. She tried working in her mother's laundry,

couldn't stand it, and talked a man into paying her $20 a week to dance in his chorus. From the headliner in his show, she got a tip about a casting call in Chicago, dropped her man and arrived in Chicago with two dollars and seventeen years growth. It was more than enough.

Her first night, she danced in the chorus at the Friars Inn, then did a week there and moved with the company to Oklahoma City and then Detroit. The other girls forced her to dress in a corner so she couldn't steal their makeup tricks, but she stole them anyway and was promoted to "end girl" even though she didn't know the steps to the buck-and-wing. She looked better than good, however, in tight trousers, loose blouses and Eton collars so they let her fake it.

A Broadway producer spotted her, put her in a chorus as a "pony," but she quickly fought and beguiled her way into the front row, caught the eyes of the men in the audience and a year later was working at Metro-Goldwyn-Mayer in Hollywood under her new name, Joan Crawford.

She arrived at Warner Bros. in 1943 after fighting the most influential mogul in tinsel town, Louis B. Mayer, until he couldn't take it any longer. When her career faltered, he fired her.

When Crawford walked on the Warner lot, however, she discovered she was up against not only a mogul, but a whole army of male employees.

Regardless of when they arrived on the lot, in the early thirties or in the forties, the actresses quickly discovered there was no help in sight. Only one woman headed a department, Jean Burt Reilly, and the one time she attended a production meeting she made Warner uncomfortable because he had to reduce his four-letter words by several hundred percent. After each speech he'd ask, "Was that all right?" She decided it was best if she didn't go again. The women writers were useless. Their ideas about art and poetry were so grand, they considered them above the means of a simple movie actress. There were men everywhere offering to help, to guide the actresses' young lives, to make them famous, but the hard facts of life at Warner Bros. were as obvious as the cement. The actresses were alone, against impossible odds.

But once they were on the lot, a few intended to stick.

"The real actor—like any real artist—has a direct line to the collective heart," wrote Bette Davis. And she was dying to touch it.

The actress would provide Warner with a little "leg art," flash her lingerie and put the threat, or promise, of a bump-and-grind in her walk if it was necessary, if it would put her in the position eventually to play the great roles, Lady Macbeth, Ophelia, Hedda Gabler, Madame Bovary and that incredible woman of such grand power, Elizabeth of England, the Queen.

All Jack Warner wanted, however, was pretty flesh that worked obediently, and he was getting it.

Loretta Young made twenty-six films between 1930 and 1933, over six films per year. At sixteen, when she arrived, she was tireless and played fallen girls, trapped wives and innocent beauties with loose sex in the dark shadows that held her large eyes. She, however, left the studio and went to 20th Century-Fox. Still only twenty years old.

Myrna Loy also left, for MGM, and left her beads and oils behind to play quick-witted, sophisticated ladies who lived in rich neighborhoods.

Ginger Rogers slithered and danced off to RKO.

Ruby Keeler, however, arrived from Broadway in 1933 and stayed. She was also a worker and looked good in satin scanties. She worked in the successful musicals and her name became associated with profits and Jack kept her in the factory until 1936.

Joan Blondell was a bargain, a solid factory employee. Warner picked her up with Cagney from the Broadway show *Penny Arcade* for a price, $250 a week. In 1931 she was only twenty-one, but already a trooper, and with curves. "God, she had a figure!" recalls Mervyn LeRoy. Her films were reasonably profitable; she would do anything she was asked to do and with gusto. During the thirties she made forty-seven films and was loaned out at a profit nine times. Jack couldn't have been more pleased. She did it without a complaint.

"We often worked through Saturday till daybreak on Sunday," recalls Blondell. "And often went without lunch and watched the directors eat their sandwiches." But there were compensations for a young beauty. "Things were made especially for you, custom-made hats, shoes, lingerie, gloves." The only time she went on suspension was when she broke the rules and took time off to have a baby. "I felt an obligation to honor the contract."

Jack tried other female stars, Dorothy Mackaill, Ann Dvorak, Glenda Farrell, Aline MacMahon, and hired dozens more for

$50 a week to see if they had what he and his supervisors wanted and needed.

Until the gangster genre became unpopular, the Talent Department would keep hunting for girls who fit the tough scripts; for dames, carhops, waitresses, gun molls and whores. On June 1, 1937, they were still looking and hired Marian Alden, Lois Chaney, Alice Connors, Bess Myers, Lottie Williams, Dorothy Varden, Sally Sage, Paulette Evans, Clara Horton, Ann Robinson, Fern Barry and Carrie Daumery, each for $50 a week. The actresses stayed at that salary for over two years. There were rumors that the Talent Department had taken the specifications of the studio bosses too literally, but they were stand-ins filled with hope.

Others contracted were Rosemary, Priscilla and Lola Lane for $500 a week, Margaret Lindsay for $1,000, Gale Page for $400, Beverly Roberts for $350, Gloria Dickson for $200 and a dozen or so others for salaries ranging from $75 to $300 a week. They all worked, had their moment on the silver screen and tried to stay there.

Lana Turner was discovered by talent scout Solly Baiano, but Mervyn LeRoy got to her before Jack, signed her to a personal contract, put her in *They Won't Forget*, then sold her contract to MGM.

Off screen, in their private lives, the actresses tried to make the traditional roles in life work and became wives and mothers, but most would have to try many times. They didn't know their parts and their men couldn't hold onto the chaos within them without chasing it away. At the studio, they began their fight for other roles, roles more suitable to their natures.

While actress Florence Eldridge was playing Queen Elizabeth in director John Ford's *Mary of Scotland* at RKO, Bette Davis was getting loud and rebellious at Warner Bros. and playing secretaries. "Our contracts were outrageous and the security I had dreamed of on Broadway had become the safety of a prison."

But Jack Warner had made a decision. After six mediocre films Ruth Chatterton was dropped in 1934 and no more actresses or actors would be allowed script approval.

Jack's rules, however, didn't discourage young Bette Davis. "My passions were all gathered together like fingers that made a fist. Drive is considered aggression today; I knew it then as purpose."

Barbara Stanwyck told a reporter during those early years:

"I worry day and night over stories. Right now I'm in the dog-house at the studio because I turned down several stories they wanted me to do which I didn't feel were right for me."

"I wanted to do the roles the way they really were," recalls Ida Lupino, but, "I never got to pick my own roles. I just kept working. I had so many pictures to do at Warner's, then two at Fox, and back to Warner's."

Ann Sheridan played, "two bad ones for every good one . . . I was under contract, it was either do it or take suspension. They were turning them out like a factory in those days, shoving everything down the public's throat." And when a good role came up at another studio, Jack refused to let her do it.

Olivia de Havilland arrived on December 14, 1934, after playing Shakespeare and working with Max Reinhardt and received costar billing in Warner Bros.' most prestigious film of the time, *A Midsummer Night's Dream.* But she was just another employee and was immediately put to work on *Alibi Ike,* a Joe E. Brown comedy in which she played a role she refuses to remember.

"Henry Blanke went to Jack and protested my casting in *Alibi Ike,* and told him, 'You've got something, so take care of it.' But Jack felt I was under contract and so I should work. They gave me a bad time and I couldn't understand why they would do that to an eighteen-year-old."

But Olivia needed discipline; she was causing problems. "They wanted to change my name and I wouldn't have it. What they tried to do was change *you*—and they succeeded to some extent. It takes years to recover from that, years to deal with it at all. But I was full of myself and thank God.

"But it was a totally male situation at Warner Bros. You were called on to be tough, but you got tired in between."

The aggressive female who fought her way to the surface at Warner Bros., however, was particularly attractive to director Howard Hawks. "They're not so aggressive as they are honest," he recalls about the women in his films. "As soon as you take away the ingenue, you have a real woman, and you have an honest one." He knew what he was after when he had the studio contract Lauren Bacall for *To Have and Have Not* in 1945.

"Bacall had a little quality, she could be quite insolent. So I told Bogart, watch yourself because you're supposed to be the most insolent man on the screen and I'm going to make a girl a little more insolent than you. He said, well, you've got a

Top. Leslie Fenton and Loretta Young in The Hatchet Man, *1932*
Bottom. What every boy hoped to find at a drugstore fountain, Lana Turner and Gloria Dickson in They Won't Forget, *1937*
Facing. Joan Blondell and Loretta Young in Big Business Girl, *1931*

fat chance of doing that. I said, you forget I'm the director and I'll tell you something that's going to happen. In every scene in the picture she's going to walk out and leave you. You're going to be left standing with egg on your face. He said, that isn't fair and I said, I know, but I'm the director and I can do that."

He did, then again in *The Big Sleep*. Bacall had it inside her to be honest, a woman, but it was up to the director, a man, to see it and photograph it. And at Warner Bros., the actresses usually had little or no idea of just what the cameras saw.

It was fun to get all dressed up, confident in your femininity, certain that all the best in you was together: the hair, clothes, skin, lips and eyes. Stepping from Wardrobe you felt you were suddenly terribly clever to be with . . . the best of you had been made physical . . . and you believed "maybe they'll see me now."

On occasion the men in the neighborhood would even deliver the attention you deserved, but then it was: "A little more shoulder, Bette." "We can't see the legs, Olivia, that's it, more, more. Perfect." "For Christ's sake, Annie, we're not selling Bibles, show us what you've got." And, "Lupe! Lupe! Remember you're a whore, not a housewife."

And suddenly it was all too physical, too crude, too male and you were certain the camera would never see what was inside.

The conflict between the delights of being a world-famous object of desire and the need to show the world your own true desires, your true female nature, drove the actresses to their expensive mirrors time after time in search of ways to fool the cameras, to make themselves both real and attractive. But they found only themselves.

The actresses weren't sure if being an actress meant you couldn't be a woman, or if it was the only way to be a total woman, an incredible creature the world had never seen before. It was up to the directors to decide. Their cameras could photograph only what they saw, but they saw both inside and outside and there was no place for the actresses to hide. But when their images reached the screen the audience liked them just as they were. They had never seen women act like that before and there was no telling what they might do. The cameras saw past the bad stories and worse dialogue, past the brocade and flower prints, past the flesh and captured

what the audience wanted most . . . the life within them—
the female, the chaos.

For centuries theater managers, impresarios, medicine men,
priests and carnival hucksters had spent their lives trying to
find ways so the wild free spirits of their "talent" would show.
They designed feathers, slippers, dances, masks, makeup and
hired magicians, physicians, astrologers, dressmakers and eyebrow pluckers to work on their performers in the desperate
hope that on one golden night that magic chaos within them
would be seen . . . so that they could tell their grandchildren
of the night that they caught a shooting star.

All Jack Warner really needed was a Mitchell camera. But
Jack Warner didn't particularly care for what was going on
inside the mixed-up employees he politely, and often impolitely,
called actresses. He kept them around until the monthly
receipts determined which ones the audience liked . . . then
dropped the rest.

Bette Davis was an early choice. She had rearranged herself,
allowed her hair to stay platinum blond, wore braless gowns
of satin and chiffon and hoped that what was inside also
showed. The public took note. "My heavily beaded lashes and
over-rouged mouth. Oddly enough, they were to become my
trademark.

"I dreamed that someday Warners would give me the glossy
productions that MGM gave its players. I felt that the girl I
was now playing would never have a hairdo by Sidney Guilaroff
or a nineteen-piece suit with a supersonic collar by Adrian."
And she was right. The public liked her as she was.

Barbara Stanwyck had made her first impression on the
audience without fine clothes, fancy hairdos and glamour. At
Warner Bros. she tried the same and made five films for "Wild
Bill" Wellman. In the first, *Night Nurse,* he roughed her up,
made her take falls and had Clark Gable sock her good. And
he let her fight back, hit people, with both fists and with a
bucket. But her fans didn't like her in gingham and flannel
roles and wrote to the studio to put her in evening gowns.

Warner immediately had Orry-Kelly wrap her like a bonbon
and gave her thirteen men to star with. Warner told Stanwyck
she needed glamour. "Everyone else has glamour but me, so
I played in *Baby Face.* Anything for glamour." *Baby Face* is
one of two films that caused the censorship code to come
into effect.

Ann Sheridan played minor roles in major films and major

roles in minor films until the studio decided to publicize her as the "Oomph Girl." It was strictly a vulgar stunt, but a national contest was conducted to find her look-alike, countless interviews were arranged with and without her consent and she spent more time in the photo gallery than she did on the screen. But the smile in the photos was real and Ann Sheridan was all girl inside and out. She became a movie star performing on 8″ x 10″ glossies.

Ida Lupino spent much of her time in the photo gallery, wore a pompadour five inches high, fluttered her big round eyes and posed in flower print dresses and a thick smear of red lipstick. "I loved having people put me in good clothes." But her fans discovered her on the screen as a gun moll in *High Sierra.* "My fan mail used to come from Brooklyn saying, 'You're one of us, baby.' It all became almost impossibly and beautifully Brooklyn and I loved that . . . oh, God, I did!"

Olivia de Havilland caught the public's attention as the lovely young girl friend of Errol Flynn in *Captain Blood.* She had wanted the part. "It was an attractive film, I wanted to do that. It was the costumes, sets which remove you from life. I guess some part of me wants the fantasy." She would play Flynn's girl friend in another seven films.

As young as she was, she became embarrassed, ashamed. "It seemed like we were little cardboard cutouts." She was intimidated by those men and women at the writers' table in the Greenroom who considered castles and swords to have nothing to do with art, with life and what was real and important. "They looked down on the kind of film I was making."

She couldn't understand why the studio didn't guide her to greater roles, build her career rather than simply let it drift. "I was a diamond and I couldn't understand why they didn't take care of me."

Blanke and Lord occasionally would suggest parts slightly different for the actresses, but they had their own male ideas of right and wrong, of reality and beauty. Warner, however, had his way. He had dropped his women in the public lap and they had liked them. And if the audience liked them, then it would get more of the same. The movies cost only thirty-five cents, they were cheap entertainment and the actresses were no different than the popcorn.

The actresses had come dreaming of playing queens, oracles, great ladies of art and music, rulers and all the marvelous whores of history, Venus, Delilah and the Witch of Endor . . . they had come to perform in the new theater, the theater of the people, of the streets, of revolution and social investigation. "Motion pictures have an advantage" recalled Bette Davis, "the chance for reality and scope. This was the road I wanted to travel."

But Bette Davis played a rich, vixenish belle . . . a soft-spoken wife . . . her first downright, forthright bitch . . . the sweet, drab sister type . . . a stenographer . . . a secretary . . . the mistress of a racketeer and . . . a typist moll.

The other actresses did worse. They ended up playing daughters, girl friends, wives and mothers . . . the roles they had run away from.

It was too much to take and at some moment in each of their careers, regardless of their diverse temperaments, the actresses decided it was time for a change. They wanted scripts with demanding, complex second acts. "Without wonder and insight, acting is just a trade," wrote Davis. And she led the parade to Warner's office.

The actresses foolishly assumed that great roles were out there someplace . . . egotistically believed that they had the wisdom to select them . . . and artistically felt that they could deliver them to the audience, by themselves. They were the medium of communications, not the camera, or the rhythmic editing, or the music of Steiner or Korngold. The actresses were completely naïve about the aesthetics of film making and their minds were set.

"I was unhappy," wrote Bette Davis, "unfulfilled and further compliance would only have destroyed the career I had so far built. Warner's seemed bent on undoing all my work. It was impossible to control their vandalism; but the least I could do was to restrain from collaborating with them.

"Much of it isn't being a woman. You've got to become a man in many areas. And, I wouldn't advocate it for any woman that lived."

Bette Davis was determined. She camped in Jack Warner's office until he couldn't stand her any more and then allowed her to be loaned out to RKO for *Of Human Bondage.* She wanted a realistic part, but after the film's completion she explained that she had wanted "the chance of showing the public what I can do with a character role. But I don't want to go too far. In *Of Human Bondage,* I feel I went to the limit." She received an Oscar nomination for her performance, but

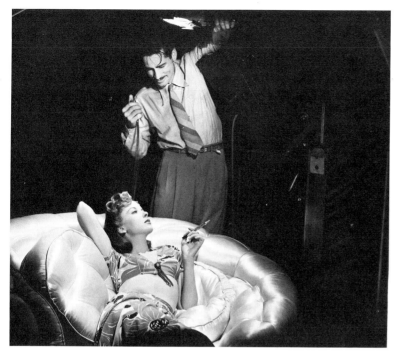

she didn't want to upset her audience too drastically and told the press, "I feel that I should like to go back to my nice, smartly dressed secretaries, lady journalists, commercial artists, and understanding girl friends. For a while at least!"

Jack Warner immediately obliged her and put her in *The Girl from 10th Avenue, Front Page Woman, Special Agent, Dangerous, The Petrified Forest, Satan Met a Lady* and *The Golden Arrow.* "I was made to trudge through the professional swamp at Warner's brimming over with frustration and rage. One skirmish after another followed *Bondage.*" Bette Davis began openly to take on the directors, supervisors and Jack Warner on a daily basis. Loudly.

Olivia de Havilland remembers Bette going after assistant director Jack Sullivan when he pushed her photographer, Ernie Haller. "She yelled clear across the set, 'You leave Ernie alone'—and some other things. It was like a volcano going off, it was that violent."

She won an Oscar for *Dangerous,* but was so furious with her parts she would only play the vapid role in *Satan Met a Lady* on Warner's personal promise of better roles. When the film was completed, she was offered the role of a female lumberjack in *God's Country and the Woman.* She promptly left for England to work there in independent productions. She was going to break her contract with the studio. Escape.

Jack Warner felt differently. He quickly and easily gathered the weight of all the Hollywood studios behind him, as they were also beginning to have trouble with independent minded performers, and on September 9, 1936, obtained an injunction restraining the actress Bette Davis from working in England for anyone but Warner Bros.

The case went to court and after prolonged testimony by Jack, Bette and others, Warner Bros. won the case. Bette Davis belonged to the factory for at least another six years, until 1942, and longer if the studio added all the times she was inactive or on suspension. The trial cost her in excess of thirty-thousand dollars and she was obliged to pay the studio's court costs. An appeal would have cost still more and she was out of money. She had lost and lost badly.

The only thing worth remembering was that at one point in the trial Jack Warner admitted "that an actress could become heartbroken if she had to play parts that were not fitted to her."

Bette returned to Hollywood, to Warner Bros., but for a brief period the fighting would pay off. The studio offered to pay their own court costs and gave her *Marked Woman* and *Jezebel,* the second with her favorite director, William Wyler, and she consequently received her second Academy Award.

Both the critics and the audience loved her, and the films made money. The vice-president in charge of production quickly made plans. As of January 1, 1938, he was paying Bette Davis $2,000 a week while Joan Blondell was receiving $2,250 and Kay Francis was up to $5,250 a week. But Bette Davis was making the money, making him rich, and her contract would run out on April 25, 1942. In only four years.

On October 1, 1938, Warner renegotiated with his actress' agents and they reached an agreement. Davis was immediately to be raised to $3,500 a week with a maximum of $5,500 per week by the last year of her contract, which was extended to September 29, 1945. She was under contract for another seven years.

At thirty-one years of age, Bette Davis had signed on with the prison again, but with reason. And without excuses. "Whatever I did, I did. My mistakes are mine. I alone am responsible."

From October, 1938, to September, 1939, she made five films: *The Sisters, Dark Victory, Juarez, The Old Maid* and *The Private Lives of Elizabeth and Essex.* She finally had parts and she had played the great woman, Elizabeth of England.

It appeared to the actresses on the lot like the fighting was almost worth it.

But the physical effort was destroying Davis. After *The Private Lives of Elizabeth and Essex:* "I weighed eighty pounds when I discarded Bess's ruff and hoop for the last time."

Bette Davis, however, was finding her style of survival. A devious woman, on *The Private Lives of Elizabeth and Essex,* she hadn't wanted the hoops and ruffs scaled down and secretly had designers Orry-Kelly and Milo Anderson make two complete sets of costumes, the first, according to the director's orders and the second according to the historical records. "I tested in the first wardrobe and played the picture in the second. Tricky is the determined female."

She also subscribed to *Vogue* magazine in Hal Wallis' name. Wallis liked the hats his wife wore and Bette hoped to change his tastes by exposing him to the current fashions. "I think he forgave me eventually."

And she kept fighting. When she heard that Irene Dunne was going to be borrowed for *Now Voyager,* "I became apoplectic.

The part was perfect for me and I was under contract to Warner's." She got the part.

On the set she rewrote lines, ran over foremen and commanded the absolute obedience of the Wardrobe, Hair and Makeup departments. "She was the queen and we all knew it," recalls a hairdresser. "She made the money not the brothers."

She trod on most supervisors, but not Lord. And to her, Henry Blanke was special, an "artist who had integrity, will for holy battle and triumph in a medium which stupidly resisted its own enrichment."

While Bette Davis was slugging it out for roles on the screen, other young actresses were finding other ways to survive. Nine young beauties, including Joan Blondell, married cinematographer George Barnes. Louise Fazenda married studio boss Hal Wallis and the Berkeley girls spread out in many directions. Virginia Dabney married director Robert Flory, Dorothy "Dottie" Coonan married "Wild Bill" Wellman, Adele Fergus married still photographer Madison Lacy, then Lois Lindsey married Madison Lacy, Victoria Vinton married the owner of the Woodland Hills Country Club, Sue Raney was dating the coach of the Green Bay Packers, Sally Haynes married Burt Wheeler and several others, another became an adagio dancer, another the "madam" at a Venice Beach brothel and still another took up work driving a truck.

Others began to show signs of wear from the constant fighting.

In 1939, following the completion of her work on *Wings of the Navy,* Olivia de Havilland went to lunch with a journalist. Halfway through she "just started to cry. I didn't know why, but I couldn't stop it." The journalist finally got her home, where she stayed for days, "simply crying. I went to bed and I wasn't going to get out of it."

A neurologist friend cared for her. "He came ten times and I cried everytime he came, out of relief. I couldn't wait for him to come back."

He finally convinced her to make out a program for each day, when to get up, what to eat, time to eat, etc., etc. "He made me an extremely simple program so I had something to live for and I did exactly that, let a day go by, then two days, then two weeks.

"Jack was totally indifferent and Flynn had become so selfish . . . did unbelievable things he didn't have to stoop to . . ."

"There was the time she found a dead snake in her panties as she went to put them on," recalled Flynn. "She was terrified and wept. She knew very well who was responsible and it couldn't have endeared me to her . . . later she told me she lived in terror of what bit of idiocy I'd spring next."

Olivia finally got out of bed to do *Dodge City* as "the girl," again, to Flynn's hero. "I had two bad times, dark depressed moods. The film had nothing to offer me and I was bored, so bored. Boredom beyond description! My nature needed something to tackle."

She got it with the role of Melanie in MGM's *Gone With the Wind,* but she had to take Jack Warner's wife Ann to lunch at the Brown Derby and solicit her help in convincing her husband to loan her out. He let her go when "I promised I wouldn't come back and be trouble."

When she did come back, however, she was put in *The Private Lives of Elizabeth and Essex,* but not as Flynn's leading lady. "My name was beneath the title. I had given my word, but it was foolish of me commercially. It was punishment and unreasonable. But I did it."

She was then loaned out to Samuel Goldwyn for a totally miscast part in *Raffles,* "my worst film," and then assigned to the third remake of *Saturday's Children* at the studio. "It was to be the third punishment, then I thought, 'Twice, okay! But not three times.' I felt I had been tried way beyond my word." She refused the role "and Jack said, 'Of course, you see!'"

After that, "I made a definite practice of taking a suspension and only took the role if it was good or big box office. I realized that if I wasn't doing what I wanted to be doing, then I had to be in an attractive film that was a box office hit. When a Flynn film came along, I did it. You had to keep yourself alive with costumes, sets, etc. I knew attractiveness was necessary to keep the career alive. And I had to preserve the career until the contract was up."

Olivia "began to read scripts in the Makeup Department, where they were sent ahead of time. I could read them before they were cast and begin to make judgments. I would sneak them out at night and bring them back the next day. That's where I found *Strawberry Blonde.*"

She also began going to films. "Not at the studio, but on Hollywood Boulevard, at the Pantages Theater. And I studied Barbara Stanwyck, she was one of the actresses who led me. And I also went to pass judgment on what an audience wanted to see."

Below. Bette Davis and Henry Blanke on the set of Winter
Meeting, *1948*
*Facing, left. Marion Davies and Jack Warner in front of the
opulent dressing room William Randolph Hearst provided her.
Hearst also supplied a bungalow, which he had moved from
MGM to Burbank*
Facing, right. Olivia de Havilland at home recuperating

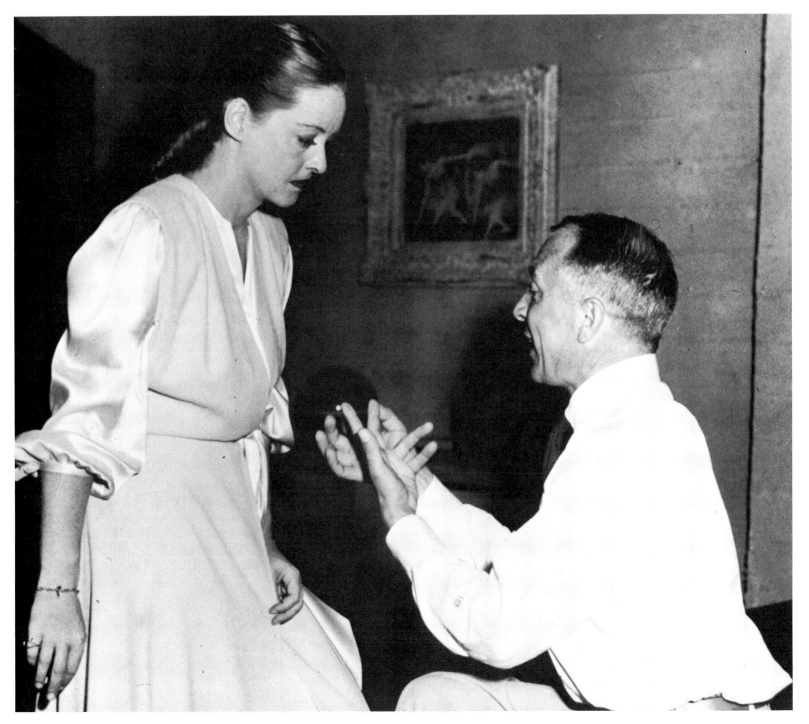

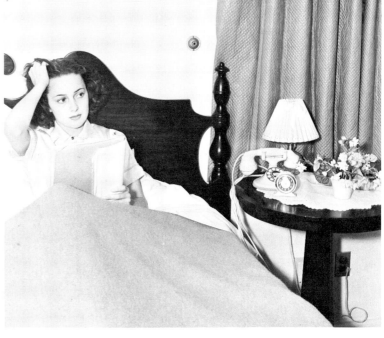

With the confidence of *Gone With the Wind* inside her, a growing knowledge of the business and a few years of growth, at twenty-five in 1941, she began to contemplate escape. In 1944 her contract came due, that would be the time. There didn't seem to be any choice: "It was ridiculous, but Jack seemed to be trying to destroy my career."

Ida Lupino fit the factory, she looked good on the asphalt streets, in cheap polka-dot dresses and alongside bearded toughs. She preferred the male world. "I'm not a woman's woman . . . I care for very few. Annie Sheridan was one that I loved. 'Lupe,' she would say, 'do you want to make it in this this town?'

"'No!'

"'Well, we'll just have to find two wonderful guys that will take care of us for the rest of our lives.'

"And then I joined her at Warner Bros. and we didn't do any of the things we said we would do."

The directors understood Lupino; she liked rough, tough men who would shove her around and challenge her. "Vincent Sherman said to me, 'Ides, how'd you like to do a story where you're really a no-good broad? You want to buy a white dress for your daughter's graduation and you whore for it?'

"'That sounds good to me.'

"'You end up in the gutter, commit suicide and your daughter goes on.'

"'That's great!'"

Lupino would try anything the directors suggested, any part, stunt, scene, wardrobe. She was strictly a "full-grown" woman, but in *The Hard Way,* where she had the role of the whoring mother, her female pride, the men, factory and world slammed down on her.

"I walked out during the film. I couldn't stand myself. Mom got mad at me, but I told Vinnie, 'I'm not right.'"

Sherman recalls she "saw herself in the rushes and she wasn't very happy about it. She was very upset. She felt that I was getting everybody in the film too downbeaten and too awful."

But there were other problems. "My dad died in the middle of it and I had a breakdown. Jerry Wald [her producer] called and said, 'You're faking.' My father was dying and I couldn't tell my mum because dad had sworn me to secrecy. I told Wald, 'This is something you can't understand! The show must

go on, to hell with that. If you don't give me two weeks off, I'll go out of my mind.'

"He said, 'Okay, Ides, you stay in the desert, we'll close down and when you're ready, we'll start again.'"

She eventually finished the film and others: *They Drive by Night, The Sea Wolf, High Sierra, Out of the Fog, In Our Time, Devotion, The Man I Love, Escape Me Never.* She fit the studio, but a real woman can be pushed only so far. Even an actress.

In a manner, however, Jack Warner was loyal to his ladies. He would continue to give Faye Emerson a chance to beguile the audience in twenty-three pictures, Margaret Lindsay in twenty-eight, Alexis Smith in twenty-four, Joan Leslie in fourteen and Jane Wyman in twenty-seven films until she entered America's heart with her twenty-eighth, *Johnny Belinda,* in 1948.

Warner also kept the major female roles for his contract actresses. Visiting actresses like Marlene Dietrich, Joan Fontaine, Hedy Lamarr and Irene Dunne came on the lot for only one picture each during the thirties and forties. Ingrid Bergman came three times, however, and stole three shows: *Casablanca, Saratoga Trunk* and *Under Capricorn.* There was good reason to keep the number of guest actresses to a minimum; they were expensive. Merle Oberon came on the lot in 1939 for *Till We Meet Again,* received star treatment and $8,500 a week, while the visiting Miriam Hopkins cost Warner $5,000 a week. Employees were much cheaper.

The Stock Talent: *female* was Warner's best bargain. As of December 1, 1939, Bette Davis was the highest-paid contract actress at $4,000 a week. Olivia de Havilland was receiving $1,250, Geraldine Fitzgerald $1,250, Priscilla Lane $750, Rosemary Lane $650, Gale Page $600, Ann Sheridan $500, Jane Bryan $300, Brenda Marshall $300, Jane Wyman $200 and Nell O'Day $125. The same month, the male talent cost Warner a fortune: Muni was receiving $11,500 a week, Cagney $12,500, Robinson $8,500, Claude Rains $6,000, Raft $5,500, Flynn $5,000 and Pat O'Brien $4,000. The salaries were kept secret, but there was little doubt in the actresses' minds who was getting the bad deal and the actresses looked each day for revenge.

Vincent Sherman recalls: "Brynie Foy came to me one day and said, 'J. L. is trying to get Kay Francis to break her contract.' In order to do that he told her that she was going

Right. Ida Lupino in the kind of makeup she wore before she came to Warner Bros.
Facing, left. Olivia de Havilland takes a call on the set
Facing, right. The studio Queen waits her turn off-camera

to have to do a picture with Bryan Foy. They felt that she would say, 'Well, I'm a big star. I'm not going to do a "B" picture.'

"But Kay fooled them. Foy talked to her and she said, 'Look, as long as they pay me my salary, they can give me a broom and I'll sweep the stage.'"

Ann Sheridan, after displaying a successful flair for comedy and warmth in *They Drive by Night* and *King's Row,* decided to go on suspension when she didn't like a role. Beginning in 1946, she stayed away for eighteen months.

When Barbara Stanwyck returned to Warner Bros. in 1944, she returned with power, confidence in her ability and a tough contract. She had approval of her makeup, her parts and could insist that costume designer Edith Head be borrowed from Paramount for her films. It was a sign of things to come.

When Joan Crawford arrived, her career was on the wane and she signed a contract that didn't give her the choices she had had at MGM. For *Mildred Pierce* she submitted to the dowdy dresses that designer Milo Anderson put on her and only protested feebly that the shoulder pads she had made famous were missing. The Makeup Department refused to paint her mouth beyond its natural outlines and when she secretly added to the sides of her upper lip one day during shooting, director Michael Curtiz promptly ordered it removed. Crawford obeyed. After the film's extraordinary success and her sudden return to fame with her Oscar-winning performance, she became instantly as disobedient as she was at MGM. She'd been handling men since she was seventeen and at forty-two she was considerably better at it. The shoulder pads went back into her costumes, the lipstick was pushed past the lip line and she behaved as if she had script approval even if she didn't.

Some of the fight was going out of Warner. It was 1947 and the century was picking up speed, racing for the halfway mark and the fighting was beginning to tell. Jack Warner had never really understood his Stock Talent: *female,* and they had had enough of his factory. They were looking for ways out and acted like they would find them.

"To fulfill a dream, to be allowed to sweat over lovely labor, to be given the chance to create, is the meat and potatoes of life," recalled Bette Davis. But the actresses were convinced they hadn't done that, not in the thirties or forties.

They had helped get a nation through a depression and a world war, provided dreams in a world that was killing them daily and encouraged a world of women to smoke the same

cigarettes, wear the same lipstick and dream of living just as courageously, loving just as desperately and being just as dangerously female as the actresses had on the screen. But those were ephemeral by-products to the actresses and had nothing to do with art, with fulfilling their true natures. They were populating the movies with two-dimensional characters, with base melodrama, escapist fantasy and with clichés, and doing it vulgarly, cheaply. At the picture show they were displaying nothing more than their flesh and faces for thirty-five cents. There had to be something better.

But the audience never noticed. Melodrama was something they understood personally, clichés were, after all, clichés because they are all too true and if the actresses could handle that kind of reality, handle pain, loneliness, death and even men, then the audience felt it could. Even if they didn't know it, the Warner actresses were doing a job, the oldest job in the theater, building dreams to live by—particularly Bette Davis.

Jack Warner surely didn't know it, but he had found her . . . found his snake charmer.

As the forties progressed, the actresses began to hunt for help . . . for a producer, director, another studio or an independent production company to front for. And they escaped.

In 1943 Olivia de Havilland took the studio to court in California and argued that it had no right to add the many months she had been on suspension to the end of her contract in 1944. It was the general practice of the studios to extend contracts in that manner and the case was fought bitterly. But Olivia won. A part of the studio system had been torn apart. Jack Warner had been beaten . . . by a woman.

Olivia left to play the great roles, to accept the challenge of her art as she saw it, and left the costumes, the sets, the cardboard castles, all the trappings of fantasy and imagination she had so artfully graced behind. She left to face reality head on in films like *Snake Pit, The Heiress* and *Not as a Stranger.*

There were boys and girls who went to the picture show after that, paid their admission price eagerly, but then began to wonder what had happened to the movies. But they weren't writing the reviews, not yet.

In 1947 Barbara Stanwyck's contract with the studio expired and she left to free-lance.

In 1949, after thirty-four films at Warner Bros., Ann Sheridan

bought her way out of her contract for thirty-five thousand dollars.

Ann's buddy Ida Lupino had already left, in 1947. "One night, towards the end of my contract, there was Hal Wallis and Jack coming out of his office. Jack saw me and said, 'Ida, why are you here?'

"'I'm about to be chewed out.'

"'Oh, Ida, Ida, Ida sweet as apple cida . . .' he sang and we went into a soft-shoe routine.

"Then he asked me to sign a four-year exclusive contract and I said, 'No, no, no! I want a home, a husband, a child and I don't want to be told someday that I will be replaced by some starlet as I was told I would replace Bette.'

"He told me, 'If you don't sign, you'll never work for Warner's again.' And I didn't.

"The beautiful thing about Warner Bros. when I was there was, I only worked with great people, actors, directors, producers. But when I left, nobody said good-bye."

In 1949 Bette Davis asked for her release during the shooting of *Beyond the Forest* and, "my brothers let me go. I never heard from them again."

Bette Davis had finally gained total power, she could now do with her career whatever she wanted to. She made the choices, had approval of script, costars, director and producer. Except for one brilliant burst of flame in *All About Eve,* however, she would burn herself out like the moth and disappear. Nothing less is acceptable to a goddess, but like all goddesses, there was the possibility of resurrection.

The actresses would not form independent production companies like the actors, but would accept the parts they felt were right for them and once again put themselves in the hands of men, writers, directors and producers, and the camera. They hadn't quite come awake, realized what they had done or who they were. Only one, the most vulnerable, would become a director. The only female director in the motion picture business, Ida Lupino.

Most should have stayed home. But as Bette Davis recalls, "If you loved it enough and you had to do it . . . you had to *do* it."

The female talent escaped, but there were performers at Warner Bros. who wouldn't, who didn't want to. Who didn't dare. The character actors. They weren't movie stars and they welcomed any chance they received to move and talk in front of the cameras. They also welcomed the weekly paychecks and eagerly provided the writers, supervisors and directors with whatever they asked for, and for a price that pleased Jack Warner. They would also give the stars the one fight they all wanted, the one on the sound stage. And with just one honest moment, the characters could steal a scene, a whole film.

The character actors knew their way through even the most difficult, complex stories. On Broadway, in the "arty" theater, they had played in a hundred second acts. But in the movies all they wanted was one . . . just one that belonged to them, one that would survive them on Celluloid.

Below. Dolores Costello, Eleanor Parker
Right. Ruth Roman
Below right. Geraldine Fitzgerald
Facing, left. Jane Wyman
Facing, right. Virginia Mayo

Facing, left. Patricia Neal
Facing, top. Marlene Dietrich
Facing, center. Doris Day
Facing, bottom. Ginger Rogers
Below. Rosemary Lane
Right, top. Lola Lane
Right, bottom. Priscilla Lane

Facing, left. Dolores Del Rio
Facing, top. Hedy Lamarr
Facing, bottom. Kay Francis
Below. Joan Leslie
Right. Joan Crawford

Below. Lauren Bacall
Right. Ingrid Bergman
Facing, left. Joan Blondell
Facing, right. Ida Lupino

250

Facing, far left. Barbara Stanwyck
Facing, left. Ann Sheridan
Below. Olivia de Havilland in three roles

Left. Bette Davis
Below. Bette Davis as Jezebel

WRINKLES AND LAUGHTER

Character Performers

"What of it? I'm going to die in Casablanca.
  It's a good spot for it."

They were born with wrinkles, born short, too tall and downright fat. They had noses shaped like snow shovels, ears the size of buckets and they laughed like mixing gravel or a boiling teakettle. They were called character actors and, on polite occasions, featured performers. In rare cases, even costar. They were either too odd or too common and would never be one of those incredible creatures of mystery and imagination, of such devastating intrigue and compelling beauty that they would be billed as stars. And paid accordingly.

When they left Broadway, the circus, vaudeville or the mortuary business and headed for Hollywood, however, they believed anything was possible. Stardom, riches, great parts, old friends, good times and one necessity. Work.

And they came. Jesters, comics, heavies, midwives, gangsters, clowns, aunts and grannies. Actors and actresses no longer dawning with youth but as real as downtown.

When they arrived in tinsel town, their jobs were to be much the same as they had been in the theater or circus. They were to supply the tarnish, the brass and the wounds, to provide the comic or tragic beasts against which the beautiful heroes and heroines would become believable . . . to supply the acting. But in Hollywood, the beauties would be billed over the performers, the animals over the clowns. With a studio contract, however, there was always a chance you'd be cast in that elusive but immortal role with a stunning second act that was surely out there someplace . . . just waiting for your wrinkles, nose and laughter.

"Everybody wanted to go, the money and the movies, that was the big thing." Allen Jenkins was working in the theater in New York with his pals Frank McHugh and James Cagney in the twenties. They'd sit at a little restaurant on Broadway and watch the girls from the other shows go by as they discussed their futures. "Everybody wanted to go. We had seen nothing but silent pictures with actors who couldn't act and that was at the time that sound came in. Oh, we wanted to get in there so badly."

Mary Astor remembers just what those early dreams were like: "It was always 'Tomorrow.' Tomorrow contained total fulfillment. 'The future' expanded in all directions, blinding glory without limit.

"Tomorrow we'll be on the train for Hollywood."

Character roles were abundant, about ten for every starring role, but the character performers quickly learned that unlike the stage, the roles were limiting. The Hollywood factories loved clichés. A character performer was asked to make a single entrance and be instantly understood, recognized and accepted by the audience as either likable, lovable, funny, sad, bad or as an aunt, uncle, grandparent, general, doctor or landlord. It saved the writers pages of exposition and the directors days of shooting time. The character performers were to be so obvious and specific that their roles didn't need a second act.

The professional trick was to find whatever your special attraction was and then sell it over and over. And if your studio contract was with Warner Bros. you were going to have to be very special.

Many of the character actors were already in their forties or fifties when they arrived in Burbank, and some wouldn't perform on Celluloid until they were past sixty, but they were tough. They had already tested their talents and done battle with men twice as vulgar, greedy and shameless as Jack and Harry Warner . . . done battle with the Shuberts, Florenz Ziegfeld, Minsky and the god of Broadway, David Belasco. And survived.

In 1932 Alan Hale, Sr., was forty-two and had been acting in the motion picture business since 1911. He and Andy Devine were friends and when one of them was working and the other wasn't, they would go to Central Casting and answer for each other when they got called. There was more than one film that billed Andy Devine when the role was performed by Alan Hale. And vice versa. In his spare time Hale invented folding theater seats, a formula for greaseless potato chips and worked as an osteopath.

Guy Kibbee was forty-eight and already round-domed and chubby. Prior to Hollywood, he had reached Broadway, from El Paso, Texas, by running away from home at thirteen to perform on Mississippi showboats.

Frank McHugh had been a part of his parents' traveling stock company since he was ten and worked in vaudeville and on the stage. He was thirty-three, one of the young ones.

Samuel Hinds was fifty-seven. He was born in Brooklyn of wealthy parents, but his family lost everything and Hinds came west to become one of the founders of the Pasadena Playhouse.

Hugh Herbert of the fidgety hands and giggling "woo-woo" was forty-five and had already been with Warner Bros. since 1926. He fit the factory perfectly, as he could double as a

Chapter opening. Joan Blondell in Gold Diggers of 1933
*Overleaf. Burbank studios in the mid-thirties . . . the streets
were turning to gold*
*Facing. Arthur Treacher, Otis Harlan, Dewey Robinson, Joe
E. Brown and Frank McHugh in* A Midsummer Night's
Dream, *1936*
Top left. Andy Devine and Pat O'Brien in Torrid Zone, *1940*
Bottom left. Aline MacMahon
Top right. Hugh Herbert and Hobart Cavanaugh
Bottom right. Boris Karloff and Peter Lorre in Arsenic and
Old Lace, *1944*

Left. Isabel Jewell
Below. Basil Rathbone as Guy of Gisbourne in The Adventures of Robin Hood, *1938*
Facing, above. Lee Patrick, Laura Hope Crews and Bette Davis in The Sisters, *1938*
Facing, below. Alan Hale and Jack Carson in Thank Your Lucky Stars, *1943*

writer and had coauthored the first all talking motion picture, *The Lights of New York*, as well as many other films.

Henry O'Neill was forty-one. He had left college in his first year to work in a traveling stock company and then served in the navy in World War I.

Peter Lorre was from faraway Vienna and had run away from home as a teenager to play bit parts in local theaters.

Dour-faced Ned Sparks from Ontario, Canada, was forty-eight and had spent a good, hard life in carnivals, one-night stands and medicine shows.

Eugene Pallette was forty-three. He had been born in Winfield, Kansas, to a couple touring in *East Lynne*, born in a trunk.

Allen Jenkins was thirty-two, keeping time with his century, and had been raised by a family of performers. "Father, mother, uncles, cousins and others." In 1919 he was a chorus boy dancing with Jimmy Cagney in *Pitter Patter*. His mom told him, "You got to get out of the chorus," and he went to the New York Academy of Dramatic Arts.

The women were somewhat younger: Una Merkel was twenty-nine in 1932, Gladys George was twenty-eight, Ruth Donnelly was thirty-six, Isabel Jewell was nineteen, Lee Patrick was twenty-one, Gale Sondergard was twenty-five, Louise Fazenda was thirty-seven and Mary Astor was twenty-six. But they knew the old rules. "You can't be a chorus girl past twenty-five." And, "The turning point in an actress's career is when she plays a mother. After that, what?"

They had wanted to be great actresses, stars, even beauties, but their mirrors argued with them.

Aline MacMahon, from McKeesport, Pennsylvania, was a young thirty-three, but already had that look of no-nonsense about her that suited the roles of loyal and disciplined big sisters and wives.

Mary Astor had read an advertisement. "Send your photograph to Brewster Publications and who knows? You too may win. You may be chosen for Fame and Fortune." She sent in her picture, came in second to the publisher's girl friend and went nowhere. Her beauty eventually made her a career, but by 1934 Mary Astor was twenty-eight and had to make a choice. "I was afraid of starring, of being too 'successful.' It sounds paranoid, but I was practical. Because starring was one hell of a gamble, and I couldn't afford to gamble."

Mary Astor was offered starring parts, even a starring

Right. "I'll wait for you. If they hang you, I'll always remember you."
"Don't, Sam. Don't say that—even in fun. Oh, you frightened me for a moment. I really thought—you do such wild and unpredictable things . . ."
"Don't be silly. You're taking the fall."
Humphrey Bogart and Mary Astor in The Maltese Falcon, *1941*
Facing, left. Dick Powell, Ruth Donnelly and James Cagney in Footlight Parade, *1933*
Facing, right. Allen Jenkins, Hugh Herbert, Rudy Vallee and Mabel Todd in Gold Diggers in Paris, *1938*

contract, but she began to look for and accept feature roles. You could play featured parts, character roles until you were sixty, even seventy and she wanted to stick, be secure.

The character performers were theatrical clichés, typical entertainers who couldn't cross a street without attempting to draw a crowd. For bread, pennies or a contract. In another time, another land, they would have been minstrels, bards, jugglers, clowns, court jesters, fools and burlesque comics. They would have worked in castle barracks, alleys, brothels and tents. Many, in fact, had. They belonged to an ancient race and Jack Warner could have hired them for pennies. And did.

Warner Bros. imported performers from Broadway by the bushel, complete with the shows they had performed in. The actors in the theater could deliver dialogue, Warner was sure of that, and if the show they had been in was even mildly successful, they must have something to offer. It was reasonable thinking and the gamble was small for the studio.

In 1932, Allen Jenkins had already watched his friends Frank McHugh, Cagney, Joan Blondell, Eddie Robinson, Glenda Farrell and Pat O'Brien go to Hollywood and take hold of success. He was performing in a comedy, *Blessed Event*, as a comic heavy and then Warner Bros. brought the property and asked Jenkins to come to Hollywood. "It was a four-week guarantee at three hundred and fifty dollars and a first-class fare on the Super Chief, each way."

Ruth Donnelly and Isabel Jewell were on the same train. They were also part of Warner's gamble.

When Jenkins finished his part in the film version of *Blessed Event*, the studio offered him another part for the same money. "All in all I went down to the Santa Fe terminal four times to change my ticket and get a reservation on the Chief for New York. And they called me back for another job. While I was in the middle of my fourth picture, *Blessed Event* was released and I got great notices."

He had found his specialty. "That kind of clown gangster they had never seen." Since the audience had approved, Warner wanted him to sign a contract for seven years at $300 a week. And Jenkins did, without an agent.

The studio signed other players in the same way, performers who had proven to be attractive to the paying customers, safe gambles. Just what their special attraction was and how they achieved it weren't Warner's concern, just so it was there. The personal preferences of the supervisors, directors, writers and executives, Wallis, Zanuck and Warner, weren't considered. If the public wanted them, the Talent Department contracted them. And didn't bother to change their names.

By 1933 the Warner Bros. contract list was already dominated by expert players from the theater. A club of actors who knew each other, who had already worked with each other and knew each other's tricks, weaknesses and strengths. "We were like a family," Jenkins recalls. "The other studios called us The Great Warner Bros. Stock Company."

Only the hardened renegades of the theater came out "on spec" in those days. Signing up in the movies was not acceptable to a proper theater performer unless the firm offer of a salary, too lucrative to be resisted, was offered. But Frank McHugh came in 1930, "on spec."

"I was advised not to go, but I went. And I had a phenomenal stroke of luck. Warner's had cast an actor for a part in a Frank Fay picture, *Bright Letters*. But they had somehow neglected to sign him and when the film started, the actor had gone to work at another studio. Warner's needed an actor immediately, and Frank Fay knew I was on the Chief bound for Hollywood. When I pulled in at the station, Warner's had a delegation waiting to meet me, and signed me up on the spot."

The Warner supervisors and directors were also quick to discover what each player had to offer that was special, then put it to use.

After several days of filming on *Bright Letters*, director Michael Curtiz commanded McHugh, "Now, in this scene, I want you should giff me ze loff."

"The laugh?" McHugh repeated. "What laugh?"

"You know, ze loff. *Your* loff. I want you should do it right here."

McHugh shook his head in bewilderment. "I don't have any special laugh. I laugh like anybody else."

"You have a loff," insisted Curtiz. "We will fix it."

Curtiz called for the sound track of a scene they had shot several days earlier and to McHugh's amazement, he heard himself do a mocking, three-note "ha, ha, ha!" that started high-pitched and then descended. A laugh he had performed unconsciously in an earlier scene.

He repeated it for Curtiz and it became his signature.

"That laugh got me a lot of pictures," recalls McHugh.

Hugh Herbert made a fortune for the studio off his "woo-

woo"; and Jenkins did his comic gangster. "In fifty percent of the pictures I did, I played gangsters. I did taxi drivers, bartenders and prizefight trainers too, but mostly I was the sidekick to Robinson, Bogie, Cagney and all the big-time hoods on the lot."

As the contract list of character performers grew, the employees in the Writers' Building began to introduce their clichéd characters in the scripts more and more frequently. Their availability and believability made the required twenty pages a day come a lot faster.

Robert Barrat, John Litel, Henry O'Neill, Addison Richards, Samuel S. Hinds, Henry Kolker and Arthur Byron played prison wardens, defense counsels, prosecuting attorneys and judges. Warren Hymer, Harold Huber, Nat Pendleton, Jack La Rue, Ed Brophy and George E. Stone, more hoods.

Barton MacLane played the boss hood of the "other gang" in the earlier years and a ruthless, cheap ranch manager in *The Treasure of the Sierra Madre*. Guy Kibbee, Hugh Herbert, Hobart Cavanaugh, Grant Mitchell and Ned Sparks were the husbands who got had by the Gold Diggers.

Ruth Donnelly, Aline MacMahon, Zasu Pitts and Alice Brady were the puritan wives and Claire Dodd, Patricia Ellis and Margaret Lindsay were the "other women."

Berton Churchill, Douglass Dumbrille and Willard Robertson played the dishonest bankers and businessmen and Arthur Hohl was their shifty-eyed underling. J. Farrell MacDonald, Wallace Ford and Charley Grapewin were the down-to-earth workingmen and the mothers and aunts were Emma Dunn, Clara Blandick and Margerie Gateson.

Frank McHugh stuck to Jimmy Cagney's side and Alan Hale, Sr., Guinn "Big Boy" Williams, Basil Rathbone, Donald Crisp, Henry Stephenson, Melville Cooper, Eugene Pallette, Una O'Connor, James Stephenson, Henry Danielle and Ian Hunter were the costumed characters that surrounded Errol Flynn.

Claude Rains arrived with the credentials of the British "theatre" in 1936 and did varied featured parts, but on special occasions costarred with Bette Davis *(Mr. Skeffington)*, with Flynn *(The Sea Hawk)* and with Bogart *(Casablanca)*.

The contracts were usually for seven years in the early days, but with the rise of agents, the signing of the Screen Actors' Guild's first contract with the major producers in 1937,

and then the arrival of World War II in 1941 and a cutback in production, the contracts were reduced to months, even weeks. The workday was Warner Bros.' normal fourteen to sixteen hours, the players under contract would do up to ten or twelve films a year and be grateful for the work. Perfect employees.

Jack Warner couldn't have been happier. The character performers couldn't complain, as their agents, when they had them, weren't strong enough politically to cause him any grief and they were such dedicated "troopers" that they didn't drink (much) and came to work at 8 A.M. every morning even when they were sick.

And, they were funny, they made him laugh. There was nothing more he could have asked for. They were both needed and wanted . . . and they, in turn, wanted and needed.

Allen Jenkins remembers a week in the early thirties when torrential rains drenched "sunny" southern California. He lived near the ocean, a long hour drive, or more, from the Burbank studios in those days. "I practically pioneered the Pacific Palisades." He awoke one morning to find his driveway and the surrounding roads were small rivers. As a precaution he roped two long wooden planks to the top of his Plymouth and set off for the studio to make his 7 A.M. call. At crossing after crossing he had to get out, take down the wooden planks, place them over a washed-out section of the road and drive across. After slow progress, he finally reached Sepulveda Boulevard, which went through Sepulveda Canyon to the valley.

There he found Hugh Herbert sitting on the roof of his Cadillac amid a sea of rushing water. An umbrella bobbed above his comic face and he waited placidly to be rescued.

Skirting the deepest parts of the flooded road, Jenkins managed to reach Herbert's Cadillac and with his ropes pulled the stalled car to safety. Unfortunately, a short way up the road Herbert's car stalled again in deep water and this time defied rescue. Herbert joined Jenkins in his Plymouth and together, using the wooden planks, pulling with the ropes and pushing, they finally made their way to Warner Bros. They arrived at three in the afternoon, drenched but ready for work, the first actors on the lot.

Others began to arrive, but they were told, "Go home, boys, we're not going to shoot anything today." After several cups of coffee, Jenkins and Herbert got back in the Plymouth and started their overland trip back home.

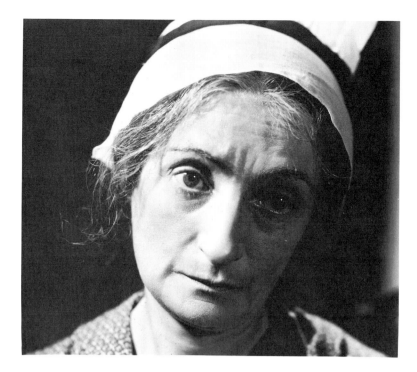

Most days, however, were good working days and Jenkins didn't miss many: "I did seventy-seven pictures in seven years."

McHugh did over a hundred. Herbert made a hundred and fifty. Hobart Cavanaugh made a hundred and twenty in seventeen years, Isabel Jewell made eighty. Charles Lane made five hundred. Edgar Kennedy worked in over five hundred, Regis Toomey made two hundred and Jenkins made over a hundred and seventy-five. They were typical.

The contract players worked their salaries up to $500 a week by the forties and a few made much more. It was good money in both the Depression era and the war years. But in 1939, 45.1 percent of all actors working were making only four thousand dollars annually. It was good for the pocketbook as well as the soul to be part of a family, part of the Warner Bros.

It was even better if you were a woman. Character actresses were hard pressed to work at all. In 1939, only 28 percent of all performers working were women.

For those not under contract, Warner's was also a desirable place to work. Its stable of performers was the best, good to work with and the studio had a policy of trying to have only the best free-lance performers, and a businesslike method of getting them that worked.

For free-lance performers, Warner Bros. offered a special deal. The top salary for many of the "B" films was $500 a week, and in order to get the best talent to work at that price, the Casting Department offered to hire free-lance performers for the $500 with the promise that they would use them in more expensive films at their normal, more expensive fees. They also allowed such performers to cancel their contract up to 5:30 P.M. on the day prior to shooting in order to take a more lucrative job if it came along. Many performers agreed to work for that price and "we made good with the better jobs when they came along. Jack Warner honored that practice every time," recalls casting director Irving Kumin.

Extras earned only from $3 to $7.50 a day, but there were people looking out for them too. Pat O'Brien recalls how he and Cagney helped their brothers in greasepaint: "Cag would say, 'Paddy, let's blow a few lines so we can get the extras some overtime.'" And director Busby Berkeley always needed more and more extras for his spectacular numbers. At least he claimed he needed them and Robert Lord didn't argue. The $7.50's added up.

Extras just managed to get by, but Warner Bros. paid hand-

Facing, above. Una O'Connor
Facing, below. Zasu Pitts
Top. Errol Flynn, Ross Alexander, Colin Kenny, Guy Kibbee
and David Torrence in Captain Blood, 1935
Center. "We are very honored tonight, Rick. Major Strasser is
one of the reasons the Third Reich enjoys the reputation
it has today." Conrad Veidt and Claude Rains in
Casablanca, 1943
Bottom. James Cagney, Margaret Lindsay and Addison
Richards in Frisco Kid, 1935

somely for its choice male character performers. As of
January 1, 1939, Frank McHugh was receiving $1,600 a week,
Hugh Herbert $1,500, Allen Jenkins $1,200, Donald Crisp
$1,000 and Humphrey Bogart, the utility man, $1,000. Performers like Henry O'Neill received $600, James Stephenson
$250 and each of the Dead End Kids $150.

Claude Rains was guaranteed four pictures a year and a
total of sixteen weeks at $5,000 a week to support Bette Davis,
who was then making $2,000, and George Brent at $1,750.
He could also work elsewhere. He had a good agent.

The female character performers didn't do as well and, by
1938, were being hired by the week or day.

When the contract performers weren't working, the studio
loaned them out to other studios. Rented them. A player like
Jenkins could draw $2,500 on the outside, but he'd continue
to draw his regular salary, and the studio took $1,300 profit.
"But I didn't mind," recalls Jenkins. "It was the deal, that's the
way it was and I was working. I got a lot of respect for Warner
Bros. now at this distance. Harry and Jack . . . they had
what it took.

"We rarely saw Harry, but Jack came on the set all the time.
Nobody liked him much in those days, he had a dictatorial
manner and every once in a while he'd really part your hair.

"But they were top financially, there never was any question
about money, about getting paid. The check was always there
or mailed to my agent when I finally got one. Harry was a
business genius and their managers were the best, of each
department. The business office was great.

"It was fun, just fun for which we got paid. The parts were
strictly assignments, but I was fortunate. They were small but
good. I think I realized my limitations . . . played some pretty
good parts . . . parts that were damn near leads."

In order to get that one good part, the character performers
found ways to discover what films were being planned and
then tried to be available when the picture went into production. They also had to learn when they wouldn't be used, when
there was no percentage in hoping.

Leonid Kinsky, who played the Russian bartender Sashka in
Casablanca, remembers: "I couldn't work with Paul Muni or
Walter Huston because we all looked somewhat similar in a
long shot. They always tested you to see if you fit with the
other players."

But they usually fit and with time their faces grew on the

Below. Sydney Greenstreet
Facing, left. Humphrey Bogart and S. Z. Sakall as Carl in Casablanca, *1943*
Facing, right. "Yvonne, I loff you, but he pays me." Humphrey Bogart, Madeleine LeBeau as Yvonne and Leonid Kinsky as Sacha in Casablanca, *1943*

audience, like recurring images of old relatives, childhood friends. Like family. They didn't make demands on the viewer, they were simply there, doing what they had to do. And each Friday or Saturday night you paid your nickels and dimes to see the stars and unconsciously waited for the character performers to fill out the darkness.

The typecasting, however, was annoying to the performers. "You got stuck into the same part over and over again. In my case it was mother roles," recalls Mary Astor. "But it wouldn't change. Even the best character performers were called upon for their simplest tricks. Sydney Greenstreet never did live down the Fat Man; in every picture he did, his evil, hiccupy laugh was exploited."

Mary Astor, however, had found starring parts even more limiting. "In the beginning I had a bit of enthusiasm—I usually did at the start of a picture—but after a while I got to the point where I'd come on the set and ask, 'Which door do I come in, where do I stand, and what do I say?' And it showed. I was as two-dimensional as the screen itself: cool, indifferent, looking lovely in close-ups.

"*Convention City,* I don't even remember what I was doing there.

"The real ee-uch ones, the bilge, the junk, the unforgivably bad," she can no longer remember. But, "resent it or not, what I was doing—and didn't realize it—was learning a craft.

"Give a little when he comes in."

"On your move, be sure to clear the 'inky.' Your look's gotta be camera right."

And she learned. "Inside of you, you've been keeping a little pot simmering on the back burner—the character, the relationships: break up the little fat chunks of emotion, and let them mix and spread. You keep up your often wordless communications with the director, you touch and exchange words with other actors. You say, 'Can I help?' If he feels crowded, if the pace is wrong; we talk and answer with few words. There is often a very high level of communications between actors, and when there is, something of excellence happens." Sam Spade to Brigid O'Shaughnessy in *The Maltese Falcon:* "I'll wait for you, angel. Unless they hang you. Then I'll always remember you."

"They were the pros," recalls John Huston. But the public didn't know the character actors' names, the press didn't interview them and at Warner's there was small if any chance

of becoming a star, of even stealing a scene. Not even when the pot was burning, when something of excellence happened.

At Fox Billy Gilbert could shuffle into a scene with star Sonja Henie, sneeze, and steal the notices. At MGM, Marjorie Main could swab the floor of a Joan Crawford set and mop up the whole picture, and they did.

But not at Warner Bros. The stars were also character actors. They knew every trick. They had played supporting roles and they weren't those soft, perfectly beautiful performers whose porcelain appearance could be made unbelievable by a realistic ugly puss.

"But don't forget," says Pat O'Brien, "the reverse of that was equally true. If the scene belonged to the wonderful Ruth Donnelly, Frank McHugh or Glenda Farrell, or that great comedy heavy, Allen Jenkins, or Henry O'Neill—any of them and so many others—then Cagney or I, or the other so-called stars had fat chance of taking it away from them. You see, for years before we came to Hollywood, they were all on Broadway, in stock and on the road with us. In many shows, they were the stars and we supported them. One of my first jobs was a bit Jimmy Gleason gave me in a play he, Lucille and Russell Gleason starred in in Milwaukee."

But generally the character performers didn't attempt to steal scenes, didn't want to.

Jenkins: "I never did it consciously. I was brought up in legitimate theater. We never stepped on a fellow actor's line, or got a laugh, or upstaged him. It was the play that counted, to hell with the personality. Stealing would only hurt everybody. I don't mean to put too much fuss on the word 'legitimate,' but you didn't bat an eye when another actor was talking."

Astor: "We were experienced, we had a sense of responsibility to each other."

Errol Flynn, however, was more insecure in his early pictures. When Alan Hale, Sr., the boisterous, brash Irishman, first worked with Flynn in 1937, he already had fifteen years experience at other studios and it showed. Flynn complained that Hale deliberately wore a gaudy costume in order to distract from Flynn's performance. The congenial Hale obligingly changed into something more drab (without appearing a whit less colorful) and he and Flynn became close friends.

Flynn recalled: "Alan Hale was the film menace, the most feared character actor in Hollywood. He was such a good actor that if he was with you in a scene he could take it away

from you, whether he was standing behind you, beside you, or in front of you.

"He was full of tricks.

"Other actors of, say, my stature, hesitated to play with Hale because he was so good. Luckily for me, he liked me, so he never pulled any of his scene-stealing with me. He could have stolen every scene, but he didn't. As a picture was being made I'd say to him, 'Alan, if you poke your nose behind me, I'll jump on your goddamn instep.'

"He taught me a hell of a lot."

Hale played with Flynn in twelve pictures.

On the lot, Bette Davis was the champion of good performers and did her best to see that newcomers Jane Bryan, Richard Travis, James Davis and Richard Erdman got their moments on film. Miss Bryan recalls, "Bette, more than one time, showed me exactly how to dominate the scene I was playing with her."

Fresh out of Hollywood High School, Richard Erdman played his first movie scene as a telegraph boy delivering a message to Miss Davis and Claude Rains in *Deception.* Bette generously gave him advice as to how he could secure the best camera angle and followed his career on the lot with enthusiasm. Erdman recalls that, ever afterward when he'd arrive at a party or other assemblage where Miss Davis had preceded him, she would call out, to his delicious embarrassment, "Here comes that sterling actor, Richard Erdman!"

McHugh and Cagney had their own methods of making the work go easily for the visiting players or newcomers. "Jimmy Cagney always had consideration for his fellow actors," recalls McHugh. "If you had a 'laugh' coming to you, he saw that you got it. If the scene was yours, he saw that you got that, too. Jimmy always felt that the 'day player' had the most tense and disciplined task in pictures. To walk on the set with a day check in your pocket, and in your first five minutes, step into the scene with the star, whom you have not met, and you are expected to be glib as he is, is a genuine test for an actor's control and confidence.

"During the shooting of *The Roaring Twenties,* there was a scene in which Jimmy was interviewing prospective employees for his movie bootlegging enterprise. One of the young actors was very good, but very nervous. Later, on the side lines, between rehearsals, we were commenting about him, and I guessed that the young actor was a victim of Jim's theory of

the 'day player syndrome.' When we broke for lunch, Jim went over to the young fellow and invited him to join us. We always had the same table with the following cast: Guy Kibbee, Hugh Herbert, Pat O'Brien, Allen Jenkins, Hobart Cavanaugh, Jimmy and myself. After listening to an hour of our funny stories and wisecracks, some pretty good but most of them very bad, the young actor relaxed and returned to the set to give a good account of himself.

"Jimmy did this on many occasions."

On the set of *The Maltese Falcon,* Bogart, director John Huston and his cast of professionals had another way of relaxing. An elaborate system of practical jokes was carefully instituted to drive the publicity men and their visiting strangers off the set. To make each performer part of the team off camera as well as on, each had his or her role to play in a gag. Each joke was also numbered, Mary Astor's was number ten. When an unwanted guest arrived, she and Peter Lorre would flagrantly intimate they had just had sexual relations in her private dressing room and the embarrassed guest would depart instantly. It was particularly effective on dowagers and dignitaries. Number five was Bogart's and Greenstreet's. As the strangers approached, the two actors would immediately get into a wild name-calling brawl that no one wanted to be a part of. The studio finally gave up and closed the set.

The *Falcon* company also had a great deal of spare time, as they were ahead of schedule and under budget due to Henry Blanke's and Huston's planning. At lunchtime they would travel to the Lakeside Golf Club and eat leisurely. Mary Astor recalled that a high-powered kidding-on-the-level went on during those lunches. She handled it for a while, but couldn't compete and finally broke into tears one day. Her tears, however, were her entrance into that male world of open competition, of ugly baiting, and constant testing. Her tears were honest.

"You're okay, baby," Bogart said. "So you're not very smart —but you know it and what the hell's the matter with that!" Although it was still on a kidding level, Mary Astor felt Bogart really meant what he said: "Be yourself. Be yourself and you're in."

Mary Astor was also accepted on the set, where it counted. And with *The Maltese Falcon* she was one of those privileged few who would be challenged artistically, asked to come to grips with a difficult second act. To be two things at once, loyal and deceitful. In love with a black bird and in love with Sam Spade.

Mary Astor had a "pot to boil" for Brigid O'Shaughnessy. The role had three dimensions, perhaps more, and the "effect getting," the "look-at-us-being-the-part kind of acting wasn't good enough." She had to become rather than act. "It was quite a bitch's cauldron. First of all, she was a congenital liar ('I am a liar, I've always been a liar!'), and slightly psychopathic. And that kind of liar wears the face of truth, although they send out all sorts of signals that they are lying. There is an unstable quality to them like nitro."

Mary Astor was put together with her share of chaos and it showed.

But it was a chaos with craft. Huston had her run around the set before each take to get that breathless quality.

The Maltese Falcon was one of those moments when the factory performed as precisely as the right kind of prison, when all the inmates came together in the right cell and that insurgent, rebellious, free-soaring chaos within them was jailed on Celluloid, so the audience could see it.

There was competition on many sets, open conflict, but that was also part of the job, part of belonging.

Alan Hale and S. Z. "Cuddles" Sakall hated each other and refused to work together. Sakall spoke such broken English that other actors couldn't get their cues and he consequently ran off with many scenes. Hale, naturally, wouldn't stand for it and Sakall, in turn, wouldn't stand for Hale's tricks. It was a standoff.

On the *Santa Fe Trail,* Ronald Reagan was playing the young George Custer to Flynn's young Jeb Stuart. On the set Flynn had the tall, good-looking Reagan placed behind two tall extras so he couldn't steal the scene. Reagan took the gesture in stride, but during several rehearsals he quietly scraped a mound of dirt up with his feet. He then waited for director Michael Curtiz to call for a take, and as he heard the countdown, "Rolling! . . . speed! . . . action!" he calmly stepped up onto his mound and stood taller than all the rest, including Flynn.

The character performers just couldn't try hard enough, each scene might be "the scene."

Director Vincent Sherman remembers Peter Lorre's efforts to make his parts work better. "There was a scene where Lorre came in to see this man to pressure him to do something. Lorre said to me, 'Brother Vince, how would it be if you had a popcorn stand outside and I came in eating a bag of popcorn during this scene. Wouldn't that be good?'

"I said, 'Yes, Peter, that's a good idea.' It gave a little color to the scene. We put a little popcorn stand outside so you could see him buying a bag of popcorn before he came in. At any rate, he came in, but it didn't stop with the popcorn. He went over and took some candy out of a bowl, and then he rubbed his fingers on a piece of cake and took the icing off. I kidded him about all of that business. I pulled that old joke on him. I said, 'Peter, I've got a feather duster for you. I want you to stick it up your behind and while you are doing all of this, you can dust the furniture too.'

"He laughed.

"He was a marvelous actor to work with. He was very inventive. As I say, he was so inventive that you often had the problem of selection and of not cluttering the scene with too many things."

As the century reached for the fifties, it finally became obvious that the character performers were ahead of it. Those who had arrived in their thirties were now in their fifties, those in their forties now in their sixties. Simply growing old. They had become better performers, but no longer as usable. And as the contracts began to disappear, the character performers were down to looking for another three weeks' work . . . another four days . . . a day. In the lines at the Unemployment Department on Santa Monica near Highland, you could see some of the best performers in the world idling away their invaluable hours waiting for their forty-dollar checks. There was television work, a little, but if you worked in television, you couldn't work at Warner Bros. Jack wasn't going to help destroy his own company, his industry . . . help destroy himself.

At Warner Bros. in 1948, after Blanke, Bogart and John Huston had waited a year, Walter Huston finally arrived to play Old Howard in *The Treasure of the Sierra Madre.* It was another job, another chance, and he had prepared like the complete professional he was.

During his run on Broadway, he had asked for the script to be sent to him and for a recording of all the Spanish-language lines so he could learn them. Blanke recalls: "When he got out

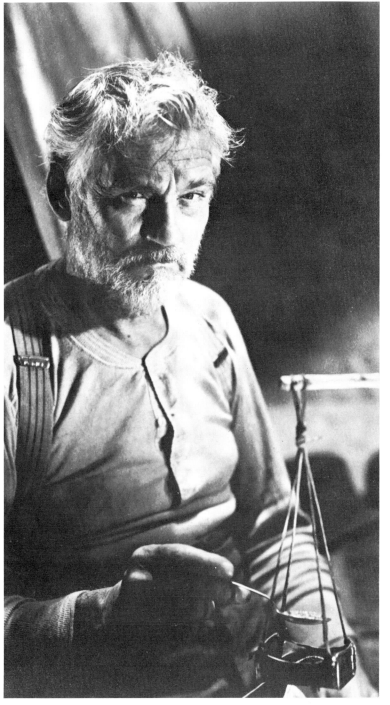

Left. Walter Huston
Facing, above. "We've wounded this mountain and it's our duty to close her wounds. It's the least we can do out of gratitude for all the wealth she's given us. If you guys won't help me I'll do it alone." Humphrey Bogart, Walter Huston and Tim Holt in The Treasure of the Sierra Madre, *1948*
Facing, below. Tim Holt, Barton MacLane and Humphrey Bogart in The Treasure of the Sierra Madre, *1948*

here, he spoke Spanish." He had learned the language so he could perform with his Mexican fellow actors, so he would be there, with them.

Walter Huston was ready. "Before the picture started, we had parties and Walter would take his teeth out and do the whole picture."

Publicist Bob Fender, who was on location with the *Treasure* company in Mexico, recalls that Huston couldn't understand the new crop of players. "He'd spent over twenty years in the business before he got his name in lights and couldn't believe the newcomers who didn't learn their lines, do their homework, know the other players' lines, every facet of their parts. He had heard that Lauren Bacall had sent back a script Warner had sent her and he was highly incensed. He was old-fashioned enough to believe he owed some allegiance and integrity to his bosses."

But his first loyalty was to the story, to the character he was performing and if there were levels within him, if there were three, four or even nine dimensions . . . a difficult second act with the promise of something excellent, of a little silver . . . then he would reach for them, play them. As a professional, an actor.

And in *The Treasure of the Sierra Madre* Walter Huston had his chance. He had the central role and the producer, star and director, Blanke, Bogart and John Huston, knew it. But when the film was released, Walter Huston won the Oscar for the best supporting role. His colleagues at the Academy of Motion Pictures Arts and Sciences hadn't noticed he had the lead. But they never really had a chance; Huston had hidden it too well with his performance.

He had the wrinkles and whiskers, he sweated and itched and he danced around like a madman, a bit of business only a character actor, a second lead, would do. He appeared to be simply Old Howard, a tireless old prospector, not the protagonist. Not the lead who makes things happen, whom the story revolves around. But he was there doing just that, acting the protagonist, right in the middle of the film. Playing God. Inciting the other characters to life, for better and for worse . . . talking about the spring harvest, about gold, greed and the mountain as if it were a woman. Talking as if a mountain was something to be cared for, patched up, its wounds closed. Old Howard was there working on the other characters with that complex and unending human conflict, with life.

When the second act culminates, Old Howard leaves his two greedy prospecting friends to their own devices and calmly goes off to a village at the local natives' request. And, for no apparent story reason he then brings a dying child back from the dead. Performs a resurrection, acts like God, nature, or whatever you choose to call it.

It was the scene in the film that revealed him, just for a moment, just a glimpse that was subtly underplayed by the camera, director and the performer. Underplayed so it could be felt rather than understood. So that it could produce an emotion that paid homage to the living.

Blanke knew the moment was there, Huston the son knew, Bogart knew and Huston the father knew. And a short old man who followed the cast around as a location guide and called himself H. Groves knew. He was the author of the novel, the mysterious B. Traven whom no one in the company would recognize until he had disappeared. But Traven had said nothing. None of them had; they were professionals. And none of them would discuss it afterward. That didn't count. What counted was that the story got onto the film and that the film got up onto the screen to light the darkness.

That is why they had come to Hollywood, to Warner Bros. and why they had stayed. For that one moment, even if one was all they were to receive. And they didn't want to destroy it with talk. Time was running out.

When 1950 arrived, Walter Huston was dead. Simply gone. Few of the public noticed at the time, but it marked the end of an era. Something fine, part of the real silver on the screen was disappearing.

Many of Huston's coworkers noticed; they were growing old too and they knew what his kind of character performer meant to that toy called the picture show. They knew what was disappearing. When Barbara Stanwyck received word of his death, she was so broken inside that she closed her set. It was prophetic. For many of the character performers all the sets would soon close. By 1954 Alan Hale, Sr., Guy Kibbee, Gladys George, Warren Hymer, Hobart Cavanaugh, Hugh Herbert, Sydney Greenstreet, Eugene Pallette, Edgar Kennedy, James Stephenson, Alan Dinehart, and many others had gone. By the sixties more would join them. Their time had come and gone and with them much of the life that filled the darkness.

Their passing made many wonder; could it all end, the

Facing. Back row, Martin Milner and James Lydon; front row, Derek Scott, Irene Dunne, William Powell and Johnny Calkins in Life with Father, *1947*

studios, Hollywood? Jack Warner? Everything? It didn't seem possible, but the thought had been planted.

The character performers kept working up till their last days and would continue to work even if there were no more contracts, not enough "day work," and only an occasional good role if you got lucky. They were sure times would improve. Tinsel town had had its slow periods before and soon it would pick up, the phones start ringing again.

The character actors were a positive, hopeful group, and they had had a good life, most of it in greasepaint. The camera had loved them, been their friend and imprisoned them. Preserved them. Watching them perform there was a tendency to think they had been trained to act in an obvious, broad and free manner. To show openly to the audience just who and what their character thought and felt. But Allen Jenkins denies it: "Hell no, there was no school. The style came from the West Side of New York, the tough side, and we brought it with us. We did our acting with the entire face, arms, hands, even the knees, you know, that's the way we talked on the West Side."

The others had also brought their local gestures with them, from Albany, Wisconsin; Wanesville, Ohio; Brooklyn, New York; Quincy, Illinois; Virginia City, Nevada; Orange, New Jersey; Shoshoni, Wyoming; Winfield, Kansas; Davenport, Iowa; and from Vienna, Vera Cruz and Munich. They were all part of America when it was big, open and simple, when it was young . . . when they were growing old. That was their style and its explanation was simple enough. It was honest.

They were exactly what you saw. And more would come looking for that one good role, for that moment when a producer would hand them a script with a second act to play, with dialogue like, "Never mind that, let's talk about the black bird."

But for the old-timers the century was closing fast.

And for the vice-president in charge of production at Warner Bros., it was a cruel time. Of all the employees in his factory, the character performers could have been considered the farthest away from him, farthest from the top. But in their own way they had been the closest and he had no jokes or four-letter words to hide his feelings. They had provided what he wanted most. Provided the laughs . . . and something more, something he would never admit to.

As the fifties began, the motion picture business was actually just emerging from its youth, finding itself. Each of the various talents had instinctively fought through the thirties and forties and shaped its particular craft . . . and on rare occasions a little art had collided, by some magic formula, with the Celluloid. And the artists were determined to work that formula out, put it down in contracts, law, union bylaws and aesthetic scripture. It was all just really beginning, but a great part of what the talent still dreamed of was already won, was already on the screen, had its run in the theaters and was in the storage vaults. Or lost, already forgotten.

The Warner Bros. story would be dragged out as long and dramatically as possible; it would be made as melodramatic and vulgar as it could, but it would not change its direction.

The story was already ending, but no one noticed.

Only Jack Warner. Now he could see things coming.

Facing. Jeffrey Hunter in John Ford's Sergeant Rutledge, *1960*
*Below. Michael Anderson, Jr., Deborah Kerr and Robert
Mitchum in* The Sundowners, *1960*

*Top. Deborah Kerr and Robert Mitchum on location in
Australia for* The Sundowners, *1960
Left. Director Howard Hawks, Dean Martin, John Wayne and
Angie Dickinson on the set of* Rio Bravo, *1959
Facing. Street set for* The FBI Story, *1959*

Overleaf. Robert Preston and chorus in The Music Man, *1962*
Below. Mona Washbourne and Audrey Hepburn in My Fair
Lady, *1964*
Facing. Audrey Hepburn in My Fair Lady, *1964*

Left. Mamie Van Doren in publicity pose a la 1950's
Facing, left. Gwen Verdon in Damn Yankees, 1958
Facing, right Elizabeth Ashley in publicity pose a la 1960's

Overleaf. Natalie Wood in Gypsy, *1962*
Facing. "I want to get out of this goddamned place—anyways
these boys will start going ripe on us by tomorrow—we got
to move—" Strother Martin as Coffer and L.Q. Jones as T.C. in
Sam Peckinpah's The Wild Bunch, *1969*
Top, right. William Holden as Pike Bishop in Sam Peckinpah's
The Wild Bunch, *1969*
Right. Jaime Sanchez as Angel and Emile Fernandez as
Mapache in Sam Peckinpah's The Wild Bunch, *1969*

Below. The Devils, *1971*

DEATH AND RESURRECTION

1950 to 1967

"The trouble with death is that you don't get two weeks notice that your contract is being canceled out," recalled Jack Warner in his autobiography. But as early as 1950 he was acting as if Hollywood, the dream factory, as if Warner Bros. had already received its notice.

"Jack was annoyed at the firings at all the other studios," recalls John Twist, who was in the Writers' Building at the beginning of the fifties turning out *Colorado Territory, Dallas, Forth Worth* and *King Richard and the Crusaders.* Warner may not have liked what was going on in his business, but he saw hard times coming and took action, started firing on Friday . . . but this time there would be no hiring on Monday.

Perc Westmore in the Makeup Department was asked to cut back on personnel, but refused and was let go. In 1952 designer Milo Anderson was asked to leave, as the studio could no longer afford lace and brocade. He left the business of movie making entirely. "I had to get out; it was all over. Everything that had made the business so great was gone."

The cutbacks in wardrobe had started in 1949 with the last of the great Warner costume epics, *The Adventures of Don Juan.* Instead of new designs, all of the extra players and some of the principals wore costumes that had been created by Anderson and Orry-Kelly a decade earlier during the production of *The Private Lives of Elizabeth and Essex.*

Director Vincent Sherman was watching another kind of decay set in as he directed Errol Flynn as Don Juan. "Up until about five or five-thirty, he would be fine. But then he would begin to take a drink. So, it was a difficult situation. And twice during the making of the picture, he became ill. He became ill the first time after we had been shooting for five or six weeks. He went home and they said that his heart was bad and he had to take a rest. We stopped shooting for like four weeks. Many of the cast had to be paid.

"Then we worked another few weeks and then we had to stop again. He was sick again. I heard subsequently that he wasn't ill. He went down to Laguna to photograph the mating of the whales with his father, who was a marine biologist."

The "laughing water," the growing independence of the established movie star and the old sounds of the sea were taking their toll on Flynn. During his world travels at that time he took to wearing false noses in Paris, Rome, London and Calcutta. "I could stand at a street corner and watch the world go by and the anonymity was blessed.

Chapter opening. Joan Crawford in Flamingo Road, *1949*
Overleaf. Warren Beatty and Faye Dunaway in Bonnie and Clyde, *1967*

Facing. Henry Blanke in the fifties
Left. Spencer Tracy and a studio crew on location for The Old Man and the Sea, *1958*

"I have been tired of this face for a long time.

"I never did like it, even when it was 'pretty.' I liked only what I hoped was behind the face, and wished for and longed to be . . ."

Jack Warner looked at that face and decided he couldn't use a drunken Robin Hood, a wrinkled and corroded Captain Thorpe, a decadent Jeb Stuart.

"Most people who work for a company for so long a time get some recognition," recalled Flynn. "My recognition, in 1952, when I was ending my service with Warner's, came in the form of a letter accusing me of breach of contract, holding up the company, and general bad behavior."

When Flynn and Warner met, Warner offered to allow Flynn to buy out his contract for a hundred thousand dollars like Bogart had. But Flynn would pay nothing and that's what they settled on. An even break.

Bette Davis and James Cagney had already departed, as had Barbara Stanwyck, Joan Crawford, Olivia de Havilland, Ida Lupino, Lauren Bacall, George Raft and other performers of the great days who had gone to other studios or were free-lancing.

John Garfield died in 1952, at thirty-nine.

Leo Forbstein had died in 1948 and the Music Department was now run by Ray Heindorf. Erich Korngold had retired in 1947, but Max Steiner was still at his piano, still scoring at sixty-five years of age in 1953. Other composers only visited the studio, on a per-picture basis.

Cinematographers Tony Gaudio and Sol Polito were gone and James Wong Howe, Hal Mohr and Ted McCord were free-lancing. Only Ernest Haller was working consistently on the studio's few important films. The big-money films were made independently of the studio system and their producers brought in their own directors of cinematography. The run-of-the-mill studio product was photographed by "bottom dollar" craftsmen.

Of the "directors," only Raoul Walsh and Michael Curtiz were still under contract. The majority of the studio work was being put in the hands of "foremen": Lewis Seiler, Gordon Douglas, Milton H. Bren, Felix Feist, David Butler, John Brahm, André De Toth and others.

Michael Curtiz was living in the famous Marion Davies bungalow in the fifties and living high. Asked to take a cut in salary for the direction of *Helen of Troy* in 1955, he refused

to do the film and was fired. Curtiz never returned.

Producer Henry Blanke was still there and Brynie Foy was back again. Edelman, Jacobs, David Weisbart and Jack's relative, Milton Sperling, were producing, but the budgets were slim.

The factory had to cut its production overhead and the most expensive item was creative talent. Vincent Sherman recalls studio boss Steve Trilling calling and asking him to go on a loan-out to Columbia Pictures and direct a remake of *Craig's Wife* with Joan Crawford. Sherman said, "'Steve, if that's the same script that Crawford asked me to read, I don't want to do that.' He said, 'Oh, gee, Vince, we've already made the deal for you.' I said, 'What happens if I say no?' He said, 'You don't want to do that. You would break your contract with us.'

"Well, it was much later that I discovered that Jack Warner had set up a new policy. The picture business was in the process of changing and Warner was trying to reduce his overhead and cost as much as possible. People were making $3,500 a week and he didn't have pictures for them, he was just ready to get rid of those heavy contracts."

The studio's production in 1952 had dropped to twenty-five films and would be down to nineteen by 1959. And four of those would be purchased from foreign film companies. Attendance in 1946 had been 85,000,000 per week, then it dropped to 45,000,000 per week in 1951 and by 1960 it would be down to 40,000,000.

Something had to be done and Jack was doing it.

By 1953 the last of the Warner writers from the golden decades would leave: Ranald MacDougall, James Webb, Winston Miller and Melville Shavelson. John Twist was brought over from Metro to write the bigger budgeted films. Independent producers brought in their own writers, like Tennessee Williams, who worked on the screen treatments of his plays, *A Streetcar Named Desire* and *The Glass Menagerie*, then swiftly left for the theater again. Young rebels Ivan Goff and Ben Roberts did their terms in the Writers' Building before leaving to populate the monster television with their creations. Niven Busch, Irving Wallace, Alan Lemay and Ernest K. Gann did their time, but then went off to a land of freedom called the novel to make their fame and fortune.

More and more options were not being picked up, recalls Stephen Longstreet. "It was a rule that a writer was fired on Friday night. Christmas was also a popular time for firing. We

Facing, above. Kirk Douglas and Jane Wyman in The Glass Menagerie, *1950*
Facing, below. Vivien Leigh and Marlon Brando in A Streetcar Named Desire, *1951*
Right. John Wayne as Ethan Edwards and Ward Bond on the set of The Searchers, *1956*

got in the habit of throwing cocktail parties every time a writer was fired. I'd say we had those cocktail parties every Friday night.

"Whenever I met a screenwriter, I'd tell him to save his money." Longstreet was the first to take his own advice. He smiles benignly now from the glass-walled living room of his eight-acre estate on top of a hill in Beverly Hills. "I decided that the picture business was over for me when I could afford this house and the Picassos on the wall. I tried television. We all did. It wasn't the same. Trying to make a story in twenty-six pages. It wasn't worth it."

For those who stayed in the Writers' Building, the story was the same. They were looking at the end of their contracts and the best were receiving only $1,000 per week.

On the screen, the writers were still no more successful than when they came. Frank Nugent wrote a brilliant screenplay from Alan Lemay's novel, *The Searchers,* a story with a baffling and moving second act. But the credit and applause were stolen by the performers, by John Wayne and the vital young actress Vera Miles. And by the director, the immortal John Ford. Nugent would go unnoticed and spend his hours drinking his scotch in Brentwood bars, alone, as his screenplay did its job. A pedestal for a monument.

There was no more trench around the Writers' Building and the gates in the fence were open continually, but it was still a long way from the parking lot and the hours were still nine to five. And Jack Warner still had his spies.

"Word reached Jack Warner that some of the writers were fornicating with their secretaries in the Writers' Building during working hours," recalls John Twist. "And he asked Brynie Foy about it. Well, those secretaries were very elderly ladies who had been with the studio since it was on Sunset Boulevard. Back then they were no doubt very pretty, but Brynie asked Jack, 'Have you looked at any of those dames lately?'

"'No.'

"'Well, if any of those writers are pleasuring those dames, you should pin a medal on them.'"

At Warner Bros. it was still all business, but the product was changing.

In 1951 Henry Blanke still had ten years to go on his $5,000 a week contract. And Jack applied constant pressure to break it. The fighting was often mean, bitter and "sad," for both

parties. But Blanke stayed. "Jack and Harry told me, 'From now on, you have to make bread-and-butter pictures. You have made enough money, now you must make our pictures.' Which, after a few years, it can ruin you . . . and it did. Look at my career . . . ah, you have looked at it, you've found me out." He bites on his lip as he talks, drawing energy to keep the smile in place, then hardens. "I knew I was going to make shit. I refused it, but they said I had to finish what they had . . . and I did them . . . I was too old to lie any more for my own purposes."

Blanke stayed to produce *She's Back on Broadway* with Virginia Mayo, *So Big* again, *The Phantom of the Rue Morgue, Young at Heart, Serenade* with Mario Lanza and *Too Much Too Soon* with whatever was left of a rented Errol Flynn. There were others, a lovely film with director Fred Zinnemann and Audrey Hepburn called *The Nun's Story.* The taste and judgment were still there, just seldom used.

In 1954 Jack Warner was sixty-two. He had already spent over fifty years going into an extra twist for the benefit of his audiences and was estimated to be worth forty million dollars. He could quit easily, but he somehow wasn't quite ready. But he was ignoring those who might have helped him.

Outside the studio gates new faces still arrived daily in Hollywood, by train, bus and by plane. And a large portion of them still came smiling and dreaming, came for the old reasons. They weren't looking back, they were looking at tomorrow. The young talent was packed with dreams built by Hollywood and they came to make them even bigger. They had been raised on *The Adventures of Robin Hood, Gone With the Wind, Gunga Din, Casablanca, Mr. Smith Goes to Washington* and all the others. And they believed them.

But they denied them. "That stuff belongs to yesterday," was the talk among the pages and mail boys at NBC's Sunset and Vine studios "They should throw all those damn old hacks out, whoever they are." And it didn't pay to find out.

They were arrogant young men who laughed at yesterday but spent their meager dollars gallantly in expensive Beverly Hills barbershops or at Sy Devore's clothing store, where they tipped the peroxided manicurist fifty cents, even a dollar, to convince the natty old-timers they belonged. They saved up to buy black mohair suits and white silk ties so they could dress just the way you were supposed to, as gangsters. At least the way the gangsters looked in the movie business.

They kept their love affair quiet, private, but they were desperately in love with the picture show. And it had made voyeurs not only of their eyes, but their hearts. As storytellers they were imitating life on the screen, not in the streets, a practice that is death for the artist. But they turned out stories, outlines, scripts and wrote game shows for television, news stories and Westerns, adventures, melodramas. Wrote but didn't sell. Others directed little theater, church theater and children's theater or performed for agents, friends and the empty night.

But whatever they did, it didn't help . . . not even when they deliberately sold themselves to old agents and producers with souls rotted by tinsel. The young talent was locked out.

If you were a relative you could get a chance, but being the boss's kid simply meant no one would listen to you.

Yesterday still ruled dreamtown and many that belonged to it wanted a bigger piece. They didn't want or need young, new competition.

There were hundreds of men who had been waiting in editing rooms, behind cameras, in story departments and elsewhere for their one chance to join the exclusive, highly paid few who actually made the picture shows. Some had what it took, most didn't, but they still got the jobs.

The only real opening was for a performer.

The young actors who arrived worked desperately to get rid of the cultivated English accents their high school drama teachers had drilled into them and spent all their money on haircuts, riding lessons at Pickwick Stables and 8" x 10" glossies of themselves. Warner Bros. was hiring beauties like Troy Donahue and Tab Hunter. The studio had forgotten where they had originally gotten their great talent and even how they looked. So, if you wanted to compete, you had to look even better than those blond superboys.

The girls arrived and found the same old problems. But with the cutbacks in production, there were fewer opportunities to get that chance no matter what they were willing to do to get it. And, "a really beautiful woman can't succeed as a writer, director or producer in this business because from the beginning . . . actually all her life . . . she has too many other things to cope with," was the standard male response to any suggestion that a girl, a woman, should do anything other than perform.

The girls got cheap apartments or stayed at the Studio Club

and waited for the phone to ring . . . but it didn't and they went to work as carhops, waitresses and secretaries.

The young men worked at NBC, CBS and ABC television as pages or in the mail room at the studios. If you thought of becoming an agent or producer, jobs were available at the Music Corporation of America if you dressed conservatively, were unmarried, and could survive on forty dollars a week while you spent six months in the "traffic" room taking telegrams from the Paris and New York offices. During that time you were either to talk one of the established agents into letting you assist him, steal his clients or find your own. If you could accomplish one of three, you were on your way. Where, was not a polite question.

Youth was locked out by nepotism, unions, guilds, age and declining production. After three or four years of daily rejection, most went into other fields, became television technicians or went home, their dreams broken by the men who had made them.

A few stuck, determined to find whatever it was that made it possible to join that silver on the screen.

Sam Peckinpah was a grip on live television shows produced at a local station, KTTV, and was hauling coaxial cables for clowns and cooks.

Stanley Kubrick was working with avant-garde films and politics at the tiny Coronet Theater on La Cienega Boulevard, taking tickets, putting up folding chairs, shooting sixteen-millimeter film.

Arthur Penn was a stage manager at the El Capitan Theater on Vine Street with a headset clamped over his ears and was ordering tumbling acts, jugglers and TV cameras about the stage for the "Colgate Comedy Hour."

For those who stuck, there were few places to learn story-telling, to learn the craft and art of making a movie. All the knowledge was in the old pictures, but in Hollywood and throughout the world only a handful took time to investigate yesterday.

In Paris a group of young men began to write criticism about American films and to analyze them, study them frame by frame on Moviolas to find just how they were made, precisely who made them and why. The young Americans considered such studies useless. It didn't take the fashionable critics of *Time* magazine and the various intellectual fan magazines to convince you the American film makers were over the hill.

You knew yourself; they were part of the group that wouldn't let you in.

Hollywood, however, had shut down on all ideas, not just young ones. Particularly Warner Bros. They didn't want anyone around who had the chance of being controversial, young or old.

The reasons went back to October 5, 1945. On that day the labor unions struck the studios and selected Warner Bros. to picket because they were using scab labor. Harry and Jack were angry because they had been singled out, and fought back, street style, naturally.

"The studio hired 'bully boys' and police dogs," recalls a white-collar worker. "Large steel bolts from the machine shop were issued to the strikebreakers and they threw them down on the strikers from the roofs of the sound stages. A hidden camera was placed next to the auto gate to photograph striking employees who would later be punished and a flag was raised or lowered on the roof of the sound stage next to the auto gate as a signal to charge the strikers or pull back." Others speak of tire chains, high-powered hoses and guns being used when the Burbank police joined the studio guards to break through the picket lines.

Joan Crawford arrived in her limousine one day, but was afraid to enter the studio: "My face is my future."

The white-collar workers slept on the lot and were issued free breakfasts, eggs, doughnuts and coffee. The strike lasted for months.

Screenwriter Howard Koch quit over the treatment of the strikers, bought out his contract for ten thousand dollars. Others were deeply upset. Jack was also bitter and declared he would "No longer make pictures about the 'little man.'"

After eight months, the strike was finally settled and the union workers received a twenty-five-cent pay increase. They went back to work to continue to build dreams, but something had changed inside them.

Jack and Harry could live with the pay increase, but they were getting too old for street fighting and the pressures seemed to be only beginning. Enemies appeared everywhere. Big ones.

On June 11, 1946, the Supreme Court of the United States handed down a decision in the form of a consent decree that, among other decisions, outlawed block booking. It gave the major companies the option of remaining in only two of their three main areas of business, production, distribution or

Above. Wardrobe shot of Marlon Brando for A Streetcar Named Desire, *1951*
Below. Marlon Brando and Kim Hunter in A Streetcar Named Desire, *1951*
Facing, left. James Dean (with camera) snaps a picture of director Elia Kazan on the location for East of Eden, *1955*
Facing, right. James Dean goes looking for his mother in East of Eden, *1955*

exhibition. The decision was fought in the courts, but in 1949 the final ruling regarding Warner Bros. was handed down, and Jack and Harry decided to get out of exhibition, to sell their theaters.

They no longer had the guarantee that the films they made would be shown to the audience. Each production now became chancy.

The next year, on October 18, 1947, in the Caucus Room of the Old House Building in Washington, D.C., the Un-American Activities Committee opened its hearings. J. Parnell Thomas was the chairman and the committee had decided to investigate the movies, to attempt to undo much that was dangerous and evil in that tinsel town on the other end of the land.

One of the first witnesses was Jack L. Warner and the committee members began their investigation with queries about how much the communist conspiracy had infiltrated the content of motion pictures. Jack, of course, replied that writers were always trying to put wrong ideas in the scripts, but that he diligently kept them out. The committee asked how the ideas were introduced and what they were about.

Jack had difficulty. "Some of these lines have innuendos and double meanings, and things like that, and you have to take eight or ten Harvard law courses to find out what they mean." He still was warring with the Writers' Building.

The questions kept coming and Jack glibly supplied names, all writers: Alvah Bessie, Gordon Kahn, Howard Koch, Ring Lardner, Jr., Emmet Lavery, John Howard Lawson, Albert Maltz, Robert Rossen, Irwin Shaw, Dalton Trumbo, John Wexley, Julius and Philip Epstein, Sheridan Gibney and Clifford Odets.

Two days later, after Warner could plainly see that the committee was working toward the establishment of an official blacklist, he became cautious and discarded his natural glib manner. He withdrew the names of Endore, the Epsteins and Gibney from his list, persisted that he could handle the writers as he always had, and on October 20, 1947, he protested against any official censorship. "I can't for the life of me figure where men could get together and try in any form, shape or manner to deprive a man of a livelihood because of his political beliefs . . . It would be a conspiracy, the attorneys tell me, and I know that myself."

Jack Warner left the stand giving the committee nothing to build their case with except the names, names that they

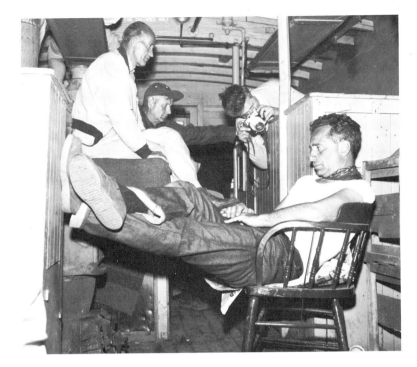

already had under consideration, names that would be reduced to "The Hollywood Ten" after ten men, eight writers and two directors were sentenced to one year for contempt of court for refusing to answer the question "Are you now, or have you ever been, a member of the Communist Party?"

In September of 1947, old Warner Bros. regulars John Huston, William Wyler, Bogart, Bacall, Paul Henreid and a mix of other Hollywood celebrities met at Lucey's Restaurant to form the Committee for the First Amendment. Their efforts to help those investigated were minimal as their collision with backroom politics and the scandal-hunting press was awesome.

On March 8, 1951, the Un-American Activities Committee began their hearings again. Between 1951 and 1954, two hundred and twelve film employees would have their politics questioned to such a degree that they would, in one manner or another, be successfully blacklisted. Wall Street was blamed for influencing the studio bosses, others felt there was a conspiracy, but one of those involved remembers, "It didn't matter what side you were on. I remember the screaming and the tears as I listened to my father and his friends downstairs fighting over politics. I didn't care what it was about, I wanted it to stop. It was ugly, so ugly it could destroy a child forever. I wanted no part of politics." Both the unfriendly and the friendly witnesses became blacklisted and in excess of five hundred film people stopped working in their medium.

Among those working, the fear also spread and the fighting over excellence, parts and ideas all but disappeared at Warner Bros.

Jack and Harry had other problems as well. In 1949, 1950 and 1951 television began to run away with the audience and Warner Bros. reacted. Television sets could not be included among set decorations, writers who worked for television were dismissed and performers were contracted in such a manner that they could not appear on television during the specified release of their films, not even to promote the films. The word "television" itself was not to be used at the Burbank studios and on a bad day, its use was cause for dismissal.

Foreign films also began to raid the audience and particularly the critics. And Warner Bros. couldn't compete. Natural locations instead of studio sets, natural lighting instead of Klieg lights and actresses with hair under their arms instead of Max Factor Number 3 were not the kind of choice the vice-president

in charge of production could even conceive of. He contracted Virginia Mayo and Doris Day while the audience chased Gina Lollobrigida, Brigitte Bardot and Sophia Loren.

Warner Bros., like the nation, had come to a standstill. It didn't trust what it had been, didn't even *know* what it had been, and was afraid to dream of what it wanted to be.

Jack and Harry considered selling the studio to a group of bankers, but decided against it. Jack still had a few twists to try.

He hired Elia Kazan, even though he suspected his politics, and Marlon Brando to make *A Streetcar Named Desire* in 1951. He paid Brando seventy-five thousand dollars to make the one film, just twenty-nine thousand dollars less than he had paid Bette Davis in 1939 to make five films. Brando did as much to change acting as Cagney and Robinson had in 1931, twenty years earlier, but Jack had him contracted for only one film.

Jack plunged again with a mumbling kid named James Dean in 1955, *East of Eden, Rebel Without a Cause* and then *Giant.* Dean was in stride with the second half of the century, with a nation growing up . . . with dreams made from switchblades and T-shirts . . . with prayers spoken with four-letter words. But he was moving too fast, drove his Porsche past eighty miles an hour and ended as a tangled mess of steel, flesh and cartilage.

In 1953 Warner tried a three-dimensional projection process with *House of Wax,* but by the time Alfred Hitchcock had finished *Dial M for Murder* in the 3-D process in 1954, the fad had passed and the film was released in the old format. The studio then turned to Cinemascope, a format "designed for photographing snakes rather than people," recalls director George Stevens.

In 1955, Warner did an about-face, got in step with tomorrow and put his son, Jack Warner, Jr., in charge of the studio's newly created television unit. Junior was thirty-nine, the same age Warner was in 1931 when all the great yesterdays had begun.

A few fine films were produced at the studio too, signs of hope, *Hondo, The High and the Mighty, A Star Is Born, The Searchers, Giant* and *Rio Bravo.* But their producers were only renting the studio or borrowing the money. The creative decisions did not belong to Jack Warner or his factory.

At the same time that the youth, the maverick ideas and the studio system were being closed out, the talent took over

creative control and with grand artistic intentions began to destroy the industry.

By the mid-fifties many producers, directors, performers, and even a writer or two, had attained their creative dreams. They had their names above the title. They had creative control, they had their own companies and could pick their subjects, roles, stories and then decide how to tell them by themselves. And with the right agent, they could find the money to get their highly personal and artistic product into a theater, with or without a studio, with or without Warner Bros.

Howard Hawks formed Howard Hawks Productions. Humphrey Bogart had formed Santana Productions. John Huston formed Horizon Pictures with producer Sam Spiegel. Hal Wallis and Jerry Wald had formed their own companies and directors LeRoy, Kazan and Hitchcock also formed companies in their own names.

The time of the truly artistic motion picture appeared to have arrived. In France, the young intellectuals were even calling the director the "author," the one personality who could dominate a film.

Simultaneously the studios divested themselves of their most expensive talent, the stars, and the agents took over. By putting the various writing, directing and acting talents they had under contract together in film packages, the agents could guarantee that a film, regardless of quality, could be made, but they could also make ridiculous salary demands and literally rewrite, recast or hire or fire directors at will. Through their agents, the talent had become the producers, the executives and the power and the glory.

The movies were just beginning, just becoming the "cinema," an art form, and the directors, producers and stars were going to prove they were the artists . . . they were finally going to tell hard, tough stories with big ideas inside them. But they found it was much easier to make a deal for a lot of money if you restricted yourself to *just* making a deal—not a great picture.

And the talent refused to formalize what they did on the screen, to argue aesthetics. They would leave that to the silly Frenchmen who would mysteriously appear from Paris asking questions about the use of the camera as a narrator, asking questions about personal cinema. The talent was too busy. They had to get to the next job, to the set where the action was.

Instinctively they still knew what counted most. "It is only

work that truly satisfies," wrote Bette Davis. "I think I've known this all my life. No one could ever share my drive or my vision. No one has ever understood the sweetness of my joy at the end of a good day's work." But in the fifties there was no one to fight with except themselves and it wasn't enough.

Jack Warner tried to stop the trend to independent films as the cost of a movie star soared every time he met with an agent. He cursed what he called "body peddlers from MCA" and had agents banned from the lot for a brief period, but that made all business dealings impossible. The agents had the power, not Jack Warner, and he had to let them back through the gates.

With the future more and more in doubt, Jack made a major decision, plunged.

In March of 1956 he sold all the films the studio had made prior to 1949 to United Artists Television. The sale shocked the industry that was dedicated either to the destruction of television or the domination of it. Again, the street kid at Warner Bros. had gone first, and the other major studios followed. Sold their libraries of films, sold the old stuff the audience had already seen to their competition. There was no going back, yesterday had been sold to secure tomorrow.

Jack Warner had made a major mistake.

"In my opinion," recalls Henry Blanke, "they thought for a long time that they were going to sell out completely. They just made films to get some more money before they did. Then they found they had all these hundreds of pictures in black and white and everything was going to be made in color from then on. So they sold them for nothing. With all the rights, of every beautiful play we had made: *The Petrified Forest, The Maltese Falcon, The Treasure of the Sierra Madre, Old Maid, Casablanca.* All of them. With only one of those plays I could be a rich man today. It was unbelievable, they behaved like idiots.

"Maybe . . . maybe they were just old . . . or tired . . . which is understandable."

In 1956 Harry Warner was seventy-five and spending most of his time with his horses at his farm. When he visited the studio, the old-timers remember he would still bend down and pick up a stray nail when he saw one on the ground. "But he could no longer straighten them with his teeth."

"Jack's denoument," recalls an old-timer, "came about the same time. He was still famous for turning out the lights and

Facing. Joan Crawford, Bette Davis and director Robert Aldrich go over a scene for Whatever Happened to Baby Jane?, *an independent feature the studio purchased in 1962*
Above. Judy Garland does the "Born in a Trunk" number from A Star Is Born, *1954*
Below. Rex Harrison, Audrey Hepburn and Wilfrid Hyde-White in My Fair Lady, *personally produced by Jack Warner in 1964*

one day blew up on a large stage and yelled for whoever left the lights on to turn them off. Someone did and left Jack in the middle of all those dark sets. It took him over half an hour to find his way out."

It wasn't an easy time for anyone. "Jack would leave town when the firing was done," recalls a studio researcher. And he had softened. "Jack was run down by a messenger boy on a bike one day and the boy was all over him with apologies. 'I didn't want to hit you with the bike.' Jack simply grinned and said, 'That's right son, never hit me with a bike.'

"There were constant rumors of Jack leaving and some of us began to think it might be better if he stayed, that it's better to have an ogre with whom you are familiar then one you don't know."

The century, however, was still moving fast, if awkwardly.

At 2:10 A.M. on January 14, 1957, Humphrey Bogart died of cancer in his sleep. He had gone refusing to discuss his illness, biting off the pain with humor, good liquor and good friends. Acting off-screen like he did on.

Erich Wolfgang Korngold died the same year, and the flag of mourning was flown over the State Opera House in Vienna.

On July 25, 1958, Harry Warner died in his Bel Air home, no longer able to fight with life or his brother.

Jack was reported dead from an auto crash in the south of France on August 5, 1958, but after intensive care, healed and returned to work.

In 1959 he fired his son. Jack Warner came to work early one morning and had the door to his son's office locked. The gate guards were ordered not to let him enter the studio and they didn't.

In 1959 Olivia de Havilland was living in Paris and decided to join the kids, go downtown and see *The Adventures of Robin Hood.* Just for fun. It had been years since she'd seen it. Afterward she was impressed with how good it was and with the way the French intellectuals took it seriously. She decided to write Errol Flynn about it. Later, however, she thought that her letter was too sentimental, unimportant, and it was never mailed.

Flynn died months later, on October 15, 1959. "I wish I had sent that letter. It would have pleased him after all those years, but I didn't." Flynn didn't make it to Jamaica, he was laid to rest on old Warner Bros. property, at Forest Lawn, in

Right. Faye Dunaway, Estelle Parsons, Gene Hackman, Michael J. Pollard and Warren Beatty in Bonnie and Clyde, *1967*
Below. Richard Burton, Elizabeth Taylor, George Segal and Sandy Dennis in Who's Afraid of Virginia Woolf?, *1966*
Facing. Paul Newman in Cool Hand Luke, *1967*

304

the Garden of Everlasting Peace. Six months later Ida Lupino's mother died and there was only one plot available in that garden for Connie—just by chance, next to Errol Flynn.

Flynn died amid scandal and "laughing water," completely unaware of what he accomplished on the screen, amid the darkness, of his compelling importance, of the need a world gone gray had for his gallant gesture.

In 1959 in Paris, there were four new French films playing on the boulevards: *The Four Hundred Blows* directed by François Truffaut, *Hiroshima Mon Amour* by Alain Renais, *Breathless* by Jean-Luc Goddard and *The Cousins* by Claude Chabrol. Films made by those young, intellectual film critics who had been prying at Hollywood's past with questions and Moviolas, who had finally come to the conclusion that what counted at the picture show was not talking about it, but the doing of it.

When those four films reached America, reached New York, the fashionable American critics acclaimed their brilliance, their invention, their newness, and used them as examples to demonstrate just how false and superficial the Hollywood product was, and always had been. Not even when Jean-Luc Goddard inserted a shot of Humphrey Bogart from *The Big Sleep* in his film would the American critics or even the film makers in Hollywood recognize where Goddard had learned his craft, his aesthetics, even his beliefs. They recognized Bogart, but gave no thought to the fact that the film came from Warner Bros., from Howard Hawks, Leigh Brackett, William Faulkner and Raymond Chandler. Or that Bogart had grown out of John Huston, Henry Blanke, Dashiell Hammett. Out of *The Maltese Falcon, Casablanca, High Sierra,* and Raoul Walsh, Mark Hellinger and W. R. Burnett. Out of what they considered false, pulpy and vulgar tinsel, out of Warner Bros. The young Frenchmen were using our yesterdays for their tomorrows, but no one noticed.

In 1960 the talent in Hollywood, reacting to the restrictions of the fifties, saw only the nudity, despair and artiness in the foreign films. They believed that anything foreign was free and personal, and they wanted the same kind of freedom, the freedom the novelists had. To have their characters speak with the vulgarities of the locker room and the gutter, to have their actresses go nude as they did in life, at least above the waist, and to investigate the dark, seamy ugly social problems that were plaguing America. It was time that the cinema be set free and be used as an art like it was intended to be. And now they could do it.

The talent was making the same sounds the screenwriters on the Super Chief had made, but their chances of making films looked slim.

Warner Bros. cut production to eighteen films in 1960, sixteen in 1961, fifteen in 1962, and fourteen in 1963. The trend hadn't changed.

In 1964 at Warner Bros. Jack L. Warner was personally producing *My Fair Lady.* An expensive, lush, happy, family picture show with songs even he could sing. He was seventy-three, still trying to get richer, but growing older.

That same year costume designer Orry-Kelly died and Jack Warner spoke the eulogy: "There's one thing I'm sure of. Orry would want me to be as honest as possible. He might even want me to make a crack or two, but I can't think of any . . . he was a man of many talents. A talent for living, for giving, for making people and the world look more beautiful."

Henry Blanke had retired in 1961, to his home in Brentwood. The bitterness was beginning to show. For ten years he had been taking the money, just the money.

In 1965 Max Steiner quit the studio after completing *Two on a Guillotine.* "They criticized the picture and I didn't like it and that was the end. It wasn't a picture, it was an abortion. There was a big mistake in the thing, the guillotine was placed in the wrong place, you know. They should have cut off William Conrad's head for producing the thing. They said I killed the picture . . . that I wouldn't take after all the years . . . after twenty-nine years."

In 1966 studio production was cut to thirteen films and Jack made up his mind. At the studio he openly and vulgarly displayed his dislike for the kind of film his studio was pro-ducing, *Who's Afraid of Virginia Woolf, An American Dream* and *Bonnie and Clyde.* He knew the characters in the films talked with the same four-letter vocabulary he was famous for, but he didn't want it on the screen and let everyone know it. He made *Camelot,* then quit.

In June of 1967 he sold the studio to Seven Arts Ltd. and took his thirty-two million dollars. He stayed on the lot for over a year, kept an office there, was seen eating in the Greenroom on occasion and was treated with respect and courtesy by the new owners. But he no longer hollered when someone left the lights on . . . they no longer belonged to him.

As he moved, his walk slowed and you could see him look back to the beginning. But he could no longer send someone up a high-tension pole to tap the wires for needed electricity when they couldn't pay the bills. It was the same but nothing was the same . . . even the secretaries in the Writers' Building were now strangers. The old-timers, those long-termers whom Jack and Harry had refused to fire even during the Depression, during the lean war years or any of the other hard times . . . those once sturdy young men like electrician Martin Murphy, Doc Solomon and Henry Blanke, who had stuck with Jack, Harry and Sam in those dark days of 1923 . . . those loyal few who had taken coupons instead of paychecks . . . they were all gone. Dead or retired. It was over.

By the middle sixties, the new moguls, the new film makers, the "artists" were sending their truth into the theaters of America. They were going to show just how ugly war, the ghettos, the language, law enforcement and the human body could be. It was honest, it was art! And many of the old-timers joined them in an effort to show that they could be modern, that they weren't worn out, corrupt old hacks like the *New York Times* and *Time* magazine claimed they were. But the audience continued to drift away.

The blacks in the ghettos, the men who had fought World War II, those who had fought in Korea and the women who had lost their men to those wars and to the ghettos were being told stories that they knew better, far better, than those self-proclaimed artists who were telling them. In time the audience realized it and more and more frequently they stayed home to watch the lame excuse for entertainment that was on their television sets.

Slowly at first, casually, then with thought, the men programming television at the local stations began to understand the need. Began to feel and know what that audience wanted to see, and then they gave it to them. At night, in the darkness, on the "Late Late Show."

All the old stars and stories of Hollywood's dream factories played in the darkness again, but it was surprising just how many of those you remembered were from Warner Bros. Tough, fast-talking, spirited street films and soaring romances filled with splendor. And the faces you knew: Bogart, Cagney, Davis, Flynn, Garfield, O'Brien, Robinson, Muni, Lupino, Sheridan, Raft. And others, those you knew but didn't know, Greenstreet, Lorre, Rains, Pallette, McHugh, Hale, Jenkins,

Dinehart, Donnelly, Herbert and all the others, faces and friends out of your past.

The audience stayed up and watched, both the young and old. Tired with the boredom of their routine jobs, sick with the eleven o'clock news and dissatisfied with the "prime time" programming, they stayed up through the late hours and let the old stories, the trivia, the vulgar product of Hollywood's uncultured youth, entertain them . . . stayed up late, very late, to let the old dreams get them through yet another day.

"Listen, this won't do any good, you'll never understand me, but I'll try once and then give it up. When a man's partner is killed, he's supposed to do something about it."

"Welcome to Sherwood, m'lady."

"If I were free, there would be only one thing I would want to do, prove you're not immune to happiness."

"You played it for her and you can play it for me."
"Well, I don't think I can remember it."
"If she can stand it, I can. Play it."

"If you know what's good for you, you won't monkey around with Fred C. Dobbs."

It wasn't over. Bogie, Bette and the others had been resurrected. And for many, they were brand new.

"Of course I watch it," recalls Mary Astor. "It's a wonderful rich memory. Of people who were friends. They all are, Sydney, Peter, Bogie. My dear ghosts."

Jack Warner had jailed their bodies, their vulgarities, their junk ideas, their sleeping beauty and occasionally caught a shooting star . . . mixed them with his thirty-five-cent shadows and put them up on the movie screen . . . with both cardboard and silver. And his Celluloid prison had preserved them, still held yesterday.

In 1967, however, Jack Warner was gone . . . and there was still tomorrow, still a story without an ending.

PIECES OF YESTERDAY

Epilogue

"I don't care what you meant to do, it's what you did I don't like."

The Warner Bros. Studios are now officially titled the Burbank Studios and both Warner Bros. and Columbia Pictures rent space there. The Writers' Building, Makeup and Wardrobe departments are all there, but many of the buildings now have different names and different functions.

Warner Bros. Pictures now belongs to Warner Communications and is presided over by Steve Ross, who resides in New York. As of January 1, 1975, Frank Wells became co-chairman of the board of Warner Bros. Pictures and John Calle president. They reside in Burbank and now make the decisions, say yes and no.

Writers now work off the lot, at home. There is no writers' table. There are no afternoon teas laced with rum, no weekly cocktail parties, no stable of stars to put into your script, no more legends to meet.

"Those old buffalo, those old picture makers who used to be pants pressers, those men of courage and imagination and *chutzpah* . . . they're all gone now," recalls Stephen Longstreet. "They've been replaced by people who don't know their ass from their elbows about movies. They all wear Edwardian suits and have twenty-five-dollar haircuts. If they make a good picture, it's an accident."

"Oh yes, I miss those days and all those people. Looking back I think of it as the best years of my career. Writers are agreeable people for the most part and writing is a lonely life." Katherine Tourney is writing a book now. She lives in what used to be called a "Hollywood bungalow." She has lived there for eighteen years. Outside there is a tree that reaches to her roof. "I remember when it started to grow. It couldn't have picked a better spot. It keeps the sun from beating in and ruining the carpets."

In 1930 John Bright was absorbed with hoods and guns. With what was happening in the streets. With one-legged men. Today he is writing a novel about yesterday. It's dedicated to his friend, Sam Ornitz, a writer who was one of the Hollywood Ten. The blacklisted. When he tells you about it, his eyes swim and he drinks from a milk glass full of Jack Daniels.

Mary McCall muses about all those scripts that lie about the Warner Bros. lot somewhere, filed, stacked away, yellowing. Scripts written during the adolescent heat of the love affair between the writer and Hollywood. "You know, each of us had one of those projects that never got made. Years spent on research and writing them. But a script is only half alive until

Chapter opening. Lili Damita, Flynn's first wife
Overleaf. "I don't care what you meant to do, it's what you
did I don't like." Scene from director Sam Peckinpah's The
Wild Bunch, *1969*
Facing. Clint Eastwood and Andy Robinson in Dirty Harry, *1971*
Below. Steve McQueen in Bullitt, *1968*

it becomes a film. You cannot put a finished script on your coffee table to be read by guests. I wonder what they're going to do with all those scripts."

Songwriter Harry Warren lives in Beverly Hills, still plays piano in his studio and rummages among forgotten songs as the remembered ones still play on every radio and in every elevator across the nation. Bette Midler's recording of "Lullaby of Broadway," Oscar Petersen's jazz version of "September in the Rain," "I Only Have Eyes for You" and so many others. But the Warren name remains unknown. He complains about it, but not angrily.

A few of the performers are still working.

In 1972, Ida Lupino went to work for director Sam Peckinpah on *Junior Bonner.* "He seemed to be the kind of man I could work with. But on the first day of shooting, in the Palace Bar in Arizona, in front of two hundred people, he shouts at me just as the shot is about to be taken . . . tries to embarrass me."

"'Ida, what's that you've got on your mouth?'

"I stopped and hollered back, 'Say that again.'

"'You heard me,' he growled.

"I said, 'I heard you . . . loud and clear,' and marched the fifty yards to where he was sitting and said, 'Now say it again.'

"He fudged in his seat and said, 'Well, they told me back at the studio that you were putting too much lipstick on.'

"'Don't back out of it, what's wrong? Why did you embarrass me in front of all those people?' Well, he didn't have much to say and I told him, 'I'm through, finished. I won't desert you, I'll stay and read the offstage lines, but you can send for Shelley Winters to replace me right now. You're not taking one foot of film of me.' And he didn't. I read the offstage lines, then walked out and told them, 'I want a car, I want out,' and I went home to pack.

"That evening my door rings, I'm all packed, everything, and does Sam show up? No. But in the hallway there are roses as far as the eye can see . . . and champagne . . . and a bucket. And a message:

Dear Shelley Winters,
As much as you would like to play this role,
we cannot have you because we already have
Ida Lupino.

Love,
Darryl Zanuck

"That bastard, I couldn't resist him. I love him. Of course I stayed, how could I leave after that?"

In 1974 Lupe is still working, answering the calls from her young agent. "Oh, Mike, well, when do I start? Oh, you son of a bitch, can't I have one evening of peace? Oh, 'Columbo'! What is she, oh, an evangelist! And I'm supposed to read it tonight! . . . Well, send it tonight. I've got a doctor mad for me coming over, but I'll have to put him off . . . and we start shooting when . . . ten days from now! All right, love, send it right over. Right now . . . I'm waiting."

Bette Davis and Olivia de Havilland are both on tour in 1974, making one-night speaking engagements . . . talking about yesterday.

Robert Lord is still writing, still working out twice a day, still a hundred and thirty-five pounds and at seventy-four, still fighting.

Allen Jenkins had a room in a warehouse in Venice, California, where he was building a houseboat from a navy tub. "I'm going to live on it for the rest of my . . . or whatever the higher power allows. Do I still work, hell yes! Did a thing at Screen Gems five or six weeks ago, 'Police Story,' played a shyster pawnbroker. It was a hell of a good little bit . . . wish they'd enlarged it." They were still editing the show when he died of cancer in July of 1974. No one had known, no one had been told and he never let it show.

At the studio a few of the old-timers are still working in makeup, special effects, editing and hairdressing. They do their jobs efficiently, professionally. "But it's not like it used to be," recalls a hair stylist. "Details are glossed over, tests or wardrobe and makeup no one has time for, or money for. Lighting setups are made too quickly, scenes aren't covered enough. There is no time for more than a few takes."

The employees no longer gripe or fight for things like they used to, no longer fight much at all. The new system has set in, been accepted, but in 1973 there was a rumor that made the rounds of the studio and persisted for months. "Jack Warner is going to buy the studio back, he's coming back, everything is going to be all right again. It's gonna be like old times."

But he didn't.

On May 19,1974, Henry Blanke and Jack Warner had lunch together at Senor Pico's in Century City. What did they talk about? "Nothing," recalls Blanke "absolutely nothing," There

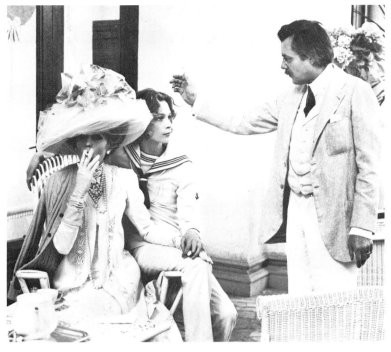

Overleaf. Bill Koenig, Darryl Zanuck, Jack Warner, Al Jolson and Sam Warner
Facing. Director Sam Peckinpah at work on The Wild Bunch, 1969
Left. Silvana Mangano, Bjorn Anderson and Dirk Bogarde in director Luchino Visconti's Death in Venice, 1971
Below. Scene from director Luchino Visconti's The Damned, 1970

Above. Gary Grimes and Jerry Houser stroll through their frustrated childhood in Summer of '42, 1971
Below. Malcolm McDowell in director Stanley Kubrick's A Clockwork Orange, 1971

was much to remember, but the habit of deceit had set in and there was too much to hide.

At the fiftieth anniversary of Warner Bros. television show in December of 1973, Jack had made an appearance. The hostess, Bette Davis, came down off the podium and embraced her "brother." They had finally found a meeting place, a neutral ground, yesterday. "I look with pride at some of the roofs of those sound stages. I am responsible for a few of them being built. I also say here I was one of the lucky ones—I had a mother and father for all those years, and they did well by me. I can't deny this. Those years were the greatest of my life."

In 1974 John Huston was working as an actor. He still wore a light tan safari jacket with eight pockets, all empty. The handsome head was now inlaid with the patina of living on uncounted sound stages, like an ancient silver vase. He two-handed a large cigar as he was asked to think about yesterday, then grinned with a smile made from quicksilver. "In the old days we could get Havanas, but no more." Then he put the cigar in between his lips, where it belonged, in the middle of his mouth.

On Henry Blanke's seventy-fourth birthday, Huston arrived for the small party "with the dullest twenty-two-year-old blond I have ever met. He passed out, cold sober, went to sleep. I thought he had a stroke and was going to call a doctor, but he was fine." Later he awoke, said, "I owe everything to Henry Blanke." Then left with his blond.

At the American Film Institute's Center for Advanced Film Studies, Raoul Walsh, after talking to the students about yesterday, grew tired and his mind drifted from the subject. "I . . . I've got a place up in the hills; I still fool around with the ranch, get some exercise and stuff. But, at my age, you have to keep the bags packed." The audience went silent for several beats as Walsh said nothing, some stared at the rug and one mumbled audibly, "They surely are."

William Wellman now lives in Brentwood and between bouts with the bottle comes out on occasion to celebrate an old friend or encourage a young film maker. Two of his children care for him, his wife and the others no longer see him since he fell in love and ran off with his partner's wife. Now he asks for forgiveness, but doesn't expect it. His hair is white, the lines deep in the battlefield of his face.

Asked about what his films were about: "I don't know anything about messages. I'm an Episcopalian and a very bad one, but

I say my prayers, and believe there is . . . I don't know. I hate getting old. I think it is the most tragic thing that happens to anybody. And when I read about growing old gracefully . . ."

Just pieces of yesterday. For some of us all that's left of tomorrow.

In 1973 the German ambassador to Japan called the Warner Bros. studios trying to locate a man who had immigrated to America from Germany back in the early twenties, a man called Henry Blanke. The studio operator checked her lists, then politely told the ambassador that there was no Mr. Blanke at Warner Bros. nor had there ever been.

As he sits in his Brentwood home and tells the story, Henry Blanke is no longer the master of his emotions. Too old to hide. He removes himself from the room for a moment, then returns with his smile back where it belongs, but his eyes still swim. "I think that's a fitting finish of my story." He laughs, then angrily wags his busy finger. "What I have just told you is perhaps the most important thing about our business. It gives you our entire motion picture history . . . in a nutshell."

Sam Peckinpah has also never heard of Henry Blanke. But he's seen *The Treasure of the Sierra Madre* a dozen times and his own Warner Bros. film, *The Wild Bunch,* openly and proudly pays homage to it: "Along with *Rashomon* and *La Strada, Treasure* just may be the best picture ever made." Like so many of us, Sam met Blanke on the screen . . . knows him well. Most of the characters in the Warner Bros. story have been met in the same place, at the picture show, and with a little magic there will be more tomorrow.

Warner Bros. is a story without a "wow" finish. Just an ordinary, clichéd, continuing melodrama full of lively people, fighters, drunks, lovers, dreamers and broken dreams. And a few that will survive. Just another soap opera, a family story about four brothers named Jack, Harry, Albert, Sam and one snake charmer. About a Mom and Pop stand-up shoe repair and a village called Krasnostow . . . a little place you can't find on the map . . . where they beat up on people. On street kids. A simple story, one of those where the writer, just in case you didn't get his obvious point, ends it with the title.

"Here's looking at you, kid."